REAPPEARING

REAPPEARING

THE WOULD-BE NOMAD KEEPS ON RUNNING
THE CHASE GETS NASTIER
MORE GUILTY PEOPLE DIE
CHINA TAKES THE WORLD TO THE VERY EDGE

CHRIS HEAL

Published by Chattaway and Spottiswood
Milverton Taunton, Somerset

Distributed by Lightning Source worldwide

www.reappearing.candspublishing.org.uk
reappearing@candspublishing.org.uk

A catalogue record for this book is available from
the British Library

5 4 3 2 1

ISBN 978-1-9161944-1-0

Design by Vivian@Bookscribe

Printed and bound by Lightning Source worldwide

For

Arran and Lisa

and

Ailsa and Murray

and

Con Coughlin, columnist,
who consistently forewarned about the threat posed
by the Chinese state:

*The conduct of China's Communist Party is not that of 'a regime that is
fit to govern. It is the behaviour of a corrupt elite that has no interest in
protecting the interests of its citizens, nor those of the world beyond'.*

For a further union, a deeper communion
Through the dark cold and the empty desolation,
The wave cry, the wind cry, the vast waters
Of the petrel and the porpoise. In the end is my beginning.

T S Eliot, 'East Coker', *Four Quartets*

We had long heard tell of whole worlds that had vanished, of empires
sunk without trace, gone down with all their men and all their machines
into the unexplorable depths of the centuries, with their gods and laws,
their academies and their sciences pure and applied, their grammars and
their dictionaries, their Classics, their Romantics, and their Symbolists,
their critics and critics of their critics … We were aware that the visible
earth is made of ashes, and that ashes signify something. Through the
obscure depths of history we could make out the phantoms of great ships
laden with riches and intellect; we could not count them. But the disasters
that had sent them down were, after all, none of our affair.

Paul Valéry, 'The Crisis of the Mind', *History and Politics*

The publisher of *Reappearing* acknowledges the permission of Faber and Faber Limited to quote from *Four Quarters* by T S Eliot.

CONTENTS

LETTER FROM THE AUTHOR, NOVEMBER 2020

I am just about to leave Timbuktu.

I had only a passing interest in visiting the fabled city, the rubbish tip of the southern Sahara. 'Passing' is the right word. I thought that I would be in and out, covering my tracks with fresh-blown sand and escaping the shadowy people who wished me ill. I expected I would be gone like a djinn in the dawn to find some version of freedom.

It didn't work out like that at all. If you read the first part of my story, *Disappearing*, you'll know that I had a bad time crossing the desert from Morocco. I would surely have died if others had not looked after me. While I lay in my sick bed, my book was published as instructed because it was thought I was dead. Instead of giving my pursuers cause for reflection, I stabbed a pen into a hornet's nest. The assassination in Brussels of those two zealots of the European Union, Jean-Claude Juncker and Martin Selmayr, set off a hue and cry for me because the murderer, hero perhaps, had never been found. The EU needed to punish someone, British if possible, to protect their dignity.

I read the leaked confidential findings of the Secretariat of the European Commission. They were explicit:

The author is taunting us with his knowledge of the unsolved murders. This was treason, a political crime of the highest wickedness. Whether alive or not, he should be investigated and brought to book in name or in person for the good of the European project.

My own country's National Counter Terrorism Security Office didn't help either:

[Disappearing] is a subversive book and we should not give it the breath of publicity ... The skills it [teaches] are best kept within the purview of government agencies.

Or the UK Home Office:

The author's manual explaining how an individual can divest themselves of identity, to go off grid and beneath the radar, and to disappear, is a danger to Western civilisation.

It didn't help, of course, that the things I criticised or foretold, like violence coming again to the heart of Europe because of the suppression of democracy, the incursion of the surveillance state, the pandemic, the unhappier, less free, new world, are now part of every day.

Nobody likes a smart arse especially if you are one yourself, like a politician or a civil servant (there's a misnomer) caught in the act or proved wrong.

But, enough of that. My own weakness, hubris, stupidity even, means that I am on the run. I am getting too old for all this intrigue. Events in Timbuktu have wrapped me in more problems. Some of my acquaintances, when it came down to it, weren't friends to be trusted.

Writing becomes a self-indulgent habit. As I write, I don't know where this story will end. My self-confidence is not as robust as in the old days. Now the virus has died down and if I get safely away, I'll send these first chapters to my publishers. If I ever find peace, I'll let you know where and what it feels like.

Snippets of my story might not be true, of course. There are people to protect. But I'll be as honest as I can be.

Chris Heal (as was)
Timbuktu

November 2020

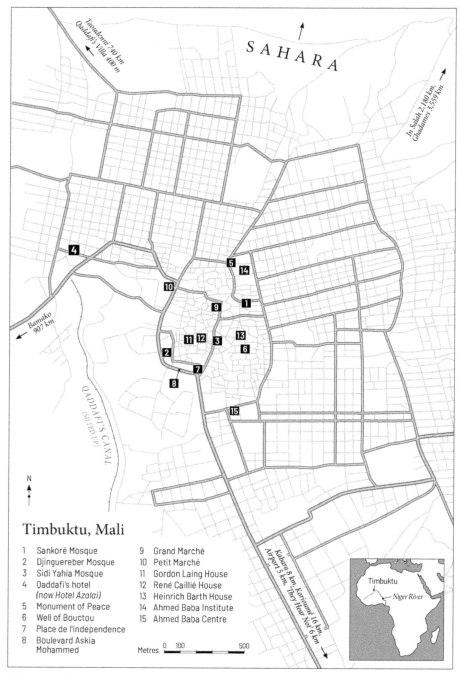

Taoudenni 740 km.
Qaddafi's Villa 400 m

SAHARA

In Salah 2,180 km.
Ghadames 3,559 km

Bamako
907 km

QADDAFI'S CANAL
(SILTED UP)

N

Timbuktu, Mali

1	Sankoré Mosque	9	Grand Marché
2	Djinguereber Mosque	10	Petit Marché
3	Sidi Yahia Mosque	11	Gordon Laing House
4	Qaddafi's hotel	12	René Caillié House
	(now Hotel Azalai)	13	Heinrich Barth House
5	Monument of Peace	14	Ahmed Baba Institute
6	Well of Bouctou	15	Ahmed Baba Centre
7	Place de l'indépendence		
8	Boulevard Askia		
	Mohammed		

Metres   0   100   500

Kabara 8 km, Koriomé 16 km,
Airport 5 km, They Hear Not 6 km.

Timbuktu
Niger River

Map 1. Timbuktu, 2020

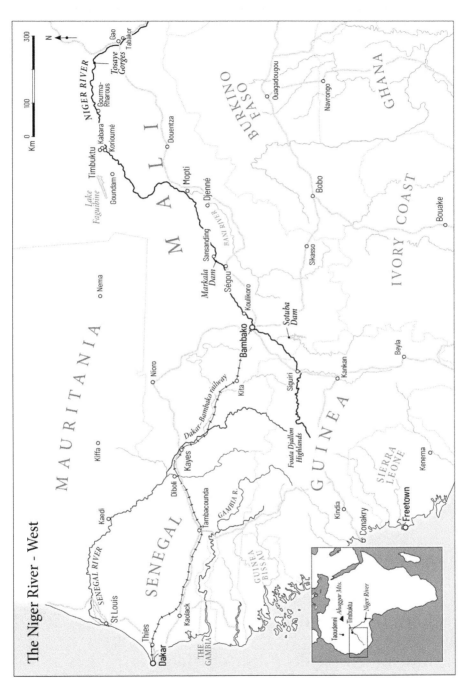

Map 2. River Niger, West, 2021

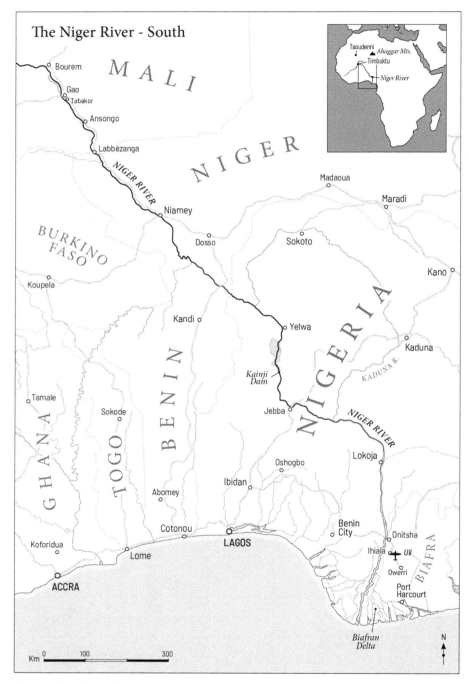

Map 3. River Niger, South, 2021

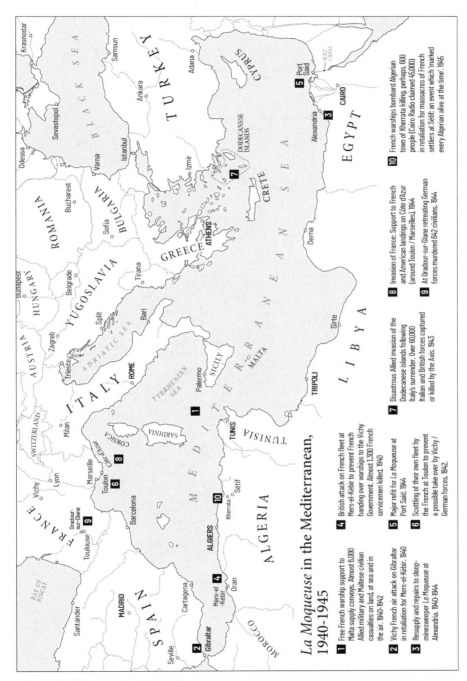

La Moqueuse in the Mediterranean, 1940-1945

1 Free French warship support to Malta supply convoys. Almost 6,000 Allied military and Maltese civilian casualties on land, at sea and in the air. 1940-1942

2 Vichy French air attack on Gibraltar in retaliation for Mers-el-Kébir. 1940

3 Resupply and repairs to shop-minesweeper La Moqueuse at Alexandria. 1940-1944

4 British attack on French fleet at Mers-el-Kébir to prevent French handing over warships to the Vichy Government. Almost 1,300 French servicemen killed. 1940

5 Major refit for La Moqueuse at Port Said. 1944

6 Scuttling of their own fleet by the French at Toulon to prevent a possible take over by Vichy / German forces. 1942

7 Disastrous Allied invasion of the Dodecanese islands following Italy's surrender. Over 60,000 Italian and British forces captured or killed by the Axis. 1943

8 Invasion of France: Support to French and American landings on Côte d'Azur (around Toulon / Marseilles). 1944

9 At Oradour-sur-Glane retreating German forces murdered 642 civilians. 1944

10 French warships bombard Algerian town of Kherrata killing, perhaps, 600 people (Cairo Radio claimed 45,000) in retaliation for massacres of French settlers at Sétif: an event which 'marked every Algerian alive at the time'. 1945

Map 4. La Moqueuse in the Mediterranean, 1940–1945

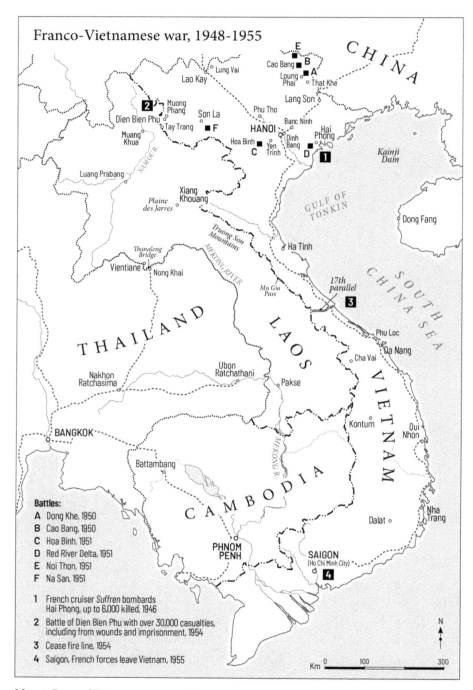

Franco-Vietnamese war, 1948-1955

Battles:
A Dong Khe, 1950
B Cao Bang, 1950
C Hoa Binh, 1951
D Red River Delta, 1951
E Noi Thon, 1951
F Na San, 1951

1 French cruiser *Suffren* bombards
   Hai Phong, up to 6,000 killed, 1946
2 Battle of Dien Bien Phu with over 30,000 casualties,
   including from wounds and imprisonment, 1954
3 Cease fire line, 1954
4 Saigon, French forces leave Vietnam, 1955

Map 5. Franco-Vietnamese war, 1948–1955

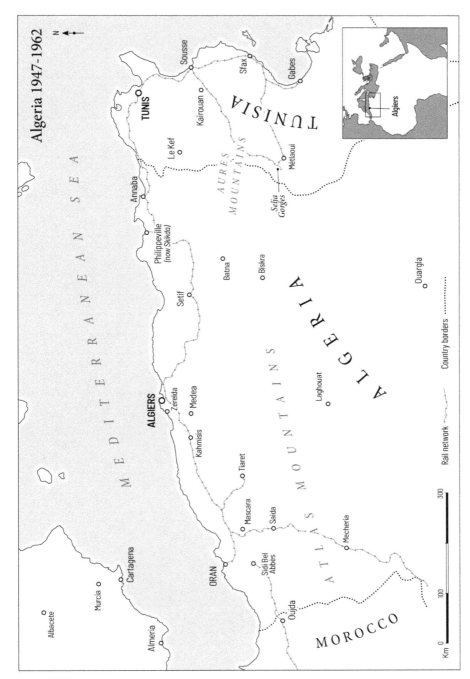

Map 6. Algerian War, 1947–48, 1955–1962

Map 7. Laos, 1963–2024

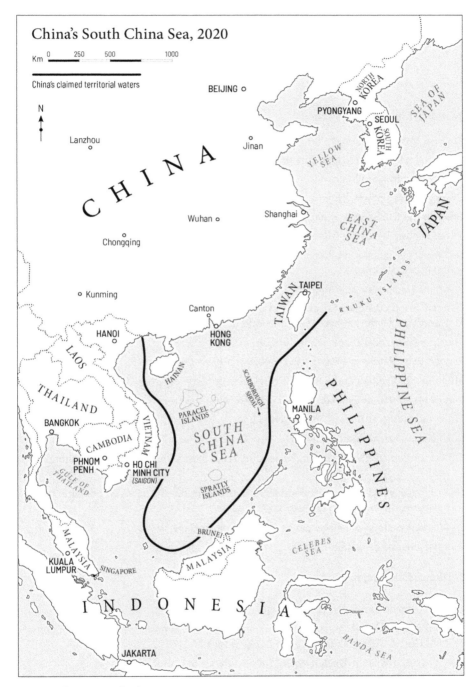

China's South China Sea, 2020

Km 0 250 500 1000

China's claimed territorial waters

N

Map 8. China's South China Sea, 2020

ILLUSTRATIONS

Section 1, following page 102:

Sankoré Mosque, Timbuktu

Muammar al-Qaddafi's canal cuts through the scrub desert south of Timbuktu

Well of Bouctou, Timbuktu

Gordon Laing's house, Timbuktu

Reading the Qur'an among the AK-47s embedded in the Peace Monument, Timbuktu

The side entrance of the Djinguereber Mosque, Timbuktu

Leo Africanus, Hassan Mohammed Al Wazzan Al Zayati, probable portrait, Sebastiano del Piombo, c. 1520

Posthumous portrait of Mungo Park by an unknown artist, 1859

General Joseph-Jacques-Césaire Joffre meets Mandarin and Vietnamese dignitaries in Hanoi in 1922 during his triumphal world tour

Martin Selmayr and Jean-Claude Juncker

Ahmed Baba 'Answers a Moroccan's Questions about Slavery', 1615

Muammar al-Qaddafi at the 12th African Union conference, 2009. US Navy

Part of Muammar al-Qaddafi's villa, Timbuktu, after the French bombing, 2013

Pinasses loading at Kabara on the River Niger

Boko Haram boy soldiers, 2016

One of the two DC-3 carcasses at Uli landing strip, 1969, which was put to another use in 2021

One of many world-wide street demonstrations in support of Charlie Hebdo after the massacre, this one in Strasbourg, 2015

La Moqueuse, sloop-minesweeper of the Free French Navy, WW2

General Charles de Gaulle, c. 1942

Section 2, following page 204:

General Jean de Lattre de Tassigny, 1946

General Raoul Salan with Lao Prince Sisavang Vatthana, Luang Prabang with Sergent-Chef Gaston Albert among the escort party, 1953

Ho Chi Minh reads the Declaration of Independence in Hanoi, 1945

1er BEP jumps into the valley of Dien Bien Phu, 1953

Aerial view of Dien Bien Phu valley, 1953

General Vo Nguyen Giap presents his plans for the Battle of Dien Bien Phu to Party and State leaders including Ho Chi Minh, second left, 1954

Albert Camus, 1950s

Viet Minh troops plant their flag over the captured French headquarters at Dien Bien Phu, 1954

Légionnaires of 1er Régiment Etranger de Parachutistes (1er REP) watch a large crowd of enthusiastic local people during the Algerian Putsch, 1961

General Vang Pao as a young man

De Gaulle's Citroen DS with marked holes from automatic weapons after the assassination attempt at Petit-Clamart, 1961

Jean-Marie Bastien-Thiry after his arrest for the attempted assassination of de Gaulle, 1963

The USS *Gabrielle Giffords*, launching a strike missile, is one of two new Littoral Combat Ships (LCS) in the South China Sea to supplement the US Seventh Fleet, 2019.

The CIA's Long Tien airbase, 1973

Cessna Bird Dogs (rear) used smoke rockets to mark targets for Hmong pilots in two-seat North American T-28s

Hmong girls meet possible suitors while playing a ball-throwing game in Laos

Hmong village

Vang Vieng

Han Zheng, 2018

Xi Jinping and Winnie the Pooh, 2018

1. FLIES IN THE CITY

Seized with disease
Halfway on the road,
My dreams keep revolving
Round the withered moor.

Bashō, *Deep North*

Flies took turns buzzing angry loops. A pair of mosquitoes meandered close by. I reasoned I was alive because I could hear the flies and the mosquitoes and I knew what they were. Unless, of course, I was in hell. The dry air around my face burned with sand from an acrid desert. Independent drops of warm water itched down my nose until they evaporated. I flickered my eyelids, but there was no light. My head would not move. I wondered where the rest of my body was for I could feel nothing. My world was full of drifting, dirty cotton wool, with no purpose, no spark of endeavour, just the insects and the sweat. I slipped back to where I had been before the flies came.

A few months later, maybe, or five minutes, the length of a prayer, the flies had gone. A sadness lapped me for they were my only company, not yet friends, but at least closer than the mosquitoes. The pungent air, still full of grit, also carried hints of half-forgotten acacia woodsmoke and the tang of slow-cooked goat. My mind fell back over fifty years to a cave high in the Atlas Mountains so that I forced open an eye to focus on a Berber symbol for freedom painted brightly on the wall. But there was no *aza* to see, only the always-swirling, wispy clouds. The scent of food quickened my stomach and my sphincter cramped instinctively.

I knew I was closer to remembering who and where I was.

In a cooler period, I heard geckos scurrying and imagined flicking tongues as mosquitoes spent their last moment. Another time, I was wakened by small wings that gave me respite as they moved through the furnace. I felt weakness in every pore. A voice, speaking educated English, cut through. The words were guttural, not unfriendly, with a deep Arabic accent tinted with something else, black Africa perhaps, close to the Igbo of Biafra that I knew so well.

'Can you hear the birds? They are finches with red throats and tails. They come into the house to escape the sun. We welcome them because they catch the flies.'

I wondered how many of my almost-friends might disappear down the busy red throats. Soon, I would be alone. I sobbed, although my tear ducts were dry. The voice continued, but I did not try to understand. In my grief, I fell back into a refuge. People aren't all the same. Often, I needed to be alone. I used to tire of explaining that I value solitude, always true when I hear news of the unexpected, especially loss and death. I thought this had happened many times.

Pinpricks of memory swam through a multi-coloured dream. I was drowning in sand, every tiny piece of stone separate and illuminated by a burning sun. I knew that each particle had been dropped by Allah onto the garden of the Sahara as he heard a careless man tell another selfish lie. Spirit Tuaregs, *djnoun*, beckoned me slyly from between the grit and, as I stumbled after them, the brilliant indigo robes disappeared to reappear and disappear again. Each time I closed my eyes against the glare, the sand clawed at my eyeballs forcing my lids apart and, as I tried to cry out, the desert trickled into my lying mouth.

I woke slimed with cold perspiration and remembered not my name, but my life. Around my head and across my eyes I felt a veil of white gauze which I unwound. I lay in blue linen sheets in a wooden truckle bed. The bare walls and ceiling were dull adobe yellow, unevenly finished. There was one strong chest of drawers, two rough doors and a shoulder-high window open to the outside, but covered with a dark blind perforated with silver stars through years of use. The whole reminded me of a flag I had seen hanging limply in Brussels. Outside, I heard children playing, boys kicking a football. I tried to sit up, but fell back, weak, alone and confused.

I knew I had gone off-grid. With three Berber companions, I had set off quietly from Mhamid across the wastes well away from beaten tracks to reach Timbuktu. We planned to shake off any chance of shadowy followers. I knew Asso had died from snakebite on the way. I recalled I had been near death from a dysentery that caused hope to die, desperate for and frightened of water, and tied to a camel's swaying hump. And, yet, here I was in this stifling room with unsoiled, if wet sheets, unbound, and hopefully free. I dozed.

Much later, I think, the door opened and a stooping old man, perhaps about my age, of burnished, creased black skin with red-scoured eyes, and wearing a dusty, worn jellaba, came through and stood over me and prised my lids.

'So, you have come back to us. Can you see me?' he asked. It was a voice I placed with red-splashed birds without knowing why, but I did not know his face. I thought I could trust him, at least for this moment.

'I can,' I said. 'You are as white as snow and have two horns. Do I owe you my life?'

He chuckled. 'Obviously the Sahara has made you colour blind, but at least you can count. If you can focus that well, you have been lucky. I thought for a while that you would never see again. So, "yes", I have saved your life and you are eternally in my debt. And, of course, the debt of my wife who has bathed you like a child each day. You have no secrets from her.'

I thought of this unknown woman who had cared for my naked and unclean body. 'Please thank her for me and I thank you, too, of course.'

'My name is Nianankoro, my wife is Attou, and you are in our house in the north of the city close by the Sankoré mosque. You will be able to thank her yourself. You have been here for almost four weeks.'

'I tried to get up,' I shared, 'but did not have the strength. Are you saying that I am in Timbuktu? Why did you take me in?'

'You should not try to talk or do too much too soon. I think you will be here for several more weeks at least till you get your strength back.'

He moved to the foot of the bed and looked down on me. He was tall and thin, his face tending to gauntness among many worry lines, but with kind eyes. 'You should know that for the first few days you all but died several times. Older men like you do not usually have the strength to come back from what you have been through. So, you will have plenty of time to ask your questions. There is no rush. For the moment you are quite safe. No one knows that you are here and, if they did, that you are a European.

'For now, I will tell you that you were brought here by Lahcen in the night. Your bag is there by the chest untouched. Lahcen stayed a few days until he knew you might live. In that time, he and his grandson, Icho, made a lot of trade. Then they took all their camels to their village in Morocco. I think Lahcen is now a rich and unhappy man. The death of his son, Asso, hurt him badly.'

Nianankoro moved to the window, tweaked the blind, and stood looking out.

'Lahcen told me that he owes you a great debt from long ago. He also said that you do not wish to be known by your real name, as some people would like to find you and kill you. Lahcen calls you *Amkssa*, the person who looks after the sheep. It is the nearest Berber word for a true nomad. You may not understand, but we find your name very funny.

'One more thing, I should say now, because of your problems. Don't do as I am doing, looking out of the window in plain sight. The jihadi army may have gone from Tombouctou[1] and before them the Tuareg fighters, but their dregs are both still here. The men in the shadows, leaning in the doorways, smoking cigarettes in the cafés, they have stayed and blended into the scenery. The fear and anger they brought lives on. There are no Europeans here now except for the French army and UN officer peacekeepers, no tourists. The French in particular are very touchy. Two of their helicopters collided up-country a few months ago while chasing militants. They lost thirteen men; that makes about forty overall killed in the Sahel.[2] Let no one see you for what you are. At the least, you would certainly be in danger of being questioned roughly which may be embarrassing and dangerous for you.'

Nianankoro said his wife would arrive soon with some food. He pointed to the second door where there was a simple toilet. 'My wife will be pleased if you use it. Otherwise, just rest, get slowly better and contemplate your future.'

I had been given enough to think about. I waited a few minutes then struggled to the window, holding onto the bed, and lifting a corner of the blind. The Sankoré neighbourhood was a labyrinth of sandy alleys where the boys kicked their ball amid the chickens and refuse. Ramshackle, sagging trucks puffed diesel clouds as they crawled past street ends. The mosque was an unlikely mud pyramid. It wore permanent bundles of palm sticks embedded in the clay to act as stabilisers and for mudding crews. There were a few dusty mango trees, fewer cars and some determined buzzing scooters. It did not look like the golden city of reputation.

A teacher's voice startled me from behind. 'You're a naughty boy. Please get back into bed.'

She was lovely to look at, aged, but with clear skin, piercing eyes and the figure of a much younger woman who had taken good care of herself. She was in such total possession of her life that I supposed only the most confident or uncaring of men could hold her gaze.

'You must be Attou,' I offered. 'I have no option but to obey you for, I hear, you know my inner secrets. One day I will cover you in flowers of gratitude.' I stumbled to the bed.

She relented and smiled. 'We have few flowers here except for the month when the rains in the west fill the Niger and the water comes up the canal to the city gates. Then we have some flowers. I studied in London and Paris a lifetime ago and it was always the red rose that I loved. We only come close to that deep colour with our blood and our silks. One red rose would be a great gift and, when it died, I could press the petals in a favourite book.'

Attou sat on the edge of my bed and stroked the back of my hand with her thumb. We said nothing for several minutes until she asked if I would like to eat. 'We can talk a little when I bring your food, perhaps in half an hour. My husband has gone out and will not be back from his books for some time when he and I will eat together as we always do.'

I managed a second, quick, quiet trip to the window. The houses in the low evening glare were boxes built of grey mud. Many of the walls sported unconnected, often enigmatic, graffiti, written in chalk in French school neatness:

Les noms de ceux qui voyagent dans la nuit sont Sidi and Yéyé.
Hélas! Les Anges de l'Enfer.
Les Touaregs ne sont pas nos maîtres.
Beauté ... Beau ...
L'esclavage est une mauvaise chose.
La poussièrer en Décembre ...[3]

My meal was a small dish of rice and goat stew with a spicy sauce. I approached it gingerly, eating in small pinches. To my relief, my stomach held although I continued anxious.

'You can have two questions this evening,' I was told.

'Thank you, my Lady. Tell me, first, how you know Lahcen.'

She clearly appreciated the title. 'Among twelve languages, there are two main races in Tombouctou,' she explained. 'The first, the Hératine, are descendants of the black *Songhai*. In their time, Tombouctou was to Africa what Florence was to Enlightenment Europe – a place renowned for its scholarly and artistic endeavours, where learning and culture reached its greatest sophistication for well over a hundred years during the Songhai Empire. My husband is a *Songhai*.

'I shall give you a history lesson, Amkssa, so that you understand my relationship with my husband. Unknown to Europeans, most of Tombouctou's wealth disappeared after 1591 when Ahmad I al-Mansur Saadi, the Moroccan sultan, demanded that the last independent king of the Songhai Empire, Askia Ishak II, surrender control of the great salt mines. When the king refused, 42,000 Moroccan soldiers and 10,000 horses and camels led by Judar Pasha crossed the Sahara and sacked our city in one day. Judar was a slave taken from Castile who had become a favoured eunuch of the sultan. The invaders were armed with cannons and *harquebuses*, a powerful matchlock gun. They faced a small force of Songhai warriors, infantrymen, fighting with only bows and arrows, and spear-carrying cavalry, men who knew nothing about mechanised warfare. The king was killed while fleeing. His brother succeeded him and pledged fealty to the sultan. Our local hero and intellectual, Ahmed Baba, called for resistance. In retaliation, troops stormed the Sankoré Mosque, just over there, and looted Baba's library of 1,600 books and dragged him in chains to captivity in Marrakech for two years.

'The second group in Tombouctou, the *Rouma*, are descendants of those invading Moors. There is also a small number of *Tolba*, people who came from all over Sudan to study Arabic and are long settled. All our races are greatly inter-married although some would pretend that this is not the case.'

Attou smiled to herself. 'Despite my dark skin, I am a *Rouma* and so the conqueror of my husband. By tradition and probably fact, my people came from Tamegroute, the same village as Lahcen. His great grandfather and mine, and those before, knew each other and traded each year when the caravans came. So, Lahcen and I are kin and we are bound to each other.'

She looked directly at me, 'We gladly carry his debts.'

All the while, the back of my hand was being stroked and I began to feel drowsy and warm and safe. I loved her way of sharing the past.

'Tell me about the canal.'

'OK, but then you must rest. Bruce Chatwin was in West Africa. You know of him?'

I nodded. 'He wanted to be a nomad. Like me.'

'Chatwin claimed that trade was a "language which prevents people from cutting each other's throats". In Tombouctou, the Songhai met with the Fulani, who travelled with the Wangara, all of them leery of the Tuareg and reliant on the Arabs and the Moors. Merchants and nomads also arrived from the Niger River with all manner of goods: weapons, cooking utensils, foods, medicine, and slaves for African owners.'

I showed off. 'The Niger is the third-longest river in Africa with a boomerang-shape that originates in the highlands of Guinea. It meanders for one thousand miles through Mali before curving south just below Timbuktu, then flowing through Niger and Nigeria and spilling into the Gulf of Guinea. I was told by Berber friends that the name Guinea was derived from their word, *aquinaou*, meaning "Negro" and identical with the Arabic word *Sudan*, the rich sub-Saharan region governed by Timbuktu and named from the Arabic *Bilad al-Sudan*, "the land of the blacks".'

'Clever boy. Between 1917 and 1921, during the French colonial period, slave labour was used to dig a narrow five-mile canal linking Tombouctou with Kabara, our port in the south. In the early 1970s, when I was a young woman, the canal was the most vibrant part of our city. It was a cool gathering point for children who fished and swam, for market sellers, and for traders in dugout pirogues piled with fruits and vegetables from the irrigated farms that flourished by the Niger. The southward advance of the desert caused the canal to dry out and fill with sand, but, in 2007, as part of the dredging project paid for by Muammar al-Qaddafi from Libya, the canal was re-excavated so that, when the Niger flooded, Tombouctou was again connected to the river ... and, of course, to Qaddafi's expensively renovated hotel, now the Azalai.

'The hotel became al-Qaeda's barracks and, nearby, the radicals' amputation and killing ground. Today, the canal is largely silted again and snakes south across scrubland. It is a dangerous place for people and animals with its steep sides.'

Attou kissed my hand and went to make ready for her husband's return. I fell into a deep sleep, smelling her scent and dreaming of her affections.

For an hour or two in the night, I found, Timbuktu was desert still. The light-hearted revellers, dancers and musicians had quit forming transitory 'joking relationships' with anyone met on the streets; the *plaisanterie* that are free of race and religion. There were no belching scooters or snorting trucks. Those who needed to be early to their work were still in bed. Questions and responses, it seemed, might be shouted the miles over scrub and low dunes to and from the boatmen on the Niger.

This first early morning of my new life, I was wakened by two men snapping insults, each beyond restraint, or any vestige of respect. The rage carried from a rooftop several alleyways beyond the Sankoré. Watching in semi-shock, I felt the visceral anger. Other windows opened. Oil lights flickered. There was the slightest pause, but the hatred returned and reached an animal peak until it ended abruptly. A single shot from an automatic pistol rapped out, a dying fall lingering on the air, carrying a memory of long ago. Then, all was silent and, one by one, the windows thumped closed and the listeners went back to their worlds.

In the morning, Nianankoro told me, the coffee shops and bread queues swarmed with rumour, but no one had answers. Fatal violence was rare in the city since 2012 when the Tuareg raiders left and the jihadis, Ansar Dine, the al-Qaeda-linked group in the Islamic Maghreb (AQIM), which had received the blessing of Osama Bin Laden, were run out of town by French and Chadian troops. There were no reports of a death in the city. Nothing.

It was another two weeks before I left my room for the first time. The routine before then was the same except that some books, English, French, Arabic, were brought to amuse me. Each morning about seven, just before the sun began to reach its strength, Nianankoro brought me thick coffee, bread and fruit and talked to me about his aged library and promised that soon I would see his collection. At noon, a silent, embarrassed young black girl wearing a *hijab* glided in, replenished my water, and left me a small round of warm leavened *tagila* stuffed with leaves, herbs and cold meat. She was careful not to meet my eyes or to touch me as befitted her position. She never answered me, although I spoke to her many times. I never knew her name.

What I waited for through the long days was the time when Attou came to me and stroked my hand before she went to fetch my food. Each visit, I asked for the next instalment. She was always free with her knowledge. Her voice had a sing-song quality that lulled me although when she had gone to meet her husband I could, even in my drowsy state, remember her every word.

I asked about the mosques and their muezzins at the heart of the city that called people to prayer, never to co-ordinated time.

'You have seen Sankoré, our oldest mosque built in the fourteenth century, when you look carefully from the side of your window,' she explained. 'It is just past that sign for Indramine's tailor's shop, the last of over thirty such places which once employed hundreds of workers. The Sankoré mosque school had 25,000 students at its peak. There are two other large mosques and, on Fridays, they are packed with the devout. All are inside the medina, which is a mile and a half around and shaped like a giant teardrop. The chants are a cry for what Tombouctou used to be. Djinguereber, the great mosque, is in the west, and Sidi Yahia in the centre. All are forbidden to non-believers.

'The spaces between the mosques are filled with houses and markets. People used to bury their relatives close to their homes and, as the city grew, the burial grounds were absorbed into the network of alleys and streets lined with 333 Sufi saints. The living and the dead, judges, poor and scholars, now exist side by side and, in the tradition of mystical Islam, the divide between them has become blurred.'

One day, I mentioned the heat.

'Desertification from the north is Tombouctou's biggest threat,' she said. 'It is our nemesis. The Sahara with seven million square kilometres of sand attacks every man-made structure, trying to bury it with even greater tenaciousness than the heat. The desert advances several miles each year. Every day, we try to sweep it back from our doorways with brooms. As the desert moved into the town and killed the mango trees which used to grow in every open space, the rainfall gradually reduced. Now, if we get 250 millimetres we are very lucky. It varies greatly from year to year. During the hottest months, from April to June, the heat is fierce, often over forty degrees. This year, we had just a month of rain, mostly while you were asleep.

'The river is our lifeline and gives us and our animals drinking water. Each year, thanks be to Allah, the rains come in the west and create a huge inland delta 500 kilometres long to a point just upstream of Tombouctou and half of that wide. As the floods recede, the land left behind is our breadbasket watered by creeks and lakes. We grow grains and vegetables and look after our cattle and goats.'

Attou leant over me to pick up my plate and I was about to close my eyes the better to drink in her perfume when her blouse shifted and I saw a breast, smooth, firm, with a deep black areola. I looked up into her frank brown eyes.

'I think you must be almost better.'

'My heart sings while I think of you.'

'Let me see how much.' She reached into her top and placed a nipple against my lips. I took it gently into my mouth and worked it with my tongue. Her hand slid beneath my sheets. 'You have certainly grown since the first time I bathed you.'

She raised her skirt to her waist and I saw that she was naked. This was a planned event. With deft movements, she pulled the bedcover back and was astride me. I thought I would burst.

'Now,' she said deliberately, an unashamed woman in control, 'I don't want you to move any more than you have to. Remember, you are a sick, old man. I will do all the work and orchestrate my pleasure if that doesn't embarrass you. It has been a long time for me.' And, then, almost as an afterthought, 'I hope that you will enjoy it, too.'

With great confidence and freedom, Attou satisfied herself. She was dedicated to the task in hand, a primal and personal indulgence that brooked no diversion. Her first release rose from deep inside the earth and the drawn-out sound spilled wantonly through the window and into the dusty street. Surely no one could have any doubt that this was a woman out of momentary control? Or that her husband was at work with his books and not at home?

As she sat on me, sated, and with the largest of smiles, she noticed my concern.

'I know, I know,' she said, 'you are worried about Nianankoro, my husband of fifty years, and the way you have repaid his kindness to you.

'Let me tell you that I have been dreaming about doing this from the first time I took you in my hands and washed you. My sexual relations with Nianankoro ended many years ago. I will not speak of it to him and he will never ask. He is my greatest friend and I would do anything for him and would never hurt him.

'What we have done was my choice. I suspected that left to you, you would have held back. But, I must tell you, that I hope you will allow me to come again tomorrow. Is that the right word?'

'Please come again tomorrow,' I managed.

Imagining something is better than remembering. She did come, every day, and it became part of my routine except that she encouraged me to many different positions and displays of energetic enthusiasm always ending in her tsunami that kept no secrets from the world outside.

---

1 Nianankoro used the city's Malian pronunciation.
2 The Sahel is a vast, semi-desert region that stretches across West Africa and is home to numerous al-Qaeda and Islamic State-aligned groups all sharing a belief in extreme Islamic ideology and which have become known for their brutality: massacring entire villages and using rape as a weapon of war. Islamic State moves fast on motorbikes and pick-up trucks. Nusrat al-Islam, formed out of AGIM and smaller groups like Ansar Dine, Katiba Macina and Al Mourabitoun and Ansar ul Islam in Burkina Faso.
3 It is Sidi and Yéyé who travel in the night. Alas, the angels of hell. The Tuaregs are not our masters. Beauty … good looks. Slavery is a bad thing. The dust in December …

2. FREEDOM OF THE STREETS

The argent streets o' the City, imaging
The soft inversion of her tremulous Domes.
Her gardens frequent with the stately Palm,
Her Pagods hung with music of sweet bells.
Her obelisks of ranged Chrysolite,
Minarets and towers?

Tennyson, *Timbuctoo*

Little mitigates the initial disappointment of Timbuktu. Authors line up to echo each other's dismay. From afar, in 1894, Felix Dubois saw the city laid out on the horizon 'with the majesty of a queen … the city of imagination … of European legend.'[1] The son of a famous chef from Provence who spent twenty years cooking for the Kaiser and who wrote best-selling cookbooks, Dubois arrived as a reporter to investigate the siren city recently captured by Major Joseph-Jacques-Césaire Joffre. On the sandy approaches, Dubois saw bones and carcasses strewn among wild animals, 'the remains of camels, horses, and donkeys that have fallen down and died in the last stages of the journey'. And then, his disillusionment – 'these ruins, this rubbish, this wreck of a town. Is this the secret of Timbuktu?'

Dubois followed the same Joffre who would save France from the massed German armies on the Marne in 1914. Ever the military man, Joffre spared not a word in the book of his West African campaign to describe the town he had freed from the Tuareg.[2] In 1879, French Sudan's governor, Louise Faidherbe, proclaimed that the territory encompassing the Senegal and Niger rivers would be the 'foundations of a new India' that would stretch as far as the Red Sea. The French occupied Bamako, then a bustling slave-trading *entrepôt*, in 1883. Ten years later, after a brutal desert march of 500 miles in forty-nine days, Joffre's column entered Timbuktu, built a fort and ushered in the French colonial era in the Malian desert. One of the paradoxes of modern warfare is that, apart from two skirmishes with badly armed desert nomads, Joffre, as well as many of his WWI German opponents, died without actually experiencing fighting at first-hand.

What had changed by modern times? Soon after the turn of this century, American explorer Kira Salak paddled alone along most of the Niger from its source to the holy city, often at risk of rape and death, and could not hide her disappointment when she arrived.[3]

'Timbuktu is the world's greatest anti-climax,' she declared. 'It is hard to believe that this spread of uninspiring adobe houses, the slipshod latticework of garbage-strewn streets and crumbling dwellings, was once the height of worldly sophistication and knowledge. The "gateway to the Sahara", the "pearl of the desert", is nothing now but a haggard outpost in a plain of scrub brush and sand. After having such a journey to get here, I feel as if I am the butt of a great joke.'

Rik Antonson, in Timbuktu for a haircut the year after the jihadis fled in 2012, announced that the city would be dismissed today if it weren't for its symbolism.[4] 'No sense of its legendary past remains in the timeworn rubbish tip of today … Timbuktu's mystique is only powerful until you arrive … I would like to pretend that it is different, but it isn't. Nothing prepares the naïve visitor for the absence of intrigue.'

The principal factor behind Timbuktu's decline from its status of capital of the Sahara to its present abject condition was the closing by the Europeans of the open slave market with its connections to the coast. But the surrounding Sahara, which started out as a Negro homeland, is still a Negro country.

I was taking a first walk with Nianankoro as my guide, faces covered, encircled from head to foot in none-too-clean white jellabas, just two old men out for a gentle stroll and sharing stories as they dodged the narrow, shallow sewers that ran down the centre of every sandy street. It was mid-morning and the heat had climbed to near intolerable. All around, amid the noise and the squalor, was a jumble of shabby concrete-block buildings and exhaust-spewing motorcycles in a city that did not get its first petrol pump until the mid-1970s. Billboards advertised *Coca-Cola* and pay-as-you-go cell phones, shoppers in jeans and T-shirts browsed the streetwear in *Almadou Dicko's Harlem Shop* and the *Victoria Emporium* with their *Pret-à-Porter Fashions*.

Our back-street shortcuts were filled with animals and their waste. Sheep, goats, cattle and chickens picked at sparse vegetation and scraps thrown without care. Boys wore Manchester United and Real Madrid strips rather than the red, green and gold of Mali. We moved north through grit alleys crisscrossed by tangles of phone wire, past teetering two- and three-storey structures of mud brick and limestone until we gained the tumbledown walls of the frail town which were half-swallowed by the greedy sand seas.

'I thought you would like to see this place,' said Nianankoro, 'because it is here that you came to the city with Lahcen and Icho. This is the start of the *Abaradiou*, the caravan suburb. One must imagine the biggest event of the year in the old days when the salt caravans trudged in, thousands of camels strong, from the mines in the desert. The animals were watered at large pools over there. Berbers and Tuareg who crossed the desert to trade also kept their animals here. We carried you in a donkey cart to my house.'

He pointed to a horizon of monotonous low dunes with many of their hollows covered by dwarf scrubby palms, mimosas and acacias, all a pale, dusty anaemic green, with trivial branches and leaves that gave grudging shade. Handfuls of weakened pack animals lazily chewed the miserable camel grass and thorns near the few dark tents. These homes, always the property of the women, were woven out of goats' hair and slouched in small family groups.

I recalled my long trip across the Sahara. Despite its eventual tragedy, the allure was the simplicity of desert life. Our small party carried all that we needed on our camels; there was no space for luxuries. It was the same with the few nomads we met, bringing with them the odours of sour milk and uncured leather. All they owned, apart from their camels, donkeys, goats and sheep, were a few cups and bowls, a rug, a linen *shesh*, a burnoose to sleep in, a saddle strewn with bags, a camel-stick, tea to flavour the water, flour, dried vegetables, dates, a silver southern cross to navigate, needle and thread, home-made ropes and hobbles, a French or American rifle and a *khanjit*, the Berber dagger.

The collection exemplified Berber freedom, their chosen way, their every-day pursuit of life. The ancient Arabs, comparable to the Kurds, Turks and others, 'chose desert life because they saw in urban settlement shame and shortcomings ... the knowledge among them (*dhawu al-ma'rifa*) declared that the desert was more healthy and more conducive to a strong, salubrious life'.[5]

'I know Taoudenni where the salt comes from,' I said. 'I was told that it is the hottest region on the planet, just over 400 miles and a week or so from here. It certainly felt like that.'

'Nowadays, the salt comes by truck rather than by camel,' mused Nianankoro. Taoudenni was still a feared place full of evil *djnoun* where the white gold was dug from the bottom of an ancient lake and cut into slabs for transportation. The mine crept across the dry bed stripping wealth as it went.

We walked back by way of the *Monument of Peace* where a roundabout also fronts the desert. In 1996, the last rebels of the Tuareg uprising that had devastated the north for half a decade surrendered thousands of Kalashnikov rifles. A patchwork of interlocking brick arches displayed colourful murals of Malian government and Tuareg soldiers shaking hands. Inside was a surreal altar to reconciliation on which children played. Weapons were buried in a pedestal with dozens of rusted and twisted barrels sticking through the concrete.

For the next few days, I rested in my room, my first excursion showing me how much more time I needed to recover. I fell into the rhythm of a community which used the sun as a clock. An hour before dawn, muezzin announced the *Fadjr* devotion when the morning light poked across the full width of the sky. The faithful washed the sleep from their eyes. On every street corner, women loaded the communal beehive ovens with flat rounds of dough, scenting the air with wood smoke and baking bread. The neighbourhood water pumps were unlocked for one hour. I could hear the donkeys pulling wagons. Sheep and goats grazed after release from overnight pens made of sticks and string and car fan belts. After midday, people went home for the *Dhuhr* prayer, to eat and then to sleep protected from the brutal heat. At *Asr*, with the sun turning orange and an object's shadow matching its own length, work began again until *Maghrib*, when the red light left the sky in the west. In the cooling evening, those without chores gossiped with friends, drank tea, made music, played games and talked politics and poetry until *Isha*, halfway between sunset and sunrise, when they would prepare for bed.

I felt ready to check my travel bag, delivered undisturbed from the desert. It lay carelessly half-hidden by the large chest in my room. It was a hard decision for me to hold it again. I had not seen Asso die painfully of viper venom, but his young son, Icho, told me in detail what he and Lahcen, his grandfather, had found. I could easily imagine the scene for that was how my own brother had died in front of me among French dunes almost seventy years before. For most of the remainder of the journey after the death, Lahcen was broken, monosyllabic. Icho became a man and slipped easily into decision-making. I could not help, but swayed between life and death tethered to my saddle. After, perhaps, two days, I realised that I still grasped a thin strip of snake meat, hardened in the sun, and this with water was all that had kept me alive. It was the same snake that had killed Asso.

My Berber companions had been true to me. My passports, cash, computer and few books were all present and untouched. Lahcen had not taken any money towards the 20,000 dollars agreed for the journey. My few clothes were scoured by the desert and not worth keeping, but there was, at least, a pair of trainers. Those stained clothes I had been wearing on arrival in Timbuktu, along with my Michelin-tyre sandals, had been burned. Atop everything, to my great surprise, was a meteorite the size of a tennis ball, one of the trio found near Asso's body. It was a generous and unnecessary gesture by my erstwhile companions.

The laptop fired up without complaint, something of a first for Microsoft. I was able quickly to enter my cloud storage and untraceable email accounts. Nothing was untoward. The storage had been accessed several times and my book telling of my journey downloaded by my publishers. There were no alerts from my credit card holders so this route for me to receive cash from holes-in-the-wall still functioned.

Attou visited me religiously every day after *Asr* with dinner and for sex, but at no other time. One evening, I woke with a start and found her already at work. A memory dripped into sharper focus from the time of my illness. I looked up at her and said, 'Garp'.

She smiled, ever in control. 'I see you have read the book.[6] I hope you enjoyed it.'

In the story, Garp's mother, a nurse, happily unmarried, decided to have a child with a dying American air force turret gunner. As he lay in his hospital bed, largely detached from the world, his main attribute was his frequent erections followed by copious ejaculations. His only uttering was 'Garp'. One time, Garp's mother straddled him and conceived her child. 'Garp' seemed the appropriate name for the baby. If it had been a woman on the bed, it would have been rape, but in reverse that was not how the world thought. I realised that Attou had used me several times before I regained consciousness, but had kept this secret.

I wanted to visit the safeguarded homes of the early European explorers who had reached Timbuktu and asked her to come with me. She declined with a sad shake of the head. 'It would not be seemly,' she said.

As if in explanation, she began to talk of Timbuktu's radio station, *Radio Communal Bouctou*. 'In the days before *Ansar Dine* and the jihadis, I would stay at home and listen as they strived to reflect the city's different cultures,' she said. 'For instance, news was in Arabic, Songhai, Tamashek and Hausa. The programme makers went into about fifty of the villages close along the Niger and recorded traditional music. When the jihadis took over, they wrecked this archive and all we heard, day after day, was from a USB stick containing the *Qur'an*. That's all they were allowed to play. It was another pleasure lost.'

Attou said that I could go out alone if I was careful and did not speak English or I could ask Nianankoro to escort me as long as I was back, she stressed, for when she brought my evening meal. As for your explorers, Attou said, you can find their books on a shelf downstairs.

'Be careful of the European conceit,' she added. 'When the Muslims came they offered salvation. You would think that people and places did not exist until some English or Frenchman found them and mapped them for their government. The British saw themselves as bringing good government to the natives; the French knew they offered a higher civilisation. Exploration is a Euro-centric pastime not usually for the Arabs, Negroes, or even the Chinese or Japanese unless for local trade. After all, the earliest travellers were moving along routes that African traders had trodden for centuries and visiting ancient cities and states that were proud of their culture. For the French and British, this was all a pretext to claim African countries for their commercial opportunities whatever the indigenous people felt.'

There was a flash of anger, the glimpse of a racial divide without a comfortable bridge. I felt our bond loosen a little.

'The connection between imperialism and exploration is explicit,' she declared, warming to her view. 'Within a generation, almost the whole of Africa was divided between the powers of Europe. Having populated their American colonies with free labour, they hid behind a philanthropic concern to extinguish the slave trade. Then they insisted on the right to protect their uninvited missionaries who tried to eradicate centuries of belief that was rooted in the earth or in Allah, God be praised.

'But you know,' she rounded on me, 'it was really all about greed and the intense rivalry between your superior nations, their desire for gain and the fear of each other stealing an advantage. Their sense of moral superiority, their self-justification as civilising nations, makes me sick.'

Perhaps it was not the best time, but I reached into my bag and took out the meteorite. Attou's eyes glittered. 'Treasures are widely believed to be governed by spells and curses,' she declared. 'Those brave and gullible enough to follow professional hunters must steel themselves to face ancient curses, monsters, death-dealing automata and lethal trapdoors.'

'That's all truer than you can know, Attou,' I said. 'I do not believe you would accept payment for looking after me at Lahcen's request,' I said, 'but I hope you will accept this treasure as a gift. It was from the desert and, before that, probably from Mars. You and Nianankoro will know better than me how to realise and to use its value.'

Attou took the rock without hesitation and nodded her head. It was a simple transaction, but its element of recompense further slipped our knot.

Ill-informed Europeans embarked, one after the other, for an African El Dorado that no longer existed. There were only two ways to get to Timbuktu, neither promising. By trying to cross the great ocean of sand from the north or by braving the malarial jungles of West Africa and then travelling down the Niger, a traveller risked enslavement, incurable disease or death. In a little over a week, I devoured the stories of the disappointed men who sought to reach the remote and mysterious Timbuktu after Leo Africanus in 1526: Mungo Park, 1795 and 1805; Robert Adams, 1813; Dixon Denham, 1822; Gordon Laing, 1825, Hugh Clapperton, 1825; Rene-Auguste Caillié, 1827; Richard and John Lander, 1830; Heinrich Barth, 1850; and Paul Flatters, 1880.[7] Scarcely known to me at the time, in just a few weeks, it was Gordon Laing who was to reach forward almost two hundred years and to change my life.

There is small pleasure in sightseeing in Timbuktu, but I set about it over the next few days, well swathed and with quiet, if lonely, determination. Little for sale on the street recognised tourists or the need for refreshment. I bought off-warm bottles of re-filled *Coca-Cola* from street vendors; sometimes there were mangoes for a few pennies to be eaten under sparse shade trees. Residents set pots of still-cooking food outside their homes or used a table to promote their desultory fried fish, individual cigarettes and old tools. Bread was stacked in front of the flat-sided mud house where it was baked. Through almost every awning, fifty-four-inch, flat-screen plasma televisions with a hundred satellite channels flickered in darkened rooms. It was a sign that few within read books.

I wanted first to find the legendary well of Bouctou. About 1100, a clan of Tuaregs made their annual summer migration 150 miles from the bleak area of the salt mines to a grassy plain beside the Niger. In Biblical repetition and in turn, a plague of mosquitoes and sand flies, an infestation of toads and the stench of decaying marsh grass made their usual encampment intolerable. They moved with their livestock to a more congenial spot a few miles north on a tributary which flooded in season. A shallow well provided clean, sweet water. When the nomads migrated north in September, they left their heavy baggage in the care of a local Tuareg woman they called *Bouctou* – 'the one with the big belly button' – and each year they returned to *Tin-bouctou*, the well of Buktou. Today, the well has nothing to celebrate it. A hand-held pulley on two rough poles with a leather bucket is hidden by a tamarind bush behind the Sidi Yahia Mosque.

That is the story, but Nianankoro firmly disabused me. There probably was a person called Buktou, he said, however, *Tin* was not a well but signified the possessive noun in the third person. I found the water less than sweet, swimming with life and good only for animals.

Whatever the founding story, said Nianankoro one morning, by 1375, Timbuktu appeared on a European map drawn by a Majorcan cartographer in an atlas made for Charles V of France. Less than one hundred years later, Sunni Ali, a warlord and animist opposed to Islam, marched from Gao in the east, captured the city, and 'killed so many human beings that only God most high could count them' before he 'put the city to flame'.

Ali built a kingdom, the Songhai Empire, Nianankoro's forebears, that stretched for 2,000 miles along the Niger.

Another day, I looked for vestiges of the old explorers. The greatest, Leo Africanus, was nowhere to be found. Africanus, Hassan Mohammed Al Wazzan Al Zayati, was a sixteen-year-old student from a black aristocratic Muslim family of Granada who settled in Fez after the expulsion of the Moors from Spain. In his book on his great African explorations, he described the markets in Timbuktu as overflowing with goods from across the world, weaver's shops filled with textiles from Europe, and a large limestone palace inhabited by the king who had gilded sceptres and many plates of gold, some weighing 1,300 pounds.

Faith and education have always provided rivers of travel. In the days of Africanus, devotees travelled to learn at the feet of their hosts. Today, most people travel to learn the rituals of other religions rather than to commit to their underlying beliefs. They want to see the holy sites.

Africanus was astonished by the scholarship that he encountered. About one quarter of Timbuktu's population of 100,000 were students who came from as far as the Arabian Peninsula to learn from the Songhai Empire's masters of law, literature and science. The University of Sankoré, a loose affiliation of homes and mosques, evolved into the most prestigious of the city's 180 educational establishments.

The leading Djinguereber Mosque does not tower physically today as it did historically when Africanus wrote that it was a 'most stately temple'. It is not much over twice the height of the surrounding buildings in the Place de l'Indépendence, a square off the Boulevard Askia Mohammed which curves around the west of the town and acts as a main thoroughfare. The mosque's modest side entrance with metal-studded wooden door lies around the corner from a large sand-earthen market place with tumbledown stalls, cast-off goods, aged food tins, open spice sacks, dried fish, hand scales and coughing vehicles. It was difficult to imagine that this mosque had once been a vast house of worship and a centre of learning and pilgrimage filled every hour with fervent adherents and devout scholars. I went inside, unrecognised as a non-believer, and plodded bare-foot along undecorated, mud corridors where the heat was a little dissipated and wood-decorated privacy hollows waited for penitents. I washed and passed into an inner court with rows of pillars where I joined a few faithful at prayer, receiving a critical look for my late arrival.

Nianankoro had explained that there was no legal entity called the 'mosque' in Islamic countries to set beside the various Western churches, nor is there any human institution whose role it is to confer 'holy orders' on its members; those Muslims who have religious authority, the *ulama*, 'those with knowledge', possess it directly from God. Those who take on the function of the *imam*, 'the one who stands in front', so leading the congregation in prayer, are self-appointed to this role.[8]

'You must understand,' he said, firmly, 'that Islam has never incorporated itself as a legal person or a subject institution, a fact that has enormous political repercussions. Like the Chinese Communist Party, Islam aims to control the state without being its subject.'

In one corner of the square, so nondescript as to be easily missed with unprotected mud bricks above the door, lies one of the most powerful offices in the city, its principal *hawala* banker. *Hawala*, 'trust' or 'change', may be strange to a European who is captive to large and avaricious international banks. Indeed, if you are not part of a Muslim community or a security agency then you may well not have heard of this way of money transfer. *Hawala* operates parallel to, but outside of, the traditional Western system. It originated in India in the eighth century and was a major component of trade between Muslims and Arabs on the Silk Road to China (where it is known as *fei qian* or 'flying money'). In the USA, India (where it is known as *Hundi*, based on 'chit', a word which is still used in English to signify an IOU), Pakistan and parts of Western Europe, *hawala* is seen as facilitating money laundering, drug trafficking, tax evasion, and the anonymous movement of wealth and can be illegal. The American government suspected al-Qaeda of using *hawala* to fund the 9/11 terrorist attacks on the World Trade Towers in New York. The system facilitated the payment of ransoms to Somali pirates. However, in Afghanistan, it is still used by NGOs for the delivery of emergency relief. It was also the financial system used in 2012 after the chaos when Tuareg and jihadist forces captured Timbuktu and much of northern Mali and left the country without an official money transfer system for many months.

For me, *hawala* was a means of transferring money across borders, avoiding traces, taxes, the need to bribe officials, or to pay high bank fees.

Moneychangers, *hawaladar*, received my cash in the UK, no questions asked, and corresponded with an *hawaladar* in another country who would dispense the money when asked. Minimal fees and commissions – about one per cent – were deducted and the exchange was effected at a much better rate than a megabank would offer with its rich employees. I went inside and, with the use only of a personal code, enabled 20,000 dollars of untraceable money to be made available in Marrakech to Lahcen or his representative.

Nearby, I stood before ruins on top of a small rise, which a sign said used to house a slaughterhouse. Some of the brick had been cannibalised from a previous building, Nianankoro told me, a palace erected by the King of Mali in the fourteenth century.

In 1824, the Geographical Society of Paris offered a reward with subscriptions of 10,000 francs and a gold medal valued at 2,000 francs to the first European who visited Timbuktu and returned to tell the story. This sparked a race to glory in which many eccentric men died of disease and the desert. In particular, there was government-backed competition between the French and British which led to ignorant risk and, probably, skulduggery. At stake, was a rumoured gold-laden empire to rival British India.

On the way back to Sankoré, there are three buildings, crumbling on the outside at least, which housed the earliest European explorers to reach the city. The nearest to Djinguereber was once briefly home to the Scot, Major Gordon Laing. I found the corner house by a dusty *Mission Culturelle* plaque placed in 1902 and stuck to the middle of a mud-brick wall below two windows of carved wood. The curved Moorish door was lodged open. Inside was silent and empty, no furniture, no evidence of occupation and nothing in the way of formal exhibits.

Laing was the first European acknowledged to have reached Timbuktu. I offer a brief account of his journey because of the great importance his expedition shortly meant to me. Laing left Tripoli in 1825 having married Emma, the daughter of the British consul, Hanmer Warrington, in bizarre fashion two days before his departure. Laing travelled 2,650 miles in thirteen months to the city, via Ghadames, In Salah and Sidi el Muktar. He sent back occasional letters, maps and drawings, which became shorter and infrequent with distance. On the way, his caravan was befriended as a subterfuge, then attacked at night by Tuaregs. Laing reported twenty-four wounds, including eighteen that were 'exceedingly severe': five sabre cuts to his crown with 'much bone cut away', a fractured jawbone with divided ear, a musket ball in the hip, five slices to his right arm and wrist which was three-quarters severed.

Near death, Laing arrived in Timbuktu in August 1826 and, one suspects, had mixed feelings about what had become a sordid and diminished slaving post and a simple salt trading river mart filled with mud-walled homes in the middle of a barren desert. He stayed for just five weeks and wrote one brief and cryptic letter to Warrington, his father-in-law in Tripoli, despatched the day before leaving. Laing stated simply that the great capital of central Africa had met his expectations in every respect except size and promised to write more fully. He had spent his few weeks searching the 'abundant' records of the town, acquiring information 'of every kind', and filling a journal with observations which he did not share, but hoped to publish later. Although warned, Laing travelled north towards Arawan on a roundabout route designed to avoid trouble. He was part of a caravan under the protection of Sheikh Ahmadu Labeida, a religious fanatic. Two days later, Laing was strangled with his own turban and decapitated by Labeida and an Arab boy companion was murdered. All valuable articles were stolen, but everything of a useless nature, like paper, was torn and thrown to the wind. The bodies were left under a tree.

Laing's great rival was French explorer René-Auguste Caillié and his home in Timbuktu was literally just around the corner from Laing when he arrived in the following year. Today, the house, number 54, with plaques above and to the right, was occupied and the residents were not greatly interested in visitors. Few men could ever have craved more for fame with ‹desperate and passionate longing› than this pair of competitors.[9]

Caillié started his trip to Timbuktu in April 1827 from the West African coast in a caravan. He was disguised as an Egyptian Arab after studying Arabic and Islam for several years, 'much to the chagrin of proper European explorers of the era'. He reached Timbuktu after a year of deprivation, including a halt for five months with scurvy, having inspected the site of Laing's murder just before arrival.

To be expected, Caillié was unimpressed with Timbuktu. 'This extraordinary city created solely for the wants of commerce and destitute of every resource except what its accidental position as a place of exchange affords.' He stayed only two weeks before returning to France by way of Morocco. He published three volumes about his travels and was awarded the Geographical Society of Paris's prize. The Germans, however, thought the book lacked authority; the British claimed it was a fake.

I rather rushed my visit to the third home, that of German geographer Heinrich Barth. This was a shame as it was well laid out. I had just paid my entry fee when I realised that I might be late for dinner and would find Attou unsympathetic. Barth, by far the most successful of the early European explorers, also found the city an anti-climax. He stayed for six months even though he was dismayed to find smoking was a capital offence. He did discover and study a copy of the *Tariq al-Sudan*, the prized complete history of the Songhai Empire written in 1653 by the scholar Ahmed Baba. Barth left Tripoli with two other explorers in 1850, both of whom soon died. He reached Timbuktu alone in 1853. He was feared dead as he did not return till two years later when he worked on five volumes of his experiences.

There was a direct back route from Barth's house to the Sankoré Mosque and I hurried along at a pace suited to my seniority. At the corner of an alley leading left to the Grand Marché, my eye caught a display of the recent arrival of a Malian French language newspaper printed in Bamako, the capital. In residual fear of *Ansar Dine* and their death threats for reproductions of the human face, portraits were seldom seen in local productions. The sight of a picture still shocked. The shock was even greater when I recognised the front-page picture as one wrongly attributed to me and used for publicity on the cover of a social history book, *Sound of Hunger*, that I wrote and which was published a few years before in London. I bought a copy, walked on a few yards and leant against a wall with an overhanging mango tree while I read.

It was a knees-to-jelly moment as I realised the enormity of the error brought about by my illness. I was probably more vulnerable to discovery at that moment than at any time since I had shipped out from Hull the previous year. During my time in Marrakech and in the desert, I had written a book, *Disappearing*, to shake off my pursuers. The instructions to my publishers were that if I had not made contact for any two-month period, they should print it. I anticipated that, by that time, I would have completed my trek to Timbuktu or have died in the attempt. What never crossed my mind was that I would end up near death for many weeks, but survive. The publishers had done their job and early copies of *Disappearing* were being circulated for review. Readers, angry chasers, distressed governments, would know that I was headed for Timbuktu. I should have been long gone, untraceable and distant. Instead, I was a sitting duck. How stupid can an old man get?

What was my position? At least, the picture was wrong. My true face was not yet identified. My name was given as Chris Heal, one that I had not used since I left England. I had plenty more passports in my bag, but not one for Heal as it had long been destroyed. My money supply was secure.

What the story announced was that Heal was wanted on suspicion of involvement in the assassinations of Jean-Claude Juncker, president of the European Commission, and his right-hand man, Martyn 'the Monster' Selmayr, the Commission's secretary general. Both had been shot dead with single bullets to the head outside a Brussels champagne bar the previous year. Their 'professional' killer had never been found. Early copies of *Disappearing* had persuaded Belgian police that I knew a great deal about the deaths. From information in my book, a 9 mm Russian semi-automatic Makarov pistol, the same as the murder weapon, and supposedly with my fingerprints, had been found buried in a field at the 1815 site of the Battle of Waterloo. One couldn't make it up, really!

The Secretariat of the European Commission accused Heal of using the book to taunt the police. An Assistant Chief Constable in British Counter-Terrorism claimed that an 'amoral mass murderer' was on the loose. 'This man is flawed, but calculating and deliberate. We should make sure we stop him dead in his tracks.' French peacekeepers in Timbuktu had been authorised to make an early capture. Belgian police and EU security personnel were expected in the city imminently.

Whatever the truth of Juncker's death, I found it sickening that the EU had set about sanctifying this dreadful bureaucrat with all of the failures of his time in office: the loss of the United Kingdom and the unfriendly threats and retaliation; over-regulation; limits to free movement of workers; failure to open the services market; the handling of the crisis over Greece, Cyprus and Italy; the illegal appointment of Selmayr; closet-politicisation; poor foreign relations with the US, Switzerland and Turkey; weakness towards Russia over Georgia and the Baltics; Germany's energy policy breaches; and, especially, a failure to stand up to Merkel over her self-imposed migrant crisis.

I supposed that there was no obvious reason for Attou to associate me with Heal other than, of course, she knew of no other Europeans in Timbuktu who freely admitted to being on the run. I arrived home, sweltering, shaken and generally not in the best condition. Attou accosted me as soon as I had crossed the threshold. She showed no interest in the newspaper I clutched.

'You're late,' she shouted as if at a slave. She made no attempt to hide her rage. 'How dare you treat me like this.' Attou sulked away into a darkened downstairs recess. There was no time to explain or to protest innocence. I realised that the problem was not the newspaper or the prepared but uneaten food. I had affronted her dignity by not being available for sex when she demanded it.

To be fair, it was the first time I had let her down. A man of seventy-plus years, I climbed the stairs like a naughty little boy, sent to bed without any dinner.

Outside, people with guns were looking for me.

1 Dubois, *Mysterious*.
2 Joffre, *March*.
3 Salak, *Cruellest Journey*.
4 Antonson, *Haircut*.
5 Al-Masudi, *Muruji al-dhahab* in Webb, *Imagining the Arabs*.
6 Irving, *World According to Garp*.
7 Adams, *Narrative*. Africanus, *History and Description*; Barth, *Travels*; Caillié, *Travels*; Clapperton and Denham, *Travels and Discoveries*; Flatters, *Mission*; Joffre, *March*; Laing, *Travels*; Landers, *Niger Journal*; Park, *Travels*, and several compendia including Gardner, *Quest*.
8 Scruton, *West and the Rest*.
9 Gardner, *Quest*.

3. TRUE WEALTH

And the great mosque which once combined
such gallantry and worship –
Withered and gone its courts and vast concourses.

Stetkevych, *Zephyrs of Najid*; Abu Nuwas (of Basra)

Nianankoro came to my room for coffee the next morning as if there was nothing untoward. From his perspective, I thought that was likely the case. Attou had not yet shared any of her displeasure with me, but, then, they did sleep apart and there was still time. The story of the search in the French-language newspaper had either not reached him or he did not associate it with me. He was a solitary man of books, trusting by nature. When we walked together, Nianankoro engaged freely, offering information. His occasional touches of humour leant towards irony. Well known in the street, people acknowledged him with an 'As-salāmu 'alaykum', but always with the respect due to an intellectual rather than a friend. He was not aloof, more preoccupied and independent, not easily approached and, as a result, heard little gossip.

Nianankoro asked if I would like to go with him that day to see his books. His library was less than five minutes, close to but separate from the Ahmed Baba Institute. As we strolled, Nianankoro spoke with admiration about Ahmed Baba al-Musufi, al-Tinbukti, the man whom Attou had told me was banished along with other intellectuals after resistance to the invasion of Judar Pasha. He was nicknamed al-*Sudani*, 'The Black One', for his eye shadow and sombre clothes. He composed a startling sixty astronomical treaties and religious texts for the University of Sankoré's library. The most famous manuscript today, *Ahmed Baba Answers A Moroccan's Questions About Slavery*, 'The Ladders of Ascent', argued that freedom is a fundamental right of human beings, except under rare conditions governed by Islamic law. The scholar said that God ordered that 'slaves must be treated with humanity, whether they are black or not'.

'One must pity their sad luck and spare them bad treatment,' he wrote.

'Just the fact of becoming an owner of another person bruises the heart because servitude is inseparable from the idea of violence and domination, especially when it relates to a slave taken far away from his country.'

In another treatise, Baba proposed methods of conflict resolution, arguing for dialogue, forgiveness and resolution.[1] This work led Nianankoro to believe that Baba was a *jihadi* in the original and best sense of the word: one who struggles against evil ideas, desire and personal anger and subjugates them to reason and obedience to God's commands.[2]

We turned a corner in a nondescript alley and stopped before an unmarked wooden door. Nianankoro used two large keys, each double-locking, and we entered a homely and efficient work area with two computers and half a dozen modern worktables. Several hand-written and illustrated books were laid about under study and comparison. He busied himself with coffee and I sat in an easy chair and looked about.

'You are wondering where my library is?'

I nodded.

I will show you after I have explained some things to you. It is important for me that you understand how much our manuscripts mean to us here in Tombouctou ... and to me personally. I will not give you a full history lesson, but enough, I hope, to capture your imagination and respect.'

When the slave-turned scholar Leo Africanus arrived here in 1506, he compared Tombouctou to El Dorado. West Africa's great Songhai Empire was home to universities, extensive libraries, Africa's largest and grandest mosque, and a population of more than 50,000 people. The city thrived off its remote but convenient location, the meeting point between the great Saharan caravan routes and the Niger River. Salt, painstakingly harvested from the desert, was traded for the gold, ivory and slaves that came from the south.

However, Africanus declared that the sale of manuscripts from Tombouctou was 'more profitable than any other goods' as he observed the flourishing trade in Tombouctou's markets. The books were made of rag-based paper sold by traders who crossed the desert from Morocco, Tunisia, Libya and Algeria. By the end of the twelfth century, Fez had 472 paper mills and was exporting south and north to Majorca and

Andalusia. Superior Italian paper soon penetrated the Maghreb, the land to the west of Egypt. By the time Africanus reached Tombouctou, most paper was being imported from Venice. Craftsmen extracted ink and dyes from desert plants and minerals and made covers from the skins of goats and sheep. Binding, however, was unknown, so loose, unnumbered folios were enclosed inside leather covers tied shut with ribbons or strings.[3] Learning and culture reached a zenith of sophistication during the Songhai Empire until its end in 1591 with the raid of Judar Pasha, a fall from which the city would never recover.

The manuscripts ranged from small fragments of paper to books and treatises running to several hundred pages. Manuscripts were imported from the Middle East and North Africa from the fourteenth to the nineteenth centuries, as well as being written and copied in the region. The thirst for works spread beyond the Qur'an to the Hadith, pronouncements of the Prophet Mohammed compiled by his companions; Sufism, the moderate and mystical form of Islam; the Maliki school of jurisprudence, the dominant legal system centred at the Great Mosque at Kairouan in Tunisia; and the Islamic sciences, including astronomy, mathematics and grammar. There were also numerous works written in the region: poetry, commentaries and historical chronicles as well as correspondence, contracts and marginal notes and jottings.

In a thriving cottage industry, scribes made elaborate facsimiles of the imported volumes for the libraries of professors and wealthy patrons. Working side by side in ateliers in the alleys of Tombouctou, the most prolific copied works at the rate of one every two months, writing an average of 150 lines of calligraphy each day, receiving their payments in gold nuggets or dust. These scribes employed proof-readers who poured over every Arabic character. A colophon, Greek for 'finishing touch', at the end of each work recorded a manuscript's start and completion date, the place where the manuscript was written, and the names of the scribe, proof-reader, and vocaliser, a third craftsman who inked the short vowel sounds that are not usually represented in Arabic script. The patron often received a mention. The scribes also produced so-called ajami manuscripts, transliterating into classical Arabic script a multitude of local languages, Tuareg, Tamashek, Fulani, Hausa, Bambara and Soninké.

Nianankoro paused to refill our cups. 'Am I boring you yet, *Amkssa*?'

'This is one of the most fascinating stories I have heard. It is also surreal because I am sitting here in a mud house in a dissolute street full of rubbish within, I believe, touching distance of many of the treasures that you talk about.'

'How many manuscripts do you think we are talking about? A rough estimate?'

'You are trying to embarrass me? The total collection over all that time since the sixteenth century, counting all those that have been lost or stolen? Impossible. How about 10,000?'

Nianankoro's eyes twinkled.

'Perhaps, my friend, one hundred times more than that. The most common estimate is 700,000 manuscripts. The Ahmed Baba Centre next door used to store 40,000 manuscripts that were a history of Africans by Africans written in Africa. Not the French, the British, nor the Portuguese, but Africans. There are many private libraries of which mine is, perhaps, the most reticent. When the jihadis took over Tombouctou and threatened our way of life, some 377,000 manuscripts were transferred to more than thirty safe houses around the city and then smuggled to Bamako. Our most prominent librarian family of Haidara had about 5,000 works. Ibn Khaldun, the greatest scholar in the Arab world, argued that there were already too many books in fourteenth-century North Africa. He regarded the profusion of commentaries as an obstacle to scholarship because it would take more than a lifetime to read all that was written on specialist subjects.'[4]

'This all helps explain,' said Nianankoro with a smile, 'why Tombouctou is twinned with Hay-on-Wye in England, the town of many bookstores. I went there with our Mayor in 2007 to help cement the relationship.'

I let out a grunt. 'That sounds like a commercial relationship to Hay's benefit rather than a true symbiosis. Most of the stock in Hay is modern and second-hand whereas what you are talking about here is fabulous. The overall value must be immense'.

'You are right, of course. Most of our "stock" is beyond price to the librarians, but not for the obvious financial reasons. It is foremost a matter of heritage. After the rape of Judar Pasha, many manuscripts were taken north to Morocco. However, the culture was not driven completely underground; it re-flourished during the eighteenth century only to vanish during seventy years of French colonisation.

'It was not until Joffre, the French general, took Tombouctou from the Tuareg that our books were rediscovered by Europeans. The journalist Dubois followed Joffre and it was his great scoop to learn about our manuscripts and he told his discovery in a way that changed Tombouctou from the tragic to the mysterious. As the French consolidated their control, the days of book exchange ended. Visiting scholars bought some manuscripts and soldiers stole others which they shipped in four chests to France where they languished in a colonial supply depot. They were then given to the Bibliothèque Nationale de France in Paris where they remained untouched for many years. Eventually, some were offered for display in government and university collections where they remain today.[5]

'To stop the theft, people hid their manuscripts all over Mali. They placed them inside leather bags and buried them in holes in the courtyards and gardens, stashed them in caves in the desert and sealed the doors of their libraries with mud.

'French became the primary language taught in schools and several generations on Tombouctou grew up without learning to speak Arabic which almost doomed the works to irrelevance.'

Nianankoro offered another coffee, but I excused myself. My recent dysentery still limited my stomach's resilience. Opening his front door, he called to a boy playing football and told him to fetch mint tea. I thought it would be interesting to try to do the same thing in a side street in Paris or London.

'You will by now have guessed, Amkssa, that I have an ulterior motive in asking you here,' he said. 'You may be taken aback by my request; two requests, actually. I need first to explain more about what I meant by "heritage".'

He poured the tea expertly from a great height out of respect for me and continued his history lesson.

You now understand that there were hundreds of thousands of the world's most valuable written sources from the so-called golden age of

Tombouctou. They have been held by experts as Africa's equivalent of the Dead Sea Scrolls or the Anglo-Saxon Chronicle. They also proved that the city and central Africa had a vibrant history: the empires of ancient Ghana, of medieval Mali, of the Songhai, and to the east the galaxy of the Hausa states and Kanem-Bornu by Lake Chad with its king-list stretching back over a thousand years. A free-thinking, sophisticated society had thrived in the Southern Sahara at a time when much of Europe was mired in the Middle Ages. According to the Tariq al Fattash, *a history of Tombouctou from the seventeenth century, the city's reputation was so great that when a famed Tunisian professor arrived to become a lecturer at the University of Sankoré, he quickly realised that he didn't qualify and retreated to Fez for fourteen years before he felt able to return.*

There has been precious little understanding or respect shown for Africa in the past.[6] Until our manuscripts were 'discovered' by the French, and long afterwards, Europe's historians and philosophers contended that black Africans were illiterates with no history.

From Immanuel Kant to David Hume, Western intellectuals cited the lack of written works from Africa as proof that the continent was too backward even to have a history. 'Only the whites were civilised,' wrote Hume in 1748. British historian A P Newton said in 1923 that 'Africa has practically no history before the coming of the Europeans since history only begins when men take to writing'. Five years later, Reginald Coupland, a professor at Oxford University, asserted that until the nineteenth century the main body of natives 'had stayed for untold centuries sunk in barbarism where human life was stagnant and the heart of Africa scarcely beating'.

European books from The Heart of Darkness *to* King Solomon's Mines *showed Africans to be brutes without a worthwhile past and therefore could be approached with the might of a white deity. Africa was a blank slate and the 'Scramble for Africa' could begin. We lived through the racial atrocities along the Congo of Leopold from Belgium, in Nama- and Hereroland of Trotha from Germany, the Dutch and the British in the Kalahari ...*

Nianankoro stopped, fervent emotion starting to well over. He poured tea, more to gain time than for the drink.

> *The French advance was a more patchwork affair often led by private traders or military officers who would use any fracas to call up gunboats or military detachments, pushing inland from the centuries-old slave bases in Senegal and the Gulf. Bit by bit, Paris took control of Guinea, Dahomey, Ivory Coast, Upper Voltaire and parts of the Niger Valley.*
>
> *Even in 1963, can you believe it, the British historian Hugh Trevor-Roper wrote that there were 'no ingenious manufactures, no arts, no sciences'. He concluded, 'Perhaps, in the future, there will be some African history to teach, but at present there is none. There is only the history of Europeans in Africa. The rest is darkness.'*
>
> *But, we now know that in the twelfth century, Roger of al-Idrisi wrote that England was a 'considerable island, in shape like an ostrich's head, where are to be found flourishing towns, high mountains, great rivers and plains. The country is fertile, its inhabitants brave, active and enterprising, but a perpetual winter reigns there.' The Arabs knew more about England, than the English knew about us in Africa.*

'I have a feeling, my friend, that we are getting close to the favours you wish of me,' I prompted?

'Yes. It is almost time, but first, I need to mention a delicate matter.'

As with all delicate matters, my heart sank.

'It concerns my wife ... and your relationship with her.'

I had been given a second's warning and knew enough to keep my mouth shut.

'You should know that there is no rancour on my side. Our only daughter was raped and killed walking near here by the Tuareg in 2012. The men were chased but escaped into the desert. This atrocity made a hole in both our hearts, which remains. We were not able to help each other. Our daughter's death drove Attou away from me. The history of this city is like the history of our family: there was closeness and even affection, but death eventually separates everyone from each other. It is only the vividness of memory that keeps the dead alive and we remember our daughter separately and in different ways.

'We have not had, what is the polite word … relations since then. Attou has found satisfaction elsewhere and, I should tell you for your own self-knowledge, this has happened many times although you are probably her most easy capture. In truth, I am now indifferent, pleased only that she has found some happiness.'

He paused and looked at me directly for the first time. 'I could only wish that she did it more quietly, but I think it is her way of letting me know that she is free.'

All that I could do was nod, a poor response given my acquiescence in the face of his hospitality and disarming honesty.

'Don't worry, Amkssa. Attou is an attractive and determined woman. She is used to getting what she wants. She decided that she wanted you.'

Nianankoro paused again, this time for almost a minute, before coming to a decision.

'I will be a little disloyal. Attou will now feel that, in some way, you are her property. You have embraced her arrangements. If you disappoint her now, she will take it as a personal rejection and react badly. You should remember that were your activities, you as a European and a non-Muslim, and she as a married local woman, to become public, you would likely both be stoned to death before you even got to court.

'What I am going to ask you to do will mean that you leave Tombouctou quite soon and suddenly which, I suggest, you need to do anyway. It will be much safer for you. If you accept my argument and my requests, neither of us should tell her that you are leaving. You might even need to continue your … contacts … for a few days as a subterfuge. Have I been clear enough?'

'Very,' I said. 'For what it's worth, I offer you a personal apology.'

While we were discussing my skin, I decided to confide my own immediate problem to him. 'In our flurry of openness, I must ask if you have read anything of me in the newspapers recently?'

Nianankoro admitted that he seldom read newspapers so I shared as much as I thought it safe for him to know and for me to tell him.

It was his turn to nod. 'So, regardless of my favours, you agree you should soon leave the city?'

'Yes. This whole conversation is percipient. However, what is killing me now is the suspense. What is it you want?'

Nianankoro explained that he had been working through his family's library, slowly and with scholarship, for many years. He had kept his work private, especially since *Ansar Dine* had taken to burning manuscripts. Just a handful of old men in Timbuktu knew of his hidden store and his studies. He had found several treasures including a treatise about Islamic jurisprudence from the early twelfth century; a thirteenth-century *Qur'an* written on vellum made from the hide of an antelope; another whole book from the twelfth century, no larger than the palm of a hand, inscribed on fish skin, its intricate Maghrebi script illuminated with droplets of gold leaf. He had also found two particular documents.

One, thought lost, was the journal of Major Alexander Gordon Laing, the first European explorer to reach Timbuktu who, as I knew, had been betrayed, robbed, and murdered after departing the city in 1826. Consul Warrington, Laing's father-in-law, refused to believe the document, known to have existed, had been destroyed. He launched a desperate search for he suspected it contained vital information about the interior which could be used to prop up any British territorial claim.[7] Warrington sent an Arab to Timbuktu to investigate Laing's death and local people freely disclosed what had occurred. The man returned to Tripoli in 1829 and reported that Laing had been warned against joining a caravan to Arawan and so took 'only a few books and trifling things' with him. He left his papers in two parcels sealed with red wax with orders for them to follow him by a safer route. This was thought to have happened, but that the manuscripts had been captured by French agents at Ghadames.

Dubois, when in Timbuktu, claimed that Joffre and the military authorities made great efforts among the leading tribesmen of the town to find Laing's papers. Privately, and under great secrecy, Dubois offered a local agent of the Mossi, a non-Muslim people who had once conquered the city, a large sum of money, but it came to no avail.

'You would like to see the journal?' Nianankoro pointed to one of the tables where two parcels lay. On one, the red wax seal had been lifted and a vellum wrapper laid back to expose a goatskin folder filled with about a hundred loose sheets of varying quality. Each page was covered in the painful, scratchy writing of a man working with his wrong hand and studded with diagrams and side notes as later information was obtained.

'Can I …?'

'Yes, but, of course, be respectful, and put on these cloth gloves. Desert heat and acidic hands are a bad combination.'

I read for about fifteen minutes while Nianankoro watched without comment. Knowing the injuries which Laing had suffered, seeing the volume of material enclosed and its meticulous research, left me in no doubt. I had a deal of expertise in old documents, particularly of this period, from my not-so-distant doctorate. This collection was Laing's lost journal and I said so.

'From a European perspective, this is a most important document,' I added. 'In its detail of Laing's journey and his observations of the Sahara and, particularly, Timbuktu, are, I think unique until the work of the German Barth over twenty years later. That apart, it is quite clear that Laing thought he was dealing with a concerted French conspiracy and it is likely that he died because of French instruction. Of course, the authorities in Paris always strenuously denied any involvement to the extent of giving Laing, the man they may have murdered, a posthumous gold medal.'

'There is one other significance, I hope,' said Nianankoro. 'Significant for me, I mean, and that is that Laing was Scottish. Scotland is a nation looking for its independence as part of the European Union away from the influence of the English. These politics are of no importance here in Tombouctou. Similarly, these observations by a European explorer matter little to us today, far less than works by native Africans written several hundred years earlier.

'I need money to further my work with my library and to keep it safe until it is handed over to the local people. I have no children, only a nephew, to take it on. Attou is not interested and you will understand that she is sometimes profligate and a drain on my capital. I believe that Scottish academics will embrace this work as showing their historic importance as independent pioneers and explorers. I want to sell it, quietly and privately, in Scotland and for the money to arrive here in Tombouctou equally discreetly. I have corresponded with colleagues in Edinburgh University who are knowledgeable about these things. My first request is that I want you to take the journal to Scotland for me as my agent and to get me the money I need without disclosing my identity. It will be our confidential arrangement.'

Nianankoro might as well have said that I owed him and this would part settle my considerable personal debt.

'You are asking more of me than you know,' I said. 'I have a complicated history and will be in danger if I return to Europe. However, before we get to any decision, I suggest you tell me of your second favour.'

Nianankoro said he needed to take me into his library. He moved to a narrow ceiling-high bookcase, touched a concealed button which allowed it swing outwards. Behind was a metal door sporting a combination lock that he dialled and we went inside. The room was large, business-like, air-conditioned, but cocooned. The walls were of metal and their shelves were filled with old manuscripts. The contrast with the cosiness outside and the squalor of the street beyond took my breath. Nianankoro closed the door behind us and moved to a central table.

'Here it is,' he said, 'my second favour. It is an unknown work by Ahmed Baba, a treatise on the treatment of women by Islamic extremists in the early seventeenth century. It is not long. It is written, of course, in Arabic so little of which was translated by Europeans after the fourteenth century.[8] The heyday for such work was in the twelfth century so that even Ibn Khaldun's twelve-volume theoretical treatise on history, the *Muqaddima*, was "discovered" very much later. One of your great modern historians said it was "undoubtedly the greatest work of its kind that has been created by any mind in any time or place".[9] My comments are not really a diversion, but show how much time has been wasted, why I needed to make a translation of Baba's work into French. This is the translation here.

'The reason that I always keep it in this room, apart from its age, is that it is a devastating critique of all of the demeaning arguments put forward by the Islamic extremists of his day and these have only worsened in present times. These counter-arguments will be anathema to the men who captured Tombouctou less than ten years ago. If they learn of the existence of this treatise, they will work to destroy it. There is nothing they fear more than the written word. It will be their fanatical religious duty. In the process, I will die, Attou will die, and it will rekindle *Ansar Dine*'s determination to try again to exterminate Tombouctou's cultural heritage.'

Nianankoro iterated the contents of Baba's denunciation:

Females were not lesser beings in the eye of Allah. They were not the property of their men. Baba denounced the forced wearing of the burka as an unwritten afront before Allah to the identity of womanhood. Men who demanded the costume on the grounds that women were to blame if men were aroused by the site of women's hair or skin were ill-controlled hypocrites. Girls should be encouraged in their education and it was the duty of parents and of the faithful to see all abilities encouraged and all promise fulfilled. If women were successful in their choice of the Almighty's work, that should be celebrated. Young women, as with young men, should be obedient to their parents, but neither should be forced into unwholesome and unwelcome marriage. Adultery was to be abhorred. When it occurred, the man and the woman should be seen as equally guilty and equally punished. To do other than these things was an aberration introduced to Islam from the minds of sick men.

Baba was particularly damning and explicit about the abhorrent practice of genital mutilation. The practice is against the law in modern-day Mali and yet Amnesty International and the World Health Organisation estimated that at least ninety per cent of Malian women still undergo the procedure.

'I can see why that wouldn't go down well with the extremists,' I offered. 'I can also see that many moderates among the faithful would be upset by parts of it.' I already guessed the answer, but I asked the question anyway. 'What on earth has this text got to do with me?'

'My second favour, Amkssa, is that when you leave with Laing's diary you take with you Baba's document and my translation. After you have been to Edinburgh, you go to Paris where I will give you the names of some powerful men who wish to combat the bullying of the fanatics. They will publicise Baba's work in the Islamic world community and use it to fight the men of death and medieval devotion.'

I started to line up my objections, chief among which were that the requests were unfair and unreasonable and that I was frightened, but I was cut off.

'I am sure, Amkssa, that you immediately see my favours as unfair and unreasonable. You have also told me that you are frightened to go back to Europe. I understand these feelings. Let me tell you why I think you should consider what I have said.

'First, if you accept my argument for taking one document, then you really have no choice but to take both.

'Second, you are impressed by my little library and what it means, a statement of African pride in heritage. Selling Laing's diary would help that process and keep my manuscripts safer for future generations.

'Third, when the Islamist alliance fighters, AQIM and Ansar Dine, seized the north of Mali, they vowed several times on television and radio to respect the libraries of Tombouctou. But their vision of a pure Islamic society challenged everything that celebrated the sensual and the secular because they bore the explicit message that humanity as well as God was capable of creating beauty and pleasure. As these men established themselves in the city, their confidence grew and their need to recognise external pressure declined.

'There is a Qur'anic law that says that a tomb must be only a few centimetres above the ground. It is forbidden by Islam to pray on tombs and ask for blessings. Ansar Dine showed Western countries that, whatever the wider world wanted, they would not let the younger generation believe in shrines. They spat in the faces of the UN, UNESCO, the International Criminal Court, and other West African states. Ansar Dine does not recognise the authority of these organisations. The only thing they recognise is the court of God, Shari'a. Shari'a is a divine obligation. People don't get to choose whether they like it or not. During their final days, before being chased out by French and Malian forces in Operation Serval, Ansar Dine arrived in pick-up trucks and took pickaxes to three fifteenth-century mausoleums of Sufi Muslim saints, destroying them.

'They then threatened the remaining thirteen heritage sites. At the same time, they set fire to the Ahmed Baba Institute. Many precious manuscripts were lost as they issued their proclamation. I have a copy here to read to you:

It is not a secret, the scale of hardship our Muslin society is suffering and the worst of it is disabling the Islamic Shari'a, which Allah has blessed us with, and replacing it with man-made laws that are taken from Jews, Christians and their followers, which result in oppression, aggression, immorality, disobedience, poverty, deprivation and only

Allah knows what ... We vow to uphold what is right, to implement the religion, to lift injustice from the oppressed, to reunify Muslims, and to unite their efforts around the [belief] that there is no god but Allah and Muhammed is his messenger.

'I want you to know clearly the new penal code these barbarians introduced following their proclamation and implemented every day in accordance with their perverted literal interpretation of the six *hadd* punishments prescribed in the *Qur'an* and *hadiths*:

For theft: amputation of the hand
For illicit sexual relations: death by stoning or a hundred lashes
For making an unproven accusation of illicit sex: eighty lashes
For drinking intoxicants: eighty lashes
For apostasy: death or banishment
For highway robbery: death

'So, again, third, the Baba treatise is a chance to fight back again against these terrible people, for the sake of the Baba Institute, for the sake of women in thrall to the Islamic extremists, and for the sake of my daughter.

'And, fourth, I know how you think you will be able to leave Tombouctou without notice. There is only one way and you will not be able to do it on your own without local help. I am the only person you know who can arrange this for you. Without me, you will certainly be caught by the French or the jihadis or fall foul of my wife's wrath.'

The fourth argument carried most weight with me.

I knew when I was beaten.

1 Baba's arguments are still being developed today. See Bunza, 'Intellectual factor in African diplomatic history', *Sociology International Journal*, 2018.
2 Hammer, *Bad-Ass Librarians.*
3 Hammer, *Bad-Ass Librarians.*
4 Khaldun, *Muqaddima,* v.3.
5 English, *Book Smugglers.*
6 Hallett, *Penetration of Africa.*
7 *PRO*, London, FO 76 (several), MPG 1/984/1; *Royal Society*, MSS 374-76.
8 Irwin, *Ibn Khaldun.*
9 Toynbee, *Study of History*, Vol. 3.

4. RIVER OF DREAMS

You have to ask the question who is the more important figure in history, the Pharaoh Rameses II, who fills the Cairo Museum with his body parts and adornments, or the prophet Moses, who led his people out of Egypt and who died in the desert within sight of the promised land, but whose features and artefacts are nowhere and is reduced by scholars today to a legendary nomad?

Shakespeare, *Chatwin*

After my day-long meeting with Nianankoro in his library, I got back home an hour later than my allotted time. Agreeing details for my departure had taken much longer than expected. Nianankoro was meticulous which, considering his chosen occupation, should not have surprised me.

The plan was that I should slip away while out for my customary morning stroll. My private bag would be handled by my host, restocked, and would be given back to me at the last moment along with my travel documents and his precious cargo for Europe. Lists of potential purchasers in Edinburgh and Paris plus my financial targets, Hawala codes and email contacts were settled. An illicit Malian permit for visiting Timbuktu and a short-term exit visa would accompany my Moroccan passport, which I had held and used for fifty years, one of eight passports, companions of my decision of two years before to shuck off my legitimate identity.[1] A North African passport suited my language skills, leading with French which was supported by an increasingly reasonable Arabic for low-level conversation. I knew Marrakech well enough to pass as a resident. My local dress, beard and skin colour, heavily tanned by the desert sun, were also assets.

When I pushed open the front door, the house was unnaturally quiet. I knew Attou was there. I could sense her in the shadows of the archways. I didn't try to make contact, but I also didn't sneak in. For the second night in a row, I climbed the stairs, a recalcitrant schoolboy without dinner.

The next morning over coffee, as agreed, Nianankoro and I avoided any discussion of my departure. We had decided not to meet again at the library so that, if Attou harboured shoots of suspicion, they would be allayed. A piece of paper containing the address of the contact who was waiting to organise my documents slid into my hand. Breakfast finished, we bade each other a casual and normal farewell.

My photograph was taken quickly with discussion limited to grunts and gestures. Outside the dingy studio, resting briefly from the heat with a dubious fizzy orange drink under a tired mango tree, I plotted my path north to the rubble of Muammar al-Qaddafi's opulent villa, reduced by French bombs seven years before; a deliberate and well-aimed insult, claimed my host. The Libyan dictator often expressed his devotion to Saharan culture and to Timbuktu in particular. He spent millions of dollars buying real estate in this 'favourite city' and in dredging the canal for guests at his luxurious hotel in the south. Qaddafi played a double game, supporting the Malian government with generous money for development projects while keeping the Tuareg insurgency in the north alive by harbouring rebel leaders, training their mercenaries and funnelling cash to the independence movement.

I was acting the tourist. The low-slung building of beige concrete sported oblong windows with turquoise ornamental Moorish trim. One corner was just a large crater, an echo of Ibn Khaldun's message from the fourteenth century. Ruins were symbols of mortality, transience, their vanity of riches the evidence of bad government and the extravagance and softness of townspeople.[2] Several fluted columns still stood, some supporting precarious canopies. Patches of gaudy mosaics surrounded the cracked and sand-filled pool. The palace had been well grubbed, the masonry chipped where the marble had long been spirited away. Every door was gone. 'Time wears us out.'[3]

One lonely cane chair with three legs sat on a tilted veranda. I wandered over and smelled harsh cigarette smoke hanging in the lifeless air. I called out in French, my words dying unanswered among the lumps of stone. A well-fed grey cat strutted a few yards from a toilet-dirty corner to acacia bushes quickly grown among the neglect. In the distance, a dog barked. There was no answer, no scuff of movement.

My slow walk back along the weed-cracked driveway to safety and the river of traffic was paced so that, at the last second, I could duck behind the lonely stump of a guardhouse sited at a bend. Resting on my haunches, I waited three minutes as my heartbeat filled my ears and the sweat ran down my neck to the small of my back. An erect man dressed head to foot in deep blue walked past following my supposed path to the main road among the pines and palms. I watched him go, noting his size and gait; for all the world he was a Tuareg.

Why was he following me? No one except Nianankoro knew where I was going that morning. We had discussed my little adventure and he, of course, had advised caution on one of my last full days in Timbuktu. Yet my watcher had been there before me, smoking while balancing in a broken cane chair. Was Nianankoro just being careful or was the encounter evidence of the beginning of a broken trust? On the way home, timed to make sure that I was back several hours before dinner, I bought a hefty *khanjit* with a slightly curved blade and a serrated edge.

I lay on my bed naked in the heat, re-reading Mungo Park's journal of his travels in West Africa, unsure whether Attou would appear with my meal. She entered the room at her usual time and sat down as if nothing had occurred. I had decided to play whatever game she wished to avoid any trouble in the short time I had left. I didn't need to concentrate hard to show her that I was pleased to see her. She had clearly planned our time and, without a word, set me a punishing schedule that mixed a degree of pain with the pleasure. When she was satisfied and felt that I had suffered and waited enough, she brought me to climax with exquisite and gentle attention. I hoped that Nianankoro wasn't nearby and listening.

'I expect you'll be hungry now,' she said. These were the first words she had spoken since she entered the room an hour before. I smiled and hoped any worries were stilled. The dinner was very good.

Timbuktu is not strong on bookshops; they tend to be an offshoot of newsagents which themselves are a corner of cigarette and candy kiosks. I decided to spend my last morning revisiting the museum at Barth's house and, on the way, bought the latest French newspaper to see whether I still featured. Next to the newspaper, I was surprised by my first sight of my book, *Disappearing*, already given pride of place, no doubt because of my notoriety which admitted the trip to Timbuktu. The cover artwork was a nomad with his camel on top of a Saharan sand dune. Just a month after printing, in a small blow to my pride, it was already at a discounted price. But then, royalties had never been the objective.

I read the newspaper first and found I was a major matter of interest on the front page. The French were looking for me. The EU had sent agents to the city. The Malians thought I had broken immigration laws and had increased security at the airport, although there were no non-military flights by which to leave, and there were extra guards on the road west to Bamako, the capital. My mistaken picture from *Sound of Hunger* was featured, but readers were assured that I was a master of disguise. I had been spotted several times and chased twice, but had the luck of the devil. It was also thought that I had already escaped the net because I had been over two months at large in Timbuktu. There were two confirmed sightings in Bamako where I was reported staying, posing as an Australian, with professional nomad, Phil Paoletta, at *The Sleeping Camel* and at the more luxurious *Hotel Le Loft*, twenty minutes from the airport.

My first sighting of my life story, *Disappearing*, easily explained the excitement. Security forces in Brussels and London had demanded advance copies of the book in order to collect opinion and evidence about the assassination the year before of Jean-Claude Juncker and Martin Selmayr, the terrible twins of European federal politics. Someone had leaked their damning report to the *Daily Telegraph* and my publisher, Chattaway and Spottiswood, had plastered the more garish extracts on the back cover to boost sales. I gave up on the Barth museum and retired to my bedroom, walking home with false confidence.

A Detective Chief Inspector from the National Counter Terrorism Security Office declared that *Disappearing* was 'a subversive book that should not receive the breath of publicity'. Among other crimes, one could learn how to kill silently, dispose of bodies, hotwire a car, make a Molotov cocktail, fraudulently extract a pension without tax, and evade mechanical and electronic surveillance. 'These are skills best kept within the purview of government agencies.'

Someone who clearly didn't mind placing guilt before trial said that I was taunting the European Commission Secretariat with my 'knowledge of the unsolved murders of Juncker and Selmayr'. This was a 'wicked crime' committed by an 'amoral, calculating, mass murderer'.

My importance grew by the minute. A high official in the International Monetary Fund explained that the book told how an individual could divest themselves of identity, go off grid and use terrorist-supporting *Hawala* to move money. 'Heal's success is a direct threat to our banking system and a danger to Western civilisation.'

I reflected that these outbursts could not have been better contrived to drive sales than if I had written them myself. The security boys and girls must have been furious when this stuff got out. Pride pricked, I could see why my naïve attempt to shake off my pursuers had turned into a continental manhunt. To make matters worse, I had told everyone I was going to Timbuktu. For the first time, I was able to read my friend Aderfi's skilful addendum and to find how Asso had died of snakebite and to appreciate how the force of personality and skill of his young son, Icho, had brought me finally to Timbuktu. Hopefully people would accept that, as Aderfi and my publishers more than hinted, I had died an unpleasant death in the Sahara.

No one knew for sure that I had survived, did they? Far from breaking free, I was now in serious fear of my life, living in a terrorist-ridden town with a woman who treated me as a wholly owned sex toy and her husband who wanted me to smuggle politically dangerous documents back to the lion's den.

When Attou arrived that evening, I confess my performance was not immediately up to scratch. There were several loud irritated exclamations in the Bambara, or was it Berber, tongue of the equivalent of 'Tut'. Toys are meant to start working when the right buttons are pressed; being a distracted human was not an acceptable excuse. Not that I shared anything, of course.

I went walking soon after coffee with Nianankoro the next morning. I gave him my copy of *Disappearing*. We had not said goodbye, but contrived an unobserved and silent man-hug. There was no plan to meet again. Within half an hour, I had quit the town and was trudging well-swathed along the main road running south from Timbuktu to the river crossing and high-water port of Kabara where I had a clandestine appointment. It was about five miles, past unexpected lakes gripped by overgrown vegetation, and would take at least three hours in the already sweltering heat. Nianankoro was insistent that I travelled alone and accepted no lifts.

I say main road because the part running to the airport turn-off was asphalt, now heavily guarded by sharp-eyed and twitchy Malian troops with French UN backup in armoured vehicles. The first attempted flight to Timbuktu set off from Algiers in 1920, became lost, ran out of fuel and the two survivors were found deranged after drinking all the liquids on the plane, *eau de Cologne*, methylated spirits, iodine, glycerine and their own urine.[4] In 2009, nomads discovered the charred carcass of a Boeing 727-200 in the Saharan sand near Kidal in northern Mali. It had become stuck after offloading some ten tons of cocaine from one of its regular flights from Columbia into the desert.

Several years after the Tuareg laid down their arms after their decades-long struggle had failed, the fruits of peace were apparent at the airport. The tourists returned and the road was made up. A fleet of four-wheel-drive taxis waited to ferry cultured and well-heeled adventurers into the dirty town and to the world-famous, big-name music festivals in the desert. Five plush hotels opened and, a sign of the times, three internet cafés.

With the misery of the resurgence of 2012, the flood of sound- and sun-seekers ceased abruptly. Military planes brought in reluctant and soon-to-be-disappointed soldiers for their two months of duty in the desert. The aircraft were interspersed with commercial charters loaded with ice cream, steaks and bottles of beer and wine. In 2019, tourists were still not allowed back as the fear of a jihadist or Tuareg resurgence was ever present. Just four years before in 2015, two warriors walked into the Radisson Hotel in Bamako, which had never been captured in the uprising. Infidels need not be guilty directly of any act of hostility against Muslims; their very existence in classical jihad is the cause of war aimed at conversion or enslaving or killing until the whole world has been subdued. About 170 hostages were taken and twenty shot dead. Foreign journalists deserted after receiving death threats. International organisations pulled out. The country was in a formal state of emergency, soldiers behind sandbags watched many roads. Police stopped cars in the streets and guards waved metal detectors over hotel guests. In the years since the French intervention, armed groups in the north reasserted themselves: tens of UN peacekeepers were killed and terrorist violence crept in and out of central and southern Mali.

Immediately past the airport, the road, still heavy with traffic, mule and truck, pedestrians, cyclists, broken-down buses all skirting animal corpses, became a gritty, bumpy nightmare. The ribbed surface, full of rain holes and rocks, took no prisoners and reduced speed so much that a donkey-drawn cart often beat the wheezing vehicles.

Largely forgotten, Malians benignly accept their diminished status and infrastructure. Their empire had long disappeared and was unknown to many. Situated on the northernmost turn of the great river, between African and Arab slave ports, the gold mines in the southern reaches of West Africa and the salt mines of the Sahara, Timbuktu became a major centre of inter-regional and trans-Saharan trade. The settlement grew from a collection of tents and mud-and-wattle houses into a crossroads of desert and river traffic. Farmers, fishermen, black Tuareg slaves known as *bellas* and their aristocratic masters, Arab and Berber traders, settled in the town. Camel caravans laden with salt, dates, jewellery, Maghreb spices, incense, fabrics and goods from Western Europe arrived after weeks crossing the Sahara. Boats sailed north from east and west to the Niger's highest bend with the products of jungle and savannah – slaves, gold, ivory, cotton, cola nuts, baobab flour, honey, Guinean spices, and butter substitute, an ivory-coloured fat extracted from the nut of the shea tree, favoured by Mungo Park, but ill-suited to modern European taste and now used more for soap and lotion.

Traders, middle-men and monarchs made fortunes in the fourteenth century. The whole expense of government was defrayed by a tax on merchandise collected at the gates of the city. An estimated two-thirds of the world's gold came from West Africa. The metal gave the city the other half of its fabled reputation alongside its priceless manuscripts. When Mansa Musa, the ruler of the Malian Empire, travelled in 1324 on the *hajj* to Mecca from Timbuktu, he took several thousand silk-clad slaves and eighty camels each carrying 300 pounds of gold dust. The emperor flooded Cairo with his 'benefactions' and dispensed so much precious metal that the value of gold was depressed for a dozen years.

Over the fifteenth and early sixteen centuries, Timbuktu gradually lost its prominence. The city was repeatedly pillaged and sacked. The long-distance trans-Saharan trade was usurped by the arrival of Portuguese ships along the coast of West Africa and then by the discovery of gold in the New World. Much of the slave trade shifted west to supply the demands of the Americas. The city existed as a depot between the desert in the north and the abundant cereals and fruit grown in the regularly flooded valleys of the south and the towns on the river to the west and to the south. By the nineteenth century, Timbuktu was so completely a town of warehouses and docks that few of its merchants owned either a camel or a boat. They were brokers, contractors and landlords. The city produced almost nothing.

I easily recognised the two Timbuktus: one the fabulous, legendary city of gold and manuscripts, today a never-never land of the mind; the other a real place, a tired caravan town near where the Niger bends away from the Sahara. Nianankoro told me of a Sudanese proverb which declared that 'salt comes from the north, gold from the south, and the treasures of wisdom are only to be found in Timbuktu'.

Today, the country vies with Bangladesh, Dahomey and Niger as the world's poorest nation. There are barely 4,000 miles of tarmac highway in a country twice the size of France. Even so, a Malian was almost seven times more likely to die in a road accident than a Frenchman.

About halfway to the port, full of historical musings, I could see the run of the canal and an infamous murder spot through the dwarf forest of palms, mimosa and acacia. It was known as 'They Hear Not' since cries for help would not reach either town. I intended to stride past the waiting djinns. I paused to take a last look and caught sight of a distant figure in blue, a Tuareg whose size and gait were familiar. Perhaps I should have hurried on, but the man was too well known to me from Qaddafi's palace. I went deeper into the scrub towards the canal bank and away from the road. It was quiet. From the absence of rubbish and plastic and glass bottles, it was also little visited. A solitary mango stood hard on the narrow track with acacia shrub growing tight about. There was enough space for me to nestle against the trunk and wait.

The footsteps were cautious, the tread of a wary man. Twice was no coincidence. This was not an attempt at robbery. The follower knew me. What could be his purpose? Who was his paymaster? Was it the French? An EU agent? Or perhaps someone connected to Nianankoro's manuscripts. I saw immediately the wisdom, from Nianankoro's point of view, if not my own, of my being alone with no baggage. The man had to be stopped before he knew of my destination.

It was a simple matter. As he passed the tree, I stuck my leg out and he fell clumsily. As he slumped to the ground, I knelt over him, shoved his face into the sand and pushed my *khanjit* with enough force to prick the skin between his ribs so that he knew not to try to fight.

'Lie still or I will push the blade all the way into your evil heart.' There was a splutter as he moved his nose sideways to breathe. He said nothing. There was that smell again, dry, cured leather, unwashed skin and old goat stew.

'You know where we are?'

There was an affirmative grunt.

'Then you will know it is useless here to cry for help. I will ask you some questions. If you want to live, you will answer them. Do you understand?' Another grunt.

'What is your name?'

He spat out some sand. 'Iklan ag El Menir.'

'You are a Tuareg?'

A grunt with a touch of irony and pride.

'From Timbuktu?'

Another grunt.

'You were at Qaddafi's palace. Now you are here. Do you know me?'

Grunt.

'Who sent you to follow me?'

Silence.

I pushed harder on the knife, breaking the skin and touching bone. 'You have one last chance. Who sent you?'

He spat viciously.

I felt I had no choice. Even if he did tell me, how could I let him go? He would guess by now that I was heading to Kabara. Kabara meant the river and the river meant a boat. There were only two ways to go by water, west and south. There would be a pursuit. 'OK, Iklan,' I said. 'You have made your choice.'

As I began to push the *khanjit* all the way home, his courage failed and he managed one word.

'Attou.'

He twitched for a few seconds, jerked and died. I wiped the blade on his jellaba, the blue and red making an unpleasant combination. I sat on his lower body. One might think that the purpose of a human being was personal welfare, but in my messy experience the crude reality of 'the entire world was trifling and futile. It ends in death and annihilation'.[5] So it was no surprise that this Tuareg was dead, his demise fixed in the *Book of Destiny*. On the one hand, why was Attou having me followed? Did she think her pet was leaving her? Was this simple jealousy, a matter of property, or did she have a deeper motive? The manuscripts? Did she know who I really was and where I came from? Was there money involved, a finder's fee, from some European agency? On the other hand, the Tuareg boast a long history of killing nearly every European traveller who ever tried to reach Timbuktu. They remained an indomitable people, never subjugated, never conquered, but at least I had levelled the score a little.

I pulled Iklan's body deep into the scrub, scratching myself as I went. He had little of value on him except for a well-worn wallet, which I pocketed. The dogs and desert foxes would soon be at work followed by the vultures. My hope was that, as there were so many animal bodies around, no one would come to investigate in this haunted place. Death does not like to wait until we are prepared for it. Death is indulgent, at least whenever I met it, and enjoys, when it can, a flair for the dramatic followed by pathos. I followed the canal bank away from the road until I came to the port.

Thanks to the inundations of the river, the largest native pirogues carrying as much as 100 tons, used to come as far as the walls of Timbuktu in the rainy season, the nearest point to the salt mines at Taoudenni. After the canal was built, Kabara was the formal port, but even here became too shallow in times of low water and Korioumé, further to the west, acted as a second quayside.

Every day, in the five months that it was accessible, I suspected Kabara was a constant market as boats arrived from Mopti a day late or a day early, only to pack up and leave many hours before travellers expected. It was bedlam, clamorous and competitive, with every conversation seeming to have an alternative motive. Owners, crew, passengers, merchants rushed each docking and argued to receive or to place their goods or themselves. Nomads from the desert brought their cattle to exchange for imports. Coal-black slaves waited to receive their orders from Tuareg gang masters. Small fishing boats unloaded their catches into wicker baskets, which were taken to waiting trucks or pack animals. One boat towed the body of a hippopotamus, inflated by air inserted through a tube down its throat. Several men with long-bladed knives immediately set about its dismemberment; the little offal that was deemed inedible left lying in the sun. The stench in places was rank. There were egrets and glossy starlings everywhere and large rats made off with pickings. All docking was informal: a beachhead here, a sloped bank over there berthing pinasses, long-used motorised wooden longboats. Three other pinasses floated offshore, holding for their turn. As I arrived one left, full of black people, black bags and black boxes, its motor puffing black smoke. Laden with its sacks and crates, would-be passengers wedged themselves as best they could.

Further out in the water, a rusty steamer with cold boilers lay at anchor, owned by COMANAV, *Compagnie Malienne de Navigation*, and a relic of happier days when tourists were plentiful. Caravans of donkeys bearing cereals waited patiently across the water for the ferry.

I sat, as instructed, at one of several empty tables in front of a brick shack with an iron roof and ordered a mint tea. I was waiting for a man with a red sash to stand near me. For ten minutes I was lost among the hubbub of colour, smells and seeming disorder. I checked out my assailant's wallet. There was a grubby ID card with a picture that added nothing to the dying words and a new crisp fifty-euro note, which I reasoned was an attractive fee for trailing me. It also suggested that the paymaster had access to fresh currency in a town renowned for its creased and soiled money.

Then I noticed my contact, red sash prominent, standing ten yards away on the edge of the bubbling crowd. He was not looking at me, but he was watching me. I stood and he immediately turned and made for the water's edge. I was meant to keep my distance. A small, well-patched, grey inflatable floated ready, a man at the engine. My guide made for the bow and sat down. I followed as if unconnected and sat near the stern. We pulled out and made for the far side of one of the waiting pinasses. The wallet, minus fifty euros, slipped through my fingers into the dirty water.

As we climbed aboard, my guide leant me a helping hand and passed me a walking stick. 'Don't forget this, Uncle,' he said in French.

This was a less-busy boat, perhaps a dozen crew and passengers, limited cargo and a patient air. I was helped as we climbed over boxes and legs to a canvas-curtained and partitioned section rigged on the starboard half of the deck near the wheelhouse where we were out of sight. We were alone.

'Would you like some tea, Uncle?' Again, memories of a Berber cave returned.[6]

'I have just had some at the café on the shore, Nephew, perhaps later. Are we able to talk freely?'

'We can if we face each other and keep our voices down. We are safe here. The captain is a distant cousin and most of the crew are his family, but people will be curious about you and money always talks. You can call me Ahmed, after Ahmed Baba. Nianankoro is my real uncle. He has told me as much as I need to know. He also told me not to ask questions about your background and so I will not. I am happy to be here at his bidding and I am to make your arrangements and stay with you as long as is necessary. I will tell you more later.'

Ahmed was a good looking, clear-skinned, fit man of about forty years. He told me he was married with four children, lived in Timbuktu, but, frankly, he was pleased to take his first break in ten years from family life. His wife was a Berber which language he spoke as well as Bambara. He had studied at Sankoré Mosque as a child and had taken degrees in French and English at the university in Fez. He followed a great tradition. The Qarawiyyin Mosque, founded in 859, was the biggest in North Africa and where, from the late thirteenth century, together with smaller mosques and supplemented by *madrasas*, or religious training colleges, wide-ranging teaching in *Qur'anic* law, *Shari'a* law and the Arabic sciences was provided. Ahmed now worked as a teacher and guide, the latter mostly today for important UN visitors. He also helped his uncle in his library and had been part of the team that had smuggled manuscripts to Bamako under the noses of the jihadis in 2012.

'We were very lucky,' he said. 'As the jihadis withdrew they started to destroy a lot of Timbuktu's infrastructure, the electricity plants which fed the water pumps, the cell phone network. It was wanton. Then they moved onto the shrines and started burning manuscripts. The French arrived just in time, but not before the jihadis had made off with all they could carry on their 4x4s and trucks, even our agricultural machinery.'

'OK, Ahmed,' I cut in. 'I believe you and understand some of what you have been through. I guess we will have a lot of time to talk. First, for now, tell me what arrangements have been made? What is my cover story?'

Nianankoro and Ahmed had prepared well. I was an elderly, educated man who had recently had a stroke, making forming sentences difficult, and could only walk with a stick. My illness left me taciturn and happy with my own company. As a dying wish, I wanted to visit family in my birthplace down river and was taking this trip under the care of my nephew. Ahmed would liaise with the crew and bring me my meals. I was not to leave the shelter without Ahmed by my side, nor to speak directly to any of the passengers.

'These papers are for you,' said Ahmed, as he handed me my Moroccan passport and travel documents. 'These are top class.'

I inspected them and agreed.

'And here,' he added, removing a blanket with a wave of his hand, is your personal bag with some extra changes of clothes and, underneath it, are two parcels from Nianankoro together in a plastic bag which he says you are expecting. All of these things, I am to guard carefully on your and his behalf.' He paused. 'Also, I was to give you this as a gift from my uncle.' It was a book, a copy of the *Qur'an* in French translation.

At that, the diesel engine juddered into life. I could hear the anchor rope being raised. The pinasse moved gently to the middle of the river. I wasn't yet sure how and where I would change craft, but I knew where I was going, first north-east and then a dramatic swing south. I was going back to Nigeria where I had flown on the losing side in the Biafran war some fifty years ago.[7]

1 Heal, *Disappearing*.
2 Irwin, *Khaldun*.
3 Khaldun, *Muqaddima*, Vol. 1.
4 Gardner, *Quest*.
5 Khaldun, *Muqaddima*, Vol. 1.
6 Heal, *Disappearing*.
7 Heal, *Disappearing*.

5. RIVER OF REALITY

I do not know much about gods; but I think that the river
Is a strong brown god; sullen, untamed and intractable,
Patient to some degree, at first recognised as a frontier;
Useful, untrustworthy, as a conveyor of commerce;
Then only a problem confronting the builder of bridges.
The problem once solved, the brown god is almost forgotten
By the dwellers in the cities …

Eliot, *Four Quartets*, 'The Dry Salvages'

It was Gordon Laing, his glory safely packed in my baggage, who disproved one of the persistent early theories as to the destination of the Niger after it left the west coast of Africa. It did not wind across the Sahara to the Nile, but, as others later found, turned south at Tosaye, our first river port, towards the southern Atlantic. The Niger begins on the eastern side of the Fouta Djallon highlands in Guinea: one of the wettest places on earth and only a 150-mile torrent away from the western ocean. Laing returned from a field trip to the sandstone plateaux and deep ravines with the latitude and longitude of the Niger's source proving that its elevation at 2,800 feet was 'not sufficient to carry it half the distance' needed to the Nile.

But Laing missed the Niger's inner secret: the river is a geological accident, a joining of two rivers that originally flowed in opposite directions.[1] More than five thousand years ago, the upper Niger, the Joliba, the 'great river', flowed north, then north-east into what is now Mali, and emptied in the lake of Juf near the Taoudenni salt mines.

The lower Niger, the Quorra, began in the Ahaggar mountains in Algeria and flowed south into the Biafran delta. The drying of the Sahara over many centuries caused the Joliba to alter course south away from the accumulating sand and towards the dying Quorra and its increasingly arid mountain source. The Niger bend is the 'elbow of capture' where the Quorra gratefully conquered the retreating great river of the west and turned it dramatically south into the Tosaye gorges, 155 miles east of Timbuktu.

The Niger and two nearby rivers, the Gambia and the Senegal, provide the names of four African countries.

Ahmed raised the awning on the side of the pinasse using a simple pulley system and we sat watching Kabara drift astern. The breeze was hot and gave little relief.

'You know,' he said, 'the dried-up beds of the two rivers can still be traced through the desert, past empty stone huts, the shells of fresh-water molluscs and the occasional bones of hippos and crocodiles.'

'I do know,' I said, 'because I have seen them.' He looked at me in surprise while I smiled as he remembered his promise to ask no questions of my history. I redirected him. 'What you can do is tell me something of the story of the two Tuareg massacres of the French as they tried to colonise Timbuktu. I heard it was the last time that spears and swords beat rifles in the hands of trained military.'

Ahmed delighted at the invitation. 'That was in the 1890s,' he explained. 'Two French officers were determined to beat each other to claim Timbuktu. A lieutenant called Boiteux, who commanded the French flotilla on the Niger, left his base at Mopti and headed for Timbuktu against orders. He wanted to show that the navy could outshine the army in the race and, of course, to take the glory of conquest for himself. Behind Boiteux were two military columns, one travelling up the river in dugout canoes and led by Lieutenant-Colonel Eugene Bonnier, the military commander of the French Sudan, the other travelling overland to the north and led by Major Joseph Joffre.

'Boiteux reached Kabara, left his two gunboats with his second-in-command, Ensign Albe. Because the river was high, Boiteux managed to get two lighters with revolving guns up a creek almost to the city's western edge. He entered on foot to a cautious welcome from a people anxious to be relieved from the Tuareg burden. Boiteux celebrated his place in history.

'Albe, kicking his heels at the river, responded to a small Tuareg raid by leaving the safety of his boats and chasing his attackers. Boiteux was alerted to the distant firing but, by the time he returned riding a horse and accompanied by fifty natives, Albe, one other Frenchmen, and his seventeen African sailors had been massacred, their munitions exhausted.

Boiteux routed the Tuareg, who left fifteen dead. The death of an officer was seen by the French as particularly insulting. The graves of Albe's force are on a mound outside Kabara where a great cross reaches to the sky.'

Ahmed recounted how Bonnier had reached Kabara and accused Boiteux of rashness and ill-discipline and accountable for the deaths of his men. After a prolonged argument, Bonnier placed Boiteux under arrest. He entered Timbuktu himself where he heard that the Tuareg were massing at Goundam, a village to the west on Joffre's overland route. Bonnier left immediately with 204 men and, finding a small party of Tuareg, took a few prisoners and captured 500 sheep, cattle and camels. That night, he camped in a clearing near the village of Tacoubao, lit fires against the January cold, and posted sentinels on the crest of dunes, ignoring warnings that the Tuareg would attack in the dark.

'Joffre said later,' explained Ahmed, 'that the Tuareg feared the power of French guns and, poorly armed, would not accept face-to-face combat. Mounted slaves could always be seen watching from far dunes. Stragglers and outliers were picked off during the day. They would "try above all to surprise us at night".'

At dawn, 'spears hissed through the camp' and soldiers numb with cold held rifles clogged with sand to face charging horsemen. Bonnier was among the first killed. One officer and about seventy survivors managed to reach Timbuktu.

'When Joffre arrived almost a month later,' continued Ahmed, 'he found the bodies of thirteen French officers and NCOs. The bodies were cremated and their ashes taken to Marseilles where a monument still stands to the "conquerors of Timbuktu". As an after-thought, Joffre said that the remains of sixty-four native soldiers were found "which we buried on the spot".'

'That's all I remember,' finished Ahmed. 'Anyway, it will soon be time for dinner. I expect we will be pulling into a bank to camp for the night. I'll go and see Yacine, the captain, and find out what is going on.'

I rummaged in my bag and found insect repellent packed for me by Nianankoro and lathered my face, lower arms and feet. If we beached, the mosquitoes would surely be waiting. The dunes of the Sahara filled the northern bank with the great desert pressing behind them. They floated down to the river until they slid to a halt at the beginning of the great boomerang of the Niger bend. There were occasional splashes of green at the water's edge. I reached for Nianankoro's gift, the translated *Qur'an*, and flicked the pages.

Death will overtake you no matter where you may be, even inside high towers. When good fortune comes their way, they say, 'This is from God,' but when harm befalls them, they say, 'This is from you [the Prophet].' Say to them, 'Both come from God.' What is the matter with these people that they can barely understand what they are told? Anything good that happens to you is from God, anything bad is from yourself. We have sent you as a messenger to people; God is sufficient witness. Whoever obeys the Messenger obeys God. If some pay no heed, We have not sent you to be their keeper.[2]

Ahmed came back trying to look calm. He leant close to my ear. 'We have a small problem, Uncle. What Nianankoro hoped would be a simple device of concealment has caused much speculation among the crew and passengers. Yacine says that people sitting nearby and passing to the wheelhouse have heard us talking in French when they had been told that you could hardly speak because of your stroke. Snatches of my stories about the Niger have confused them.'

'How did you handle this?'

'I said that your brain and speech had improved quickly, no doubt because you were a devout old man and were also blessed by a river djinn. I said I expected that you would be able to join the *Maghrib* prayer and I hoped that you would be able to go ashore to do so.'

'Very good. Then that is what we should do.'

'You will use your walking stick, Uncle?'

'Of course,' I replied.

Ahmed reached to his side and passed me the shaft. As I took it, he pressed carefully at one end of the ivory handle and twisting, pulled on it. It was a swordstick of some strength. Ahmed pushed the blade back home. 'It is another of Nianankoro's presents.'

There is no hiding place from the curious mind. I was adrift in a society that was full of myth and where belief required ritual. My rejected world was secular where individuals were in unremitting competition for material supremacy and resources. Isolated societies, like this unknown place where the water was taking me, were seen as dream-bounded and only fit to be exploited. Within the progressive society I had shunned, every vestige of the ancient human heritage of morality was in full decay. Today, mankind can no longer rely for truth on the comparatively stable periods of great co-ordinating mythologies. They are proven lies. Today, individuals, personalities, use technology to hold ephemeral sway over the mass. As a result, few consider their destination or what propels them.

'The lines of communication between the conscious and unconscious zones of life have all been cut and we have been split in two.'[3]

Boats working the river were busy enterprises: older children pulled on their nets with one hand and waved with the other. Our pinasse slid through the fixed traps staked close to the right-hand shore. As we pulled into the bank, I saw younger children watching silently. The pinasse jumped to a muddy stop. The shy youngsters ran away, but soon crept back to watch from behind skinny trees. The more isolated children, the ones who tended cattle or goats, were the most reluctant to wave. None called for *cadeaux*.

After the bulk of the passengers were ashore, I made a performance of hobbling to the bow where I gratefully accepted the willing hands that helped me to the mud. I sprinkled '*Shukrans*' and '*Merci beaucoups*' to left and right and paused to get my footing. Then, with my stick in one hand and an arm linked to Ahmed, we made our way to the spot he had chosen for our prayer mats. The mooring place gave way to wizened grass between a handful of independent huts. Circular mud walls about four feet high carried conical roofs of thatched bamboo cane; all looked tired in the draining sunlight. I sank to my knees, laid back my *shesh* disclosing my grey hair and beard, and tried to wash my hands and feet.

Ahmed took over. 'It is fitting work for a nephew,' he said. Yacine led the ritual in a clear, accustomed voice and I felt the cloak of peace.

The crew went back to the pinasse to eat while most of the passengers sat down by the fire to share rice and a pot of Nile perch with their pop-eyed heads bobbing on the surface. It is sometimes easier to eat in the dark when food is obscured and especially when the cooking smoke keeps the worst of the mosquitoes at bay.

Ahmed started to talk, almost to himself, about the Timbuktu manuscripts. I wondered whether he knew what was in my package from Nianankoro.

'If you look around a place like this,' he worried, 'it is difficult to accept the general view that the manuscripts point to a vibrant written history. The Sahara and the area south of the Niger is still a land of the black African. The written history of West Africa begins with the arrival of the Arabs who brought with them an alphabet, a book, the habit of writing, and the profession of scribe.

'Writing has never occurred among these people or in these huts. They see their first words printed on scruffy football T-shirts. In the black African tradition, events were handed down in a similar way to the French *chanson de geste*, but from much earlier times. Men were trained to commit to memory the story of their people and to recite for hours the accomplishments of their tribe.

'No West African Rosetta Stone will ever be found.'

We made our way back to the boat where I left Ahmed discussing plans with Yacine while I stumbled to our quarters. As I opened the canvas, I heard a scuttle and a little light fell amongst the shadows on a man in stained singlet and shorts. I thought I recognised him as one of the passengers. Several of my passports were lying open on a pillow and he had a wad of my money in one hand. I looked hard at him and wondered how to keep him quiet. If he shared his new knowledge, there was no hope of the clean get-away I craved.

'Put everything back where it was,' I instructed, but there was a glint of easy profit in his eye. He did put the money down, but it was only to pick up his long knife. It was a lot easier when people made the decision for me. He moved forward.

'Prepare to meet your ancestors.' I flicked off my cane sheath, took one step, and skewered him through the heart at just the moment when Ahmed joined us. He caught the body and lowered it to the deck.

'It's a good job I trained as a librarian,' he offered. 'I would put your passports away before I see them.'

I wondered whether this was an impromptu theft or this man was also under orders, in which case our difficulties may just be beginning. Perhaps it was the late hour, but, for the first time, amid the gentle rocking of the boat, a weariness crept on me. I had not sought any of this, but violent death was becoming a grubby companion. Ahmed and I discussed our immediate problem and decided that the corpse had to go at once in case a search was made or there was an accidental discovery. It was best to act while the pinasse was almost empty. Ahmed slid into the dark water and I lowered the would-be thief into his arms and off they went up-river. He was back half an hour later after he had jammed his burden under some rocks. The body might work free in a day or so after attention from some river creatures, but we would be long gone. With luck, no association might ever be made.

No place is safe. Safety itself is an illusion. Neither individuals nor the state can ban all risk. Accepting that made it easier for me to keep going. While I don't advocate tempting fate, I guess that after all I have been through, I don't worry about it much either. All that I was looking for when I left the UK was some ill-defined personal freedom.

The next morning, Ahmed took down our canvas sides so that we were at one with the other passengers. Everywhere, roof awnings were raised against the coming sun. Even at eight o'clock, it was over one hundred degrees. Great dunes met the river on either side, little adobe villages half buried beneath them. It was the land of the Tuareg and the Moor, fierce nomadic peoples who crouched down close to the shore and stared at us from their indigo wrappings. Mungo Park admitted fearing these people most, nightmares of his time as their prisoner plaguing him long after he was captured and managed to escape.

I read the *Qur'an*, reciting and reflecting on chance selections. I doubt many, even among the devout, read it straight through, but rather visit it as an old friend or trawl for comfort or direction or insights into the problems of the day.

You are accountable only for yourself. Urge the believers on. God may well curb the power of the disbelievers, for He is stronger in might and more terrible in punishment. Whoever speaks for a good cause will share in its benefits and whoever speaks for a bad cause will share in the burden: God controls everything.[4]

Even in the heart of the Sahara, relics of Western wars, ancient living and travel are never far away. Something was strange about being on the river now and it took a few moments to understand. It was not an erudite revelation, but it was unsettling. Accuracy had become unimportant. I had long given up on a watch; I had learned to tell the time well enough by the position of the sun. There were no signs of Western civilisation. No electrical wires, no phone lines, no aerials, no cars, no roads. No sound of engines, except our own. The buildings were constructed from earth and thatch, rather than cement, brick or steel. I saw only adobe or woven grass mats where there were people. There were no hotels, restaurants, filling stations, flushing toilets, running water. It was a reflection offered by Kira Salak as she paddled alone in her canoe for 600 miles downstream from Old Ségou to reach Timbuktu.[5] It was repeated by Norwegian adventurer Helge Hjelland in 2005 when he became the first person ever to travel alone down the Niger's entire 4,178 kilometres, albeit mostly in a powered inflatable.[6] He was not the first, however, as two Frenchmen completed the journey in 1947.[7]

Timbuktu marks a rough halfway point and I was sad to miss the beginnings of the epic journey. After falling untamed and overgrown from the mountains in Guinea, two great dams, the Sotuba and the Markala near Sansanding, bracket Mali's capital, Bamako. The river travels north-easterly towards the Sahara and for 1,600 kilometres its bed becomes free from impediments. At Mopti, the Niger is joined on the right by the Bani, its largest tributary, after which it enters a region of creeks, backwaters and lakes, the greatest of which is Lake Faguibine, nearly 120 km long, 25 km wide, and more than 50 metres deep. Here, the Niger is more like an inland ocean. Its waters break upon its banks with monotonous waves often swollen by violent winds from the desert which evaporates two-thirds of its flow.

By the end of the dry season, large tracts of river are dead. When the rain falls again and immense volumes of water pulse their way downstream, the dried-up channels and lakes refill. Floating grasses and wild rice explode; fish and insects hatch; egrets and spoonbills arrive joining hippopotamuses and crocodiles. Cattle herders drive their animals to the grass that has grown along the river's edge; farmers harvest rice, sorghum and millet. Irrigation and cultivation along the middle Niger is as easy as along the Nile with even greater munificence. The Nile carries its fertility to a few hundred or a few thousand feet on each side while the Niger due to its immense plains reaches more than 60 miles without the aid of man.

Our second night's destination was the town of Gourma-Rharous, 110 km from Timbuktu, an intellectual centre at the height of the Songhai Empire, a meeting point for poets, scientists and marabouts. The boatman motored the pinasse past beaches and low dunes, devoid of vegetation except for patches of desiccated grass and the occasional acacia tree. We passed the dugout canoes of Songhai fishermen, known as Bozos, who lived in box-like mud huts lined up against the olive-green water.

We prayed and ate in the shade of a small natural wood of shea trees. Shea is a product that has established itself almost unnoticed to the Western world as a base in lotions and soaps, often as a replacement for the now derided palm oil. The kernels, looking like olives with a thin green rind and unripe above our heads, would be dried in the sun and the sweet pulp then boiled in water. Two hundred years before, Mungo Park noted that it was much prized as a substitute butter that kept for the whole year without salt. 'It is whiter and firmer and of a richer flavour than the best butter made from cow's milk.'

Ahmed said he had a serious matter to discuss. 'It is a personal duty,' he began, 'to dispel evil spirits from our lives and have good fortune. Many evil spirits might lurk around the next corner. They build up around a person, so it is important to rid yourself of them periodically. In your case, Uncle, you are bothered by a bad aura and have clearly not been cleansed for a long time by a top holy man. In Gourma Rharous, you are lucky that there is such a person. I have made an appointment. It is time to go.'

Consultations with sorcerers and witches are routine for most West Africans, Muslim or not. Fetishism and superstition are as alive and well in the twenty-first century as they were during Park's time. Nearly everyone wears *saphies*, or magic charms, meant to ward off misfortune and ensure success in myriad adventures. Park noticed that '*saphies* are prayers, or rather sentences, from the *Qur'an* which the priests write on scraps of paper and sell to simple natives who consider them to possess extraordinary virtues'. The *Qur'anic* verses are sewn inside little leather pouches, made by special *saphie* makers, and there is such a demand that these craftsmen have made a good living for centuries.

'It may even be,' continued Ahmed as we made our way among the huts, 'that the reason why that robber attacked you last night was because he noticed that you were not wearing a *saphie* and, therefore, were not as protected as you should be.'

'Well, he got that wrong,' I suggested. 'His *saphies* did him no favour. Perhaps I have an in-built protection?'

'This is not something to joke about, Uncle.'

'Don't get me wrong, Nephew. I will take any help I can get and I am grateful to you.'

Ahmed knocked on the post of a ramshackle hut that begged for repair and pushed, without waiting, through hanging, grubby fronds into a gloomy and smelly interior. 'You should sit here,' he said, and with one hand I reached into the dark and found the seat of a rickety stool. 'It is not proper to see the holy man or to gaze into his eyes,' I was warned.

We sat for a few minutes until there was a rustle and I was aware of the odour of a never-washed goat. A hand, much older than mine, seized me by the wrist. It might have belonged to a lizard. Ahmed passed over some money. A chant began, high-pitched, ethereal, disconcerting even. The effect was hypnotic and I felt my eyelids joining. There were a few sharp words, another rustle, and then we were alone again.

'Uncle, it seems we have come just in time. The holy man said that you have recently faced death and that more danger of the same kind is waiting for you. The common purpose of his amulets is to hold off diseases, to prevent hunger and thirst, to guard against the bite of snakes or crocodiles. They can even be used in time of war. However, in your case, the danger is extreme and greater conciliation is needed from superior powers. The holy man has gone to find a revered colleague so that together they will be able to provide the level of protection that you need.'

'I know this will upset you,' I replied, 'but I suspect more money will be required. You are sure that these are top of the range holy men and not a couple of country cousins taking the townies for a scam?'

'It is important to show respect, Uncle.'

And, so, I found my eyes closing again as each wrist was held in a reptilian clasp and the wailing intensified. There was a long consultation, mostly monosyllabic, and three pouches were produced containing my special *saphies* and added to a single string and placed around my neck. More money changed hands and we were out into the night.

'I feel much better now,' said Ahmed. 'I have done my duty to my uncle and increased your protection.' He paused. 'There was one small problem, though.'

'Tell.'

'They both knew that you were European. They could smell you. But I gave them extra money and said that we would be coming back this way in a few months.' I paid up.

Late the next afternoon, black clouds took over and leapt upwards in columns. A whirlwind passed by with such violence that it threw up waves that jeopardised the pinasse. These whirlwinds are common and come from the desert; that morning I had seen five of them at the same time. They carry sand to such a great height that they seem at a distance like pillars of smoke. The air became insufferably hot. We struggled to reach shore at some tiny fishing village. Then the rains came.

The first expected downpours around August had seen only clear skies. Now, in November, the gods remembered their duty in a torrential thunderstorm during which several centimetres of rain fell in an hour. Run-off was intense; the dry sandy beds of the *oueds* were transformed into raging torrents within minutes. Despite the danger to both humans and livestock, these late rains were much appreciated by nomads and farmers as they ensured fresh winter pasture that would see off famine.

As I stood close against a hut while Ahmed sought shelter and food, a wind nearly knocked me over. Thunder was continuous and consumed the entire world with noise. The rain stung my skin. I had to guard my eyes from the vortexes of dust that swirled and twisted through the passageways of the village like genies come to life. Cattle were so tormented by the particles lodging in the eyes and ears that they ran about like mad creatures and I was in danger of being trampled. Then, my adobe refuge began to lose a great part of its wall, clay falling away in brown floods of water.

Ahmed waved at me from a distant hut and I moved towards him almost ignoring my cane. As quickly as it started, the rain stopped. The sky 'fearfully rolled with thunder and flashed with lightning'.[8] In a final statement of control, forked juddering lightning struck two trees. They both roared into flame and fell towards me, landing one on either side. The air was full of smoke and static. Those of the crew who were witness used the event to raise me to high spiritual status as men and women living in the forest and, hearing a clap of thunder, invented God and heard his voice.[9] When men are ignorant of the natural causes producing things, they attribute their own nature to them. 'Men had a terrible fear of the gods who they themselves had created.'[10]

The women of the village immediately got to work, fetching large pails of river clay to patch the parts of their homes that had washed away.

I reached Ahmed and he dragged me inside as the rain began again, seeming even heavier.

'You see,' he shouted, 'how effective those *saphies* are. If this had happened yesterday, you would surely have been killed.' I didn't bother to respond, but slumped to the floor and began brushing off the last vestiges of the ashes. Surprisingly, a woman arrived thirty minutes later with a pair of grilled carp wrapped with rice in large palm leaves as protection against the rain.

The next day, we made Bamba and, at noon two days later, Tosaye. The vertical sun was backed by a scorching wind from the desert; the ground too hot for bare feet. At the dock, scores of merchants gathered along the shore to sell their specialist wares. There were large slabs of greyish Sahara salt, mangoes, bananas, fried rice cakes, kola nuts, pots and pans, flip-flops, writing supplies. 'All that is needed, truly needed, is there.'

A clutch of boys gathered around us with an incessant clamour. '*Cadeau, Monsieur, Cadeau! Cadeau! Argent!*' always shouted and angry because they thought us rich and obliged to share. Ahmed flung a handful of small coins into the sand and we were left alone to take mint tea.

To pass the time, but also because I was interested and we would be entering an area occasionally festering with elements of *Boko Haram*, I asked Ahmed about the connection between this terrorist group and the jihadi of the Sahara.

'I suppose everything comes back to this question,' shrugged Ahmed. 'There is a connection, but people assume that it is slight because of the collapse of the jihadist invasion of Timbuktu in 2012. The reason the French and the UN are in Mali is to keep it that way. Perhaps more importantly the reason the Americans, French, British and everyone else are in Nigeria is to protect the oil and to stop *Boko Haram* from linking with *al-Qaeda* in the Gulf States. The relationships are so complicated, on-off, fighting then not fighting, that nobody really understands. It's all egos, personalities and corruption.'

I decided to share a small part of my background. 'The vision of an independent Tuareg homeland inspired three generations of rebels, including Berber and Arabs,' I said. 'I had some experience of it in Morocco in the early days. I know that nomadic Tuareg wander over an area roughly defined by Algeria, Ghadames in Libya, Timbuktu in Mali and Zinder in Niger. Traditionally, tribesmen remain in territories defined by the leaders of their federation. The leaders assign grazing so that its members remain peacefully apart for most of the year. Even today, Tuareg respect these boundaries; national borders mean less to them. When the Tuareg lost their dream of *Azawad*, an autonomous Tuareg state, they also lost their ability to keep the radicals' most extreme impulses in check.'

'That's right,' agreed Ahmed. 'What a lot of people don't realise is that in 2003, the Algerian jihadists fighting a war against their own government took refuge across the border in Mali and soon afterwards adopted the name *al-Qaeda* in the Islamic Maghreb (AQIM) led by Mokhtar Belmokhtar. They put down deep roots in the desert, taking a cut from the smuggling trade, but their biggest money came from kidnapping. Between 2003 and 2010, AQIM made tens of millions of dollars by ransoming Western diplomats, energy workers and tourists who strayed into the wrong territory.

'In 2011, an extra ingredient was added to the simmering stew. The rebellion in Libya, backed by NATO jets and cruise missiles, toppled Muammar Gaddafi and hundreds of Malian Tuareg who had been employed in the dictator's armies returned home with all the weapons and ammunition they could carry. In Mali, they joined with a political movement that had been campaigning for *Azawad* and the National Movement for the Liberation of *Azawad* (MNLA) was born. The MNLA declared war on the Bamako government. They sought to create a caliphate in northern Mali in which they would impose *Shari'a* law, train terrorists, and steadily expand their Islamist state across northern Africa. This is when the group made an alliance with *Boko Haram* in northern Nigeria.

'Fast forward to when the MNLA was kicked out of southern Mali. AQIM, and their supposed-offshoot *Ansar Dine*, the Defenders of the Faith, led by Iyad Ag Ghaly, felt free to turn the clocks back 1,400 years. It was a terrible time. Three Malians joined the rebels in 2012 and were given prominent roles in Timbuktu's jihadist administration. One of them, al-Mahdi, joined the Islamic police as head of the morality brigade, *Hisba*. Houka was made a judge and told to enforce *Shari'a* law.

'MNLA members got out of hand with many complaints of looting and were told to return private property and then forced to retreat in 2012 from Timbuktu by the jihadists. AQIM criticised *Ansar Dine* for their over-enthusiastic pursuit of *Shari'a*. AQIM accused them of "foolish policies" that didn't consider the length of commitment of the local people to other standards of Islam which, experience had shown them, often led to rejection and the failure of the sacred experiment.'

The rain had ceased, the sky was black with troubled cloud, and the pathways were deep in mud. Ahmed stood up.

'Time we got back to the pinasse, please Uncle.'

---

1 de Gramont, *The Strong Brown God*.

2 *Qur'an*, 4:78–80.

3 Campbell, *Thousand Faces*.

4 *Qur'an*, 4:84–85.

5 Salak, *Cruellest Journey*.

6 Amehn Production & Norsk Dokumentarfilm, *Den Grusomste Rejse*.

7 Former French colonial civil servants Jean Sauvy, Pierre Ponty and filmmaker Jean Rouch set off walking from the source at Kissidougou on 24/10/1946, then used various local craft as the river broadened. Ponty left the party at Niamey. The other two reached the ocean on 25/3/1947. Rouch's documentaries, *Au pays des mages noirs and La chasse a l'hippopotame*. Rouch, *La Niger En Pirogue*. Sauvy, *Descente du Niger*.

8 Joyce, *Dubliners*.

9 Lucretius, *On the Nature of the Universe*.

10 Burke, *Vico*: Epicurus argued that the origin of religion was fear and that the universe was not created by design, but was merely the combination of a chance combination of atoms; a working atheism, but always open to new ideas and proofs.

6. SLAVES AND FAMILY

But the deeds of disbelievers are like a mirage in the desert: the thirsty person thinks there will be water but, when he gets there, he finds it is nothing. There he finds only God, who pays him his account in full – God is swift in reckoning. Or like shadows in a deep sea covered by waves upon waves, with clouds above – layer upon layer of darkness – if he holds out his hand, he is scarcely able to see it. The one to whom God gives no light has no light at all.

Qur'an, 24:39–40

On the southern fringes of the Sahara, the Niger threads between the rust-coloured, low cliffs of Tosaye. As if realising that it has no business in the desert, the river veers south almost at a right angle and bisects the mile-long gorge. Its narrow bed contains a rocky ridge that endangers navigation at low water. However, with the recent rain, the river hummed along with a depth of more than 30 metres until it widened considerably across a floodplain 5 to 10 kilometres wide. We reached Gao on the left bank, the end of the line for the tourist river steamers from Koulikoro, west of Bamako, in a not-so-distant time.

Gao, the ancient capital of the Songhai Empire, was another great trading city, like Timbuktu a link between river and desert peoples. It was also briefly the terrorist capital of *Azawad*. As a result, the streets were no less tense than Timbuktu, both of which had been captured by the MNLA in March and April 2012 and then lost to *Ansar Dine*, in the case of Gao in a major street battle in June. Despite the French recapture in 2013 when the airport and town were bombed, there was still a heavy and alert troop presence at road intersections dripping in the appalling heat. This was no place for a casual walkabout. Less than two years before, a suicide bomber drove a vehicle filled with explosives into a military camp housing the Malian Army and former militants who had signed a peace agreement, killing seventy-seven and injuring over a hundred. Belmokhtar, leader of

AQIM and former Gao resident, claimed responsibility through his al-Mourabitoun affiliate, yet another of the groups seeking to implement *Shari'a* law in the Maghreb. Belmokhtar said the bombing was 'punishment for Mali's cooperation with France'.

Notwithstanding, Ahmed felt it imperative to leave the pinasse for an hour to find a restaurant and a change of diet. There was a clean and suitable place opposite the Wabaria bridge, built by a Chinese state company to replace the cross-river ferry. As is their way, the Chinese imported their own labour, brought their own food and finished more or less on time. Less than ten per cent of local labour found only the most menial of work. When the Chinese left, almost overnight, they took with them large debt pledges which promised the likelihood of later control of the project.

The floodwater from the Guinea mountains and upstream tributaries had slowly, but, finally, reached the town and the Niger looked over 3 kilometres wide. It was still sluggish.

The captain of our pinasse joined us. He spoke in Bambara which Ahmed translated. Most of the passengers from Timbuktu had left to conduct trade in the town or to visit family. Over a mint tea, it was at last time to decide how much further the captain would travel. There was an unpaved road, the N1, going south through Niger into Nigeria, but it was considered too dangerous. Buses were frequently attacked. Ahmed thought Yacine could pick up a cargo and a few people who preferred to go the 100 kilometres by boat to Ansongo, once the limit of travel of the smaller ferries. However, Yacine had received a surprise offer, the chance of a lucrative cargo of salt and dates which needed moving to Niamey, the capital of Niger, another week away. It was a journey he had made once before from his home port of Mopti, altogether a twenty-one-day voyage. Despite the family connection, it was, as always, a question of money. Yacine's cargo would not quite cover the expense. Would we be prepared to make up the difference? I nodded.

Agreement reached, departure was delayed a few hours to allow the sacks to be loaded. I told Ahmed that I wanted to use the time to visit the Askia Tomb, built at the end of the fifteenth century by a Songhai emperor. We made our way through the markets of canvas stalls, many selling vibrant spices, and down the *Marche Wellington*, the cloth and clothes quarter. *Ansar Dine* had beaten us to the tomb, constructed to ape the Great

Pyramids which Mohammed had seen on his pilgrimage to Mecca, and bore comparison with Sankoré in Timbuktu. Despite Askia being a working mosque, the jihadis had destroyed much of the outer clay fabric and palm struts declaring it 'idolatrous'. The real reason, the caretaker suggested, was that Askia was a UNESCO World Heritage site and this western intrusion needed rejection.

We took a straight line back through the older side streets to the pinasse. Rounding one corner into a sand-filled and decrepit square, Ahmed stopped dead. 'This cannot be,' he declared.

I knew that slavery had been abolished in Mali in 1971, but continued, something Malian officials and anthropologists denied. Thousands of people, black African Bella or Billat, work for their Arab masters as unpaid labourers, unable to end their servitude for myriad economic, social and psychological reasons. Tuareg slave owners, *terché*, with their olive complexions, believe themselves Caucasian and therefore superior to the dark-skinned sub-Saharans.

But, here, we faced an out-an-out market, supposedly one of the most secretive of the old institutions. There was a wooden box; reminiscent of platforms I had seen in pictures of sales of Negroes in the West Indies. A line of a dozen black men, women and children, *aklini*, were waiting in rope shackles to take their turn on display. One young woman had her teeth examined, her breasts were pulled out from her singlet, and then her skirt raised to show her hips, presumably to assess them for childbirth. The buyers were a mix of nomadic Tuareg, Arabs, and some Fulani cattle dealers.

I also knew some of the history. Slavery had been one of Timbuktu's, indeed all Mali's, most lucrative operations, the Arabs giving the Niger the name *Neel el Abeed*, River of Slaves.[1] Arabs and Europeans aggravated the problem by providing local traders with the most lucrative and unquenchable market for slaves with perhaps ten millions of black Africans being shipped on the infamous Middle Passage to North, South and Central America and its islands. The number taken across the Sahara to North African homes and Middle Eastern harems was reputed to be as great. The European hunger for slaves was such that West Africans widely believed that the white men considered African people a delicacy and were shipping them away to eat them.

Mungo Park relied on slavers for his Niger voyages and found among the population that 'three-fourths are in a state of hopeless and hereditary slavery, and are employed in cultivating the land, in the care of cattle, and in servile offices of all kinds'.[2] Park's assessment that abolishing the Atlantic trade would do little to affect slavery in Africa proved entirely accurate. When export markets dried up, masters put their slaves to work in the production of palm oil which was declared 'legitimate commerce' by the Europeans. 'The poor Africans,' wrote Park, 'whom we affect to consider as barbarians, look upon us, I fear, as little better than a race of formidably ignorant heathens.'

Laing arrived in Timbuktu at the height of the anti-slavery movement in Britain. He was horrified to be offered on two occasions, by mothers, child slaves for thirty shillings each. When he refused, he was abused 'as being one of those white men who prevented the slave trade and injured the prosperity of their country'.

The Europeans who visited West Africa were far from being the most impressive representatives of their various nations.[3] 'Most of them had a stake in the slave trade, a traffic that coarsened its participants. Harsh judgements were passed on these hard-drinking seamen, those seedy European factors.' John Newton, captain of a slave ship, wrote, 'With a few exceptions, the English and Africans reciprocatively consider each other as consummate villains, who are always watching opportunities to do mischief. We have, I fear, a very unfavourable character upon the coast.'

Kira Salak was so disgusted by what she anticipated at Timbuktu in 2005 that she took with her from the USA two large gold coins. After a covert meeting with a Tuareg master, working through an intermediary, she succeeded in buying and freeing two of his Bella. I immediately and instinctively decided to do the same. What was the worth of my long journey across a third the depth of the world to seek my own freedom from repressive states and rapacious international companies if I stood by and did nothing?

Ahmed looked at me with something like horror in his eyes when I shared my thoughts. 'No, no, you can't do this, Uncle. This will never let you get away.'

'Look, Ahmed, this is an auction. It's all about money. It doesn't look like anyone here is that wealthy. Translate for me and do what I ask.'

We moved closer to the front. I made a play of using my walking stick. Some of the potential buyers watched us closely, talking loudly and looking displeased.

'And what will you do if you are successful. We must leave in less than an hour. What are we going to do with a slave? You just can't let them go. They will be recollected and sold again. These people have no experience of living independently. You will have responsibilities. It is not a game for a bleeding Western conscience.'

'Trust me to do the right thing.'

As the sale of the young woman was completed to an indigo-wrapped Tuareg who looked even older than me, I was badly jostled from behind. I turned angrily, pointed my cane at the perpetrator and roared, '*Keef Tajaru*', 'How dare you?' I edged closer and the aggressor melted back into the crowd. 'A little more respect, now, I think?'

Ahmed shook his head sadly, reduced to a bystander.

'How much did the woman go for?'

'Just about 120 US dollars, Uncle,' answered Ahmed. 'She was expensive for these days because she will be good for sex and will produce other slaves. Modern slaves are not considered investments worth maintaining. If someone gets sick or injured, they are simply dumped or killed.'

'Well, Nephew, in the Americas 200 years ago they could pay upwards of 10,000.'

A good-looking boy with frizzed, tight hair of about twelve years with ripped and stained T-shirt and shorts shook off the rough hand that tried to pull him onto the box and stepped up proudly on his own. He was unbroken. His teeth were good, his penis in order, but his eyes were angry and the buyers were wary of buying a package that needed arduous training. The bids staggered to fifty dollars and halted. Almost over, I nudged Ahmed who bid sixty. The slave-master looked delighted. There was a rustle of discontent which after a brief discussion at the back, brought sixty-five. I suspected a ring was at work and that might well mean trouble. Another nudge. 'Seventy', and the boy was ours, handed over with tied wrists and a rope lead. He was reticent to move until I hit him across his back with my cane and forced him to sit on the ground.

Two women produced lively auctions before a boy of perhaps ten, was shoved onto the box. He was thin, frightened and sobbing. The acquisition at my feet stirred and, for a second, the boys' eyes met, one with compassion, the other pleading. I nudged my boy with my cane and I looked at him for an answer. He nodded. I held his gaze for a second and nodded in return. Fifty dollars later, I had a pair of young slaves.

Two older men were the last waiting their turn. Ahmed whispered, 'I think that this would be a good time to leave, Uncle.'

I picked up a short length of rope and tied the two hand shackles together and we moved deliberately out of the group. The slave-master stopped his work and two odorous henchmen barred our way, one palm outstretched. 'Commission, I think,' said Ahmed and handed over ten dollars.

We moved around the corner and Ahmed pushed the boys in a trot. I think they sensed that all was not normal. At the next corner, we heard the slap of chasing sandals in the sand. We reached the first of the market stalls before the pursuers were in sight and there stood a ramshackle Citroen taxi with barely-treaded tyres and darkened rear windows, its driver with cigarette in hand leaning against the bonnet. He barred us from the back seat with a complete lack of interest. I pushed ten dollars at him, he hesitated; another ten sealed the contract. As we piled in, the driver shouted to us and made off into the crowd.

'He's gone to get his wife. She's doing the shopping,' explained Ahmed.

The anti-climax happened quickly. I saw three Tuareg from the slave auction appear at pace. The boys were squashed to the floor of the car with Ahmed and I on top of them, all of us hopefully out of sight. The taxi driver returned talking urgently to his wife who had her arms full of vegetables and a new metal cooking pot. The pursuers looked left and right and, not seeing their prey, questioned the driver. He gesticulated with incomprehension while his wife opened the boot and placed her purchases inside. The Tuareg moved towards the Wabaria bridge while the couple got into the front seats. I passed another ten-dollar bill up front which disappeared in the wife's paw and suggested we drove first to the port.

As Ahmed and I sat up, keeping the boys underfoot, I asked where was the first quiet village south on the river where the taxi could go in under thirty minutes and the pinasse could easily pick up passengers. There was a brief discussion: the answer was Tabakor.

'Right, Nephew, don't argue. We'll drop you near the pinasse and you get aboard as discreetly as you can. I will drive to Tabakor with the boys and you will pick us up there in the boat. Give me your phone. If there is any difficulty, I will call you on Yacine's number.' He looked at me like I was mad, but decided against arguing.

The boat was moored opposite a sand mountain, known locally as *La Dune Rose*, which was beginning to glow pink in the dropping sun. 'Best of luck, Uncle,' and Ahmed was gone.

On the way south, while still in the town limits, I saw to my surprise the yellow archways and big 'M' of a McDonald's drive-in. It was an opportunity to cement friendships and I requested a stop. The driver had little French and no Arabic so it was a matter of sign language. My hosts were more than happy to order at the counter as they were included. I hauled the boys up, took off their ropes and gave them each their first taste of Western civilisation: a 'Big Mac', fries and *Coca-Cola*. On such small arrangements are long-term friendships formed. It seemed like they hadn't eaten well for a week. I didn't think they would make a run for it.

Tabakor took about twenty minutes. It was never going to feature on a tourist map of Mali. I negotiated briefly with the driver and, in the end, paid him what he asked while passing my fingers like a zip across my lips. He understood, spat on the ground, said, 'Tuareg. *Terché*,' and then drove off with a window wave.

The landing place was a muddy indentation among semi-derelict huts, the main village further inland. Two old men sat on a porch gazing sightlessly into the river breeze, scratching themselves without stopping. We joined them.

Everyone knows of AIDS. Who has not heard of malaria? I had seen river blindness on our journey, but this place epitomised its worst effects. The blindness crawls from behind the eye. First the parasite strikes old Africans. Eventually, it invades the children who lead their sightless elders by hand. Fewer villagers can work in order to support those infected people who sit out their days. The village economy falters and then disappears. The disease is seldom noticed outside Africa. Mali recognises the worms only too well. It is *oncho*, their abbreviated word for the intruder: *onchocerciasis*.

Disease makes West Africa the deadliest place in the world for Europeans.

In the early nineteenth century, between twenty-five and seventy-five per cent of any company stationed on the West African coast in the eighteenth century, known as the 'white man's grave', could expect to die. The interior was even more deadly with first year survivors dying at about ten per cent a year – roughly four times higher than in India or the West Indies.[4]

Villages along the Niger have their own wells for drinking water; everyone knows not to drink from the polluted river which acts as a washing place and communal toilet for thousands – if not millions – by the time it reaches Nigeria.

The region boasts a rich ecology of burrowing parasites, viruses, bacteria, and insects that no explorer could escape. These included the Guinea worms, whose larvae entered the body through drinking water, migrating to the tissue beneath the victim's skin, where they grew over several months up to three feet long. If the host survived this agony, immensely painful pus-filled blisters would appear on the lower leg a year later, then rupture as the giant worms forced their way out. The blood-sucking tsetse fly, meanwhile, carried sleeping sickness whose initial symptoms of fever and weight loss gave way to personality changes and narcolepsy as the disease entered the brain, killing its host only after several years. Intestinal infections such as amoebic dysentery were often lethal, too.

The most dangerous sickness by some margin was malaria. The commonest form of this parasite in West Africa, *plasmodium falciparum*, is also the deadliest. It still kills hundreds of thousands a year. The mosquito that carries it thrives about humans and its larvae can grow in a puddle as small as an animal's footprint. Once injected into the body, malarial microorganisms enter the bloodstream and are carried to the liver where they grow inside cells that pop eight to twelve days later, releasing tens of thousands of offspring which then start to invade the host's red blood cells and eat them from inside. When each cell implodes, the parasites move on until the host's blood is being eaten on a massive scale. Victims begin to vomit bile and their skin, fingernails and eyes take on a yellow hue. Their stools and urine turn black by which time death is not far away. Then, there is bilharzia, yellow fever and sleeping sickness ...

I was woken from my reflections by the sound of the boys chatting amiably with the two old men. I heard enough to know they were speaking a variant of Soninké, the tongue of the masters of the river, which suggested the children might have lived some distance from the tribe's centre around Mopti. The boys were describing with obvious knowledge the antics of helmeted turtles with their olive shells. These animals were emerging from muddy holes with the advent of the rainy season and were about to hunt aggressively for small crustaceans, snails and fish. They also work together to drown small reptiles and mammals making them favourites for fresh-water tanks in Manhattan apartments. The boys excited stories moved on to their exploits with spears, I assumed in taking crocodiles and hippos.

My pinasse had sailed past many Bozo bamboo huts during the trip from Timbuktu. Rock drawings link the Soninké language and the Bozo people as far back as 6,000 years when they were reputed to be founders of the cities of Djenné and Mopti.

I reached for Ahmed's mobile to call and see where he was. Scrolling through the phone, I realised that it was out of range. It was no surprise to see Nianankoro's name. There was every reason also why Auntie Attou's name should be there, but it still gave me a turn. It was automatic for me to check the call logs. Ahmed had called Nianankoro every few days since we left Timbuktu, no doubt progress reports, but contact with Attou every day made me very nervous. I was about to move over to the boys to see if I could find out more of their background when I heard a familiar motor. The pinasse crawled into view on the sluggish current and we three climbed aboard, the boys happy and in their element. They shouted farewell to their two old friends.

Nothing untoward had happened at Gao. Ahmed put up a canvas screen after he had updated Yacine and laid low while he waited for the dates to arrive and be loaded on top of the salt. He checked frequently, but there was no sign of the Tuareg slavers.

My original plan was to get to Niamey and find a flight to Lagos. I had heard that there were direct flights to Paris, but the arrival of the boys put paid to that option. Could I find their home or some village elders with whom they would be happy? If not, it looked like Lagos was the best bet. I would also get easier connections to London and then to Edinburgh. I told Ahmed about the boys' probable Bozo heritage and asked him to investigate their background. He readily agreed, but as he turned to find them, I told him there was one more thing. I handed back his phone. 'Why are you calling Attou every day?' I asked.

He was taken aback, clearly embarrassed. 'I cannot tell you, Uncle', he replied.

'I have to know, Nephew,' I pressed. 'This is important to me and to our trust in each other. I thought you were here at Nianankoro's bidding. I did not know that Attou knew what was going on.'

'She does not know, Uncle. Believe me, I have not told her, but she is very curious and very angry. She thinks I know something, but she doesn't know that I am with you. She makes me ring her every day.'

'Why would she do that?'

'Perhaps, you think that you know her, but I don't believe that you really do. She frightens me badly. She is not someone to upset.'

'There is something that you are not telling me, Ahmed.'

'Yes, there is, Uncle, but it has nothing to do with you.'

I let it lie and watched Ahmed made a quick retreat to talk to the two boys. The pinasse pulled into a quiet piece of shore. There was no need to find a village to ask for food as Yacine had bought fresh supplies in Gao. I watched as the smaller fires were lit to keep the hippos and mosquitoes away. I sat with my *Qur'an* and read in the falling light and listened to the sounds of the bush. Far away, I thought I heard a lion proclaiming territory.

> *If any of your slaves wish to pay for their freedom, make a contract with them accordingly, if you know they have good in them, and give them some of the wealth God has given you. Do not force your slave-girls into prostitution, when they themselves wish to remain honourable, in your quest for the short-term gains of this world, although, if they are forced, God will be forgiving and merciful.*[5]

When Ahmed came back the worry that I had piled on him had multiplied. 'You know how to find trouble, Uncle,' he said. 'One of the crew is also a Bozo and, between the two of us, we have got somewhere near the truth. Now, everyone knows this except you and people are waiting to see how you will react. They have decided that you are more important than they first thought and they want to be careful in case you have some special powers given to you by the *saphies* that you always wear around your neck. If it was left to the men, the boys would either be killed or left behind in the morning.'

'OK, Ahmed. Tell me the boys' story.' He gave a deep sigh and told me what he had learned.

Their names were Kabu and Tabu, brothers, aged, they thought, eleven and nine. They had lived in a small fisher community east of Timbuktu, which regularly uprooted and moved to a fresh spot. They reckoned themselves expert at using spears to kill crocodiles and hippos asleep on the tide. They were used to taking catfish, carp and perch with nets. One evening, Fulani herdsmen with Kalashnikovs and machetes came and demanded food. They had strong drink with them and began to abuse the women. The boys' father and some of the men argued. There was a fight. Tempers were lost and wild shooting began. Some people ran off in the dunes. When the fighters realised what they had done, they began killing all the survivors. Only Kabu and Tabu were left alive inside the village and the men decided to take the boys with them. They were taught how to use guns. Both had raided villages and been forced to kill innocent people. After about a year, the Tuareg surprised the camp, captured the Fulani and tortured and executed them. Kabu and Tabu were kept as slaves for a few months and then sold on to a slave-master who took them to market in Gao.

I sat and thought for a while then called the boys over where they knelt before me. The crew silently gathered to hear my decision. I took off two of my *saphies* and pressed one each against the boys' foreheads and then placed them around their necks. 'Tell them, Ahmed, that they are forgiven all they have done. These *saphies* have the power of the strongest djinn and will protect them against evil.' My words had a strong effect amongst my other listeners. The boys fell to kissing my feet.

'Tell these men, also, that if we all reach Niamey unharmed, I will pay everyone a good bonus in US dollars.' That went down very well.

The Niger River is navigable to small craft during normal high water as far downstream as Ansongo, a small antimony and uranium mining and farming centre, and gateway to the Ménaka animal reserve. Below there, navigability is interrupted by a series of gorges and scattered rapids until the Niger reaches Labbézanga close to the border with Niger. Interrupted, that is, apart from about five weeks every few years, normally around December, when the river is abnormally high and the water sluggish, most rocks below the keel of a pinasse, and the river slow enough to allow men with poles to edge the boat's way through: difficult, occasionally dangerous, but not fraught. At Gao, Yacine talked with a Nigerien trader who had just made the trip upriver from Niamey, pronounced it passable with care and hence our cargo of dates and salt.

It took three days to work our way slowly through the obstructions, using every hour of daylight with Kabu and Tabu, now known collectively as the 'BuBu', perched high on the bow and shouting instructions against rocks near the surface to the men armed with poles. The river was relatively clear because of its rocky headwaters, carrying only a tenth as much sediment as the Nile. In one of the calm stretches, we came against a sleeping crocodile and BuBu asked me if I would like some fresh meat. It was a remarkable demonstration of skill as we floated alongside the inert creature. BuBu waited their moment and both stepped on the horny back and rammed their spears simultaneously into the crocodile's eyes. Nimbly, they stepped back into the pinasse as the animal twitched, rolled over, and was dead. With considerable shouting and delight, the boat pulled the carcass to shore and the boys and the Bozo crew member directed the skinning. It was a mighty feast, yes, tasting like chicken, but pleasantly fishy with olives, the whole saddened by the bones of a small, decayed human hand in the stomach. Yacine decided to keep the leather coat, towing it behind, to make a later trade.

We passed the blue-domed towers of the Labbézanga mosque without incident and soon monkeys screeched without pause from behind creepers fronting a madness of animal sound. The river was dense with hippo and crocodile. One moment, I was reading my *Qur'an* and reflecting, the next my body was sheathed in sweat, I felt I was aflame, my strength drained, and I knew my time had come. Ahmed told me later it was heatstroke and that he had bathed me continuously for twenty-four hours to try to bring the fever down. I remembered nothing, certainly not the passing of the border into Niger, which happened at dusk. The police post was empty when we moved in close and so we carried on, BuBu hidden under some date sacks. A minute after, there was a crack like a rifle shot.

Everyone was nervous. This was bandit territory. In late 2017, *Islamic State in the Greater Sahara*, ISGS, laid an ambush 20 kilometres from the border killing four US soldiers and five Nigerien troops, the largest number of American lives lost in combat in the sub-Sahara since the 'Black Hawk Down' incident in Somalia in 1993. Other US vehicles had hit landmines. In May 2019, just seven months before our visit, twenty-eight Nigerien soldiers were killed in an ambush and, in a ten-day retaliation the next month, eighteen IS terrorists were killed and five captured in a US, French and Nigerien joint operation.

I came to as weak as a well-used tissue and wondered where I had been. BuBu sat at the foot of my bed. My thoughts drifted to Timbuktu and my last illness. Every time I fell asleep, an avenging Attou reared over me. Near my right hand, I found a *kalimba*, a crudely fashioned thumb piano made from a gourd, bought to amuse the BuBu. I started to twang the flattened nails. What followed was surreal. My haphazard strumming produced a pop tune I recognised from many years ago. I concentrated and corrected and then heard a 'Woohoo, woohoo' from the wheelhouse behind me. The song came flooding back: the *Walk of Life* by Dire Straits. 'Woohoo' was picked up around the boat and someone unseen contributed a Bambara-inflected chorus:

He got the action, he got the motion
Oh yeah, the boy can play
Dedication devotion
He turnin' all the night-time into the day

Then, I recognised Ahmed, with a heavily French-accented version:

There's just a song in all the trouble and the strife
You do the walk, do the walk of life
Hm, you do the walk of life.
Woohoo
Woohoohoo[6]

South into the country of Niger, the riverbed broadening again, its banks teeming with livestock and small villages, this grubby pinasse motored with its crew, four passengers and my small family. Someone whipped up a percussion accompaniment to my terrible *kalimba* thumbing. Those who could sang near-verbatim snatches of a 'Top Ten' hit from the 1980s about a busker in the London Underground passageways. BuBu were jigging stylishly without restraint. 'Woohoos' rebounded everywhere. It seemed the monkeys joined in although out-of-tune. It was a very un-Islamic episode.

The river rippled down a series of rapids until it reached Niamey, Niger's capital and a semi-modern city of almost a million people. The river cuts it in half as the Seine does Paris, the south bank almost entirely residential. The mud and sand banks were dotted with the rusted hulks of turn-of-the-century paddlewheel steamers which could no longer compete with trucks.

Tuareg, Sonuri and Fulani thronged to the *Grande Marché* of 5,000 stalls in narrow, shaded aisles in a grid pattern, a third of them under cover. Early morning was the busiest time, packed with both river transients and land-based sellers. Narrow side stores stocked what the main market might not: peanuts, *Singer* sewing machines, plastic seats, mattresses, cigarettes, clothes, mountains of multi-shaped pots, handicrafts. The *Petite Marché* in the town centre provided fruit and vegetables of every variety, with pestering crowds and inflated prices for visitors and as hassle-laden as its bigger brother was calm.

I recalled that Bruce Chatwin, who had been a partial guide on my nomadic journey since leaving England, had visited Niger to make a short film about nomads. He spent time at the aesthetic market at Bermou and enjoyed the tribal variety: Tuareg, Bororo, Peuls and Hausas with their camels, cattle and goats that might have come from Egyptian tomb paintings. Chatwin was captivated by Ibn Khaldun's argument that desert people who lack grain and seasonings in their food are found to be healthier in body and better in character than the hill people who have plenty of everything. 'Their complexions are clearer, their bodies cleaner, their figures more perfect and better.'[7] Eating too much caused excessive moisture to circulate in the body creating 'putrid humours, pallor, obesity, ugliness and stupidity'.

But it was about this time that Chatwin also started to fall out of love with the concept of the noble nomad who wandered free and eternally, morally superior to town-dwellers. He recognised the French lie that invented historical antagonism between nomads and sedentary peoples, between Arabs and Berber. Chatwin was told bluntly that if there was 'more pasture for our animals we would not move so much'. Others noted that, all over the world, nomads were moving less and were not noticeably unhappy about it. 'Nomads have a strong sense of home and place. The notion of them moving around randomly is false.'

Yacine unloaded the pinasse, completed his transactions and, with bonus pocketed, decided on a rapid return to Timbuktu before the river fell and the stretch to Ansongo was closed to them. It was a sad and unreal moment. My home of many weeks pulled out in the mainstream and chugged slowly upriver. Ahmed, who said his job was not yet done, stood next to BuBu and me on the quayside and we all waved. A few lonely 'Woohoos' reached the shore.

1 Cleaveland, 'Ahmed Baba ... racial slavery in the Maghrib', Journal of North African Studies.

2 Park, Travels in the Interior.

3 Hallett, Penetration of Africa.

4 Hallett, Penetration of Africa. English, Book Smugglers.

5 Qur'an, 24:33.

6 Knopfler, Universal Music Publishing Group.

7 Khaldun, Muqaddima, Vol. 1.

7. JUDGEMENT DAY

Perhaps some of us have to go through dark and devious ways
before we can find the river of peace or the high road to the soul's
destination ... and each one who was dared to harken to and follow
the secret call has known the perils of the dangerous, solitary transit.

Campbell, *Thousand Faces*

My dawdle across Europe and Africa to shrug off the trappings of identity, to lose the chains of national state and big business, had got me where exactly? I was standing in jellaba-drenching heat on the bank of an inhospitable river in one of the poorest countries of the world surrounded by American, French and Nigerien troops dealing with a hit-and-run jihadist insurgency. In the small pile at my feet were two valuable documents: one the diary of a long-murdered Scottish soldier-explorer that would prove historic French duplicity to the English, the other an early-seventeenth century treatise that rejected basic tenets of today's vicious Islamist revolution. Adversaries, once they knew of the documents' existence, might work to keep them quiet and, in the case of the latter, quiet could require my death. To escape this, I had to conduct covert negotiations in countries that were hunting me for the assassination of a saint-or-sinner European president. Somewhere behind me was a vengeful and dangerous ex-lover who might have corrupted the man by my side, but who claimed to be my guardian. Against all notions of discretion, I had acquired two war-shattered and enslaved young black boys, without official papers of any kind, who saw me as a benevolent and courageous djinn. I had arbitrarily taken responsibility for their lives and they trusted me as an adoptive father. The sole airport was closed to us as we had no entry permits or vaccination certificates. We didn't even have a place to stay.

I remembered a conversation with an ex-intelligence officer back in the days when I had a name, a car, a bank balance and a house. 'You might be able to hide for a while,' he advised, 'but, if we want you badly enough, we

Muammar al-Qaddafi's canal cuts through the scrub desert south of Timbuktu. *Atlas Obscura*

Sankoré Mosque, Timbuktu. *Baz Lecocq*

Well of Bouctou, Timbuktu. *Alamy*

Gordon Laing's house, Timbuktu. *upyernoz*

Reading the Qur'an among the AK-47s embedded in the Peace Monument, Timbuktu. *JoaolLeitao.com*

The side entrance of the Djinguereber Mosque, Timbuktu. *JoaolLeitao.com*

Leo Africanus, Hassan Mohammed Al Wazzan Al Zayati, probable portrait, Sebastiano del Piombo, c. 1520. *National Gallery of Art, Washington*

Posthumous portrait of Mungo Park by an unknown artist, 1859. *Wikipedia*

General Joseph-Jacques-Césaire Joffre meets Mandarin and Vietnamese dignitaries in Hanoi in 1922 during his triumphal world tour

Martin Selmayr and Jean-Claude Juncker

Ahmed Baba 'Answers a Moroccan's Questions about Slavery', 1615. *Mamma Haidara Memorial Library*

LEFT: Muammar al-Qaddafi at the 12th African Union conference, 2009. US Navy. *Wikipedia*

BELOW: Part of Muammar al-Qaddafi's villa, Timbuktu, after the French bombing, 2013. *Paul Hannaford, The Sun*

Pinasses loading at Kabara on the River Niger. *F. van der Kraaij Collection*

Boko Haram boy soldiers, 2016. *Financial Tribune*

One of the two DC-3 carcasses at Uli landing strip, 1969, which was put to another use in 2021

One of many world-wide street demonstrations in support of Charlie Hebdo after the massacre, this one in Strasbourg, 2015. *Claude Truong-Ngoc*

La Moqueuse, sloop-minesweeper of the Free French Navy, WW2. *Association Aux Marins*

General Charles de Gaulle, c. 1942. *US Library of Congress*

will find you. It will be you who will make the mistake. For some reason, you will pop your head above the parapet and we will see the movement. Then we will have you.'

I stood visible and vulnerable in the sun. With a rush of *kamikaze* traffic at my back and a far shore dotted with crocodiles feeding on human waste, I thought I might have made a mistake or two.

Ahmed gave a last wasted wave as our pinasse chugged under the Kennedy Bridge, recipient of more Chinese funding. 'What's the plan, Uncle?' he said, his leadership role relinquished.

'Local cash first, McDonald's second, I think.'

A private taxi took us to the *Grand Hôtel du Niger* where for a small and necessary bribe, locally called *dash*, the front desk exchanged US dollars for 440 Central African Francs, a challenging rate. The clerk also threw in the addresses of an *Hawala* banker, where I popped in and set up a money transfer, and a recommended burger restaurant, the *Fast Food de L'Année* on the road that leads from the *Rond Point Grand Hotel* to the bridge. BuBu approved the choice so I left them there with Ahmed scouring the menu for a second assault and went in search of accommodation.

Street naming is a recent endeavour for many West African cities. The road to the south of the bridge is known as *Boulevard de l'Université, Pont Président Kennedy* over the bridge, then *rue de Gaweye* after *Place des Martyrs, rue de Commerce* for a couple of blocks, in turn followed by *rue de Kailey*, until, in less than 2 kilometres altogether, it ends at the *Grand Marché.*

I won't disclose the cosy auberge I found for fear of causing trouble for the charming, part-French, lady owner. Let's call her 'Michelle'. At first, she turned her nose up at my dirty clothing, but I assured her that a visit to the shower and a clothes market were my next stops. She was, perhaps, fifty with elfin black hair. Her simple yellow dress discreetly accentuated her figure and her light-coffee skin. Over *Lady Grey* tea, I handed her my French passport and explained that I was part of a small group with some official difficulties. We needed a week's respite to sort ourselves out before moving on. It would be best if my companions provided no papers and that none of us came to the notice of the hotel police.

I told Michelle of the BuBu's race from slavery in Gao. She was instinctively indignant and protective and replied with a story, in which she had been tangentially involved. Hadijatou Mani, a twenty-four-year-old woman was sold when twelve by her Berber Tuareg family as a sex-slave, a *sadaka*, to a master in the Hausa community. Slavery was made illegal in Niger in 2003. When Hadijatou was set free two years later, she married, but the courts declared this bigamy because she was *de facto* already married to her previous master, a man who never gave up on the chase. She was jailed for six months. The case was taken up by the anti-slavery campaign group, *Timidria*, 'solidarity'. Eventually, judges from neighbouring countries decided in Hadijatou's favour.

It was a serious embarrassment for the Nigerien government, ordered to pay ten million CFA (about 20,000 US dollars) compensation, made worse when set against Timidria's survey of the country's hereditary slave caste which claimed that 870,000 people, seven per cent of the population, lived in forced labour, 40,000 of whom were slaves.

It was a simple matter to enlist Michelle's help in taking BuBu to the market for a T-shirt expedition. Of course, an up-front cash payment in dollars for three rooms for a week helped. By the time I left to collect my charges, I wondered if the third room might be unnecessary.

That evening, BuBu attacked the small hotel swimming pool. It was their debut in water away from the river. As they said in amazement, there were no fish. It was also the boys' first time alone in purpose-made beds in a room with a door and a hard roof. This city was a living example of the yawning gap between the few in their plush hotels who have and those in the hovels and doorways who do not. In the morning, I noticed that one of BuBu's beds had not been slept in.

Breakfast was lengthy after BuBu had been scooped from the pool. Michelle took the boys to the market for conservative clothes, suitable for a Hausa Muslim community, all blood and religious supporters of my previous enemy in the Biafran war. It was hard, as Freddie Forsyth kept saying, to shake off the disgust at barbarous behaviours of fifty years ago. In my case, it was where my distrust of cynical government, particularly my own, became a deep part of my psyche.

After morning prayer, BuBu went hand-in-hand with Ahmed to the Musée Nationale and Zoo in the *Avenue Mitterrand*. In truth, I wanted them out of the way. Michelle had arranged a confidential interview with a contact at Timidria. Immediately, I had passports, visas and vaccination certificates to think about, as well as a return to my Hawala banker. For the future, I had to decide what was best for the boys and where and with whom to try to settle them. It was clear they could not stay with me. After I had been to Edinburgh and Paris on a possibly dangerous trip, I had my own nomadic journey to continue. If I could get the boys to Nigeria, I wondered whether I could find them an educational establishment which would care for them with my financial support. I did not see them prospering back in Mali, but I needed to talk through my ideas and then get BuBu's agreement as young, free men, albeit in need of guidance.

The meeting with Timidria was in a small park in the centre of a busy roundabout of sand holding large, isolated acacia trees. I visited first a smart men's clothes shop and in a pleasurable mirror of Lee Child's 'Jack Reacher' emerged in crisp, hot-weather clothes with my old wear in the bin, swiftly recovered by the staff, I guessed, and sent for cleaning. Ten minutes after I arrived at the nominated bench, a woman sat next to me. I noticed two men lingering some distance away. Was this a set up? Was there a microphone? I was in no condition to run.

My contact was best described as 'plump', her figure straining at her startlingly coloured costume. Her turban was violet and not designed for undercover operations. She sat with her hands in her ample lap and looked to the right, away from me. I had to strain to hear her above the raucous Chinese and Japanese trucks in the traffic that swirled around us.

'As-salāmu 'alaykum. My name is Asibet. Our office is not safe now. Our founder, Ilguilas Weila, is in hiding.'

I nodded to an acacia.

'He has been falsely accused of stealing money from two foreign donors, including Anti-Slavery International in London. I hear from a mutual friend that you would like to understand more about slavery in Niger.'

'That would be very helpful.'

'You should understand that the government has said that slavery does not exist in this country. To say that it does, to say that the law that prohibits slavery is not being enforced rigorously, is to criticise the government, to call them liars. In a Muslim country, this does not sit well.

'Foreign governments frequently announce that there are no slaves in Niger and this proves that the local authorities are correct in their denial. Any slavery that used to exist was a cultural hangover from colonial rule. You will understand, therefore, that slavery is a Western problem, not African. Some falsely say that Islam assisted in the indoctrination of slaves by preaching, for example, that if you disobey your master, you will not get to paradise. If this were true, paradise would be in the hands of your master. But Islam also says that no Muslim can be a slave. These are difficult times.'

'Can I tell you a hypothetical story about two young Bozo boys from Mali?'

'I would be happy to listen, but I cannot countenance anything illegal.'

And so, I shared the tale of BuBu, boys without parents, without family or village, and only recently free of the jihadis. I also shared my plans in an imprecise way.

'Am I right that in a case like this, BuBu, love their name, would need no financial assistance to get to Nigeria.'

I said I thought that was the case. In fact, additional funding might be available for wider purposes.

'So, hypothetically, BuBu would need travel documents and vaccination certificates to allow them to leave Niger and enter Nigeria. Their companions would need stamps in a Malian and a ...'

'English European passport.'

'... and would also appreciate assistance with travel arrangements.'

'In our pretend world, that would all be most helpful.'

'It has been a most interesting story. Of course, I cannot help you. I must leave now; I have been here long enough and I have meetings.'

'It was a pleasure to meet you, Asibet. *Wa alaykumu s-salām.*'

Asibet rolled away, followed shortly by her two guardians. After a satisfactory visit without stress to my dingy hawala office, I returned to the hotel, took up my *Qur'an* and prepared to wait.

Let those of you who are willing to trade the life of this world for the life to come, fight in God's way. To anyone who fights in God's way, whether killed or victorious, We shall give a great reward. Why should you not fight in God's cause and for those oppressed men, women, and children who cry out, 'Lord rescue us from this town whose people are oppressors? By your grace, give us a protector and give us a helper!'[1]

Mid-afternoon, Ahmed and BuBu came back, excited by the Hausa-styled pavilions at the museum containing the bones of prehistoric animals, and displays of primitive native tools, utensils and instruments, all of which were intimately known to the boys. 'It wasn't real because there were no chickens in the huts.' BuBu were unimpressed by the crocodile and hippo pools in the zoo. They were also sad to see lonely elephants and giraffes in captivity. 'Why not let them be free?' The swimming pool was the best antidote.

That evening, Michelle accepted my invitation to dinner providing she chose the restaurant. The *Maquis Africa Queen* was tucked away off the street near the *Rond Point Maourey*. The patron was a delightful Cameroonian lady and, clearly, a good friend. They chose the dishes between them and, when they were served, I applauded. BuBu were constantly entertaining as they experimented. Their first taste of ice cream was a time of wonder. In bed, that night, I heard Tabu scream and, trying not to disturb Michelle, slid out and padded into his room. He was wide-eyed, standing, shaking, bathed in sweat and fast asleep. I hugged him, dried him off and carried him back to Michelle's bed where the three of us snuggled down. The patter of feet soon announced Kabu's arrival. All Tabu would tell me later through Ahmed was that he was 'shooting children'.

For a man seeking to quit all responsibilities, this was a lot of commitment.

'You must not go out before ten o'clock this morning,' announced Michelle at breakfast. 'The boys must be out of the pool and in their new clothes.' She took us a street away to an antiseptic room in a private house where a nurse gave vaccinations and a photographer set up facing a blank wall. We were all posed for official pictures. On the way back, Michelle told me that the price for the arrangements, including travel and food, was 1,000 US dollars to be paid in cash to her. With my dash, I should offer 1,500. 'Is this satisfactory?'

I told her I would collect the money later that day. Afterwards, I went with BuBu to see the *Grande Mosquée* where we took the tourist tour and, after some street food, to see a wrestling match at the *Stade de la Lutte*

Traditionelle. Fighters in leather loincloths faced each other across the ring. The losers were the first to fall, or even touch a knee to the ground. Bouts could last over ten minutes. BuBu were entranced and, by the third wrestle, stood on their seats cheering on their new heroes. That night, after much wrestling around the pool and without discussion, the boys went straight to Michelle's room and, when I checked, were fast asleep.

Of all things, there was a soft rain falling over Niamey. We said our farewells in the early chill dawn, grey before the sun. Everyone clung to Michelle and promised to try to return one day. Even I said that, despite my rule never to go back. Our bags had gone ahead during the night to our new pinasse. We had one subterfuge to conduct. I went aboard first, helped by Ahmed, and settled into a seat. Ahmed then went back to the taxi to assist the third member of the party in a sheesh and long jellaba, in reality Tabu perched on Kabu's shoulders. 'BuBu has arrived,' declared Ahmed to much stifled giggling.

The Niger made a series of short, sharp bends in the shape of a 'W' as it crossed the large game park to where the river acts as an 80-mile border between Niger and Dahomey. I was not bothered by the slow pace of the boat, preferring to end the journey alive. Yet, time seemed to have no value or meaning to this crew. I guessed that they did not even know their own ages. They were quiet and uncommunicative without a potential 'yahoo' anywhere. There seemed little understanding of a man who could undertake a long journey and carry little but the hair on his head. After half an hour, well away from Niamey, the captain cranked the engine and we began to create bow waves. Every time the river curved, I looked ahead for the sight of men lying in wait in canoes. I realised, without surprise, that I had lived with constant fear on this trip, fear of being chased, assaulted and robbed.

It took two nights, almost three full days, to reach the border. We beached each evening in a routine that was now familiar to me. The villagers were always friendly, their hair greased with shea butter, the men with pronounced bad teeth, while the women moved with stunning poise as they carried buckets, pots or firewood on their heads.

At the first stop, we were offered bowls of locusts with red peppers, okra and chilli cooked in peanut oil. The meal ended with a small bowl of honey which attracted the attention of a few passing bees. 'They want their honey back,' explained Ahmed.

At the next camp, the horizon to the east was thick and hazy and a sandstorm was expected. It started the next morning and lasted for two days. The force of the wind was not great, a stiff breeze, but the quantity of sand and dust carried before it darkened the sky. The constant stream swept along so that the air was at time so dull and full that it was difficult to discern people nearby. It adhered to our skin, moistened by perspiration, to form a cheap and universal hair powder. It coated our rice and fish, taken with ease from a river with nearly 250 species, twenty found nowhere else.

Finally, we slipped under the Malainville Bridge and entered Nigeria, the last of the Niger's host countries. Our first encounter with the Nigerian Marine Police passed smoothly after a small amount of dash disappeared from my passport. I encouraged BuBu to play noisily about the pinasse and to jump into the water as we waited for our stamps. There were police outposts seemingly around every corner. Mostly we were left alone, but were occasionally called over if the men were short of cash to buy beer and cigarettes.

We had another three days to go to reach Yelwa at the start of the 500 square miles of the lake formed by the Kainji Dam, the fourth largest in Africa. The dam's giant lock could lift 49-metre barges past 280,000 cubic feet of water per second roaring down to be converted by turbines into electricity for nine of Nigeria's twelve states. The dam was completed in 1968 after four frantic years by an Italian consortium to British and Dutch designs. The Chinese were suggesting repairs and enhancements. The lake supplies Nigeria with an abundance of fish and a vast irrigated hinterland. Passing Yelwa, we saw white crowds of little egrets nesting on the tops of submerged trees. All along the shore, men were stooped over the rock-hard earth, loosened with Sahara dust and ash from constant controlled fires. The fields were studded with shea, silk-cotton and tamarind trees. Farmers were double cropping, scooping water in calabashes from grid channels to runnels to feed a plethora of mixed vegetables, but concentrating for the market on their famous red onions.

Watching the sorghum, millet, peppers, cassava, tobacco, tomato and sugar cane and, impressive though the lake promised to be, my thoughts turned to the village of Old Boussa, now far below this artificial lake. There, in 1806, Mungo Park, the great beard, *Bonci-Ba*, a Scottish doctor, was ambushed. His expedition of dozens of Europeans and natives had all died or abandoned him. Park had several fearsome battles with the Moors for whom killing a white man was a sacred duty. At the last, alone, sick and probably a little mad, Park tried to escape the spears and rocks. The earliest European 'Timbuktu and Niger' explorer slipped over the side of his schooner after it became stuck in the rapids. He was drowned and his body never found.

The Lander brothers, Richard and John, in 1830 made a more successful attempt in two native canoes with enough provisions for a month, including two sheep. They survived the rapids and reached Old Boussa after five months where they found relics of Park's exhibition: his logarithm tables, the hymnbook of his brother-in-law, both carefully preserved, a tailor's bill and an invitation to a dinner party in London's Strand. Shortly afterwards, the Landers were captured by Igbos, but they did reach their destination and return home. Richard died on the island of Fernando Po from a stomach wound incurred in an ambush on a later trading mission; five years afterwards, John succumbed to an 'African illness' in London. I felt a connection with this pair because of my own experiences on the river and in Fernando Po and Biafra. I also found the brothers' journals, written by two Cornishmen brought up 'well away from the centre of things', full of verve and among the best of their kind.[2]

Modern travellers in Africa move encased in the shell of their own culture, moving too fast, eating their own food, sleeping in their own sort of bed. Young men, like the Landers, moved slowly, alone and unprotected, exposed to all the pressures of African life, an experience as exhilarating as it must have been exhausting.[3]

At the back of my mind, I began to imagine that the river would never stop. 'Never stop, Niger stop,' became a whirling mantra. When Park asked a local man where the Niger went, he was told that it ran 'to the world's end'. At least, I thought, Park's story had taught me the importance of patience and the acceptance of fate, no matter how difficult life was at the time.

In the emptiness of the man-made lake, miles from safety, our cosy progress halted. Three pirogues, unkempt, hacked from tree trunks, pushed along by powerful outboards, came out of the morning mist. They might as well as had loudspeakers blazing Wagner's *The Ride of the Valkyries*.

At first, we ignored them as they seemed headed for New Bussa, but their curving wake clearly set them to intercept. Tabu stared and then began to shake as he pointed and screamed, '*Boko Harem.*'

To a warrior believer, infidels were not respected human beings because they did not obey the Muslin God. Thus, infidels were benighted natives, rebels or outlaws, who had to be brought to heel. It was impossible to conceive of them as being endowed with rights as all rights came from God, as conceived by Muslims.[4] What right could one have to hold out against the only force and power in the universe? 'Submit willingly or unwillingly', it was all the same.[5] It was likely that we would all be killed out of hand. Armed men, four to a boat, in football T-shirts and ragged shorts shouted at us to stop and two fired unmistakable AK-47s in our direction, the warning bullets falling short.

Boko Haram, literally 'fake' in Hausa, meaning 'fake education', and 'haram', 'forbidden' in Arabic, was beyond any pale, publicly tied to the murderous cells of al-Qaeda. Their attacks varied between young, mainly female, suicide bombers and sleeper groups, blending in with local communities or hiding in the vast bush, before more conventional armed assaults on civilian and military targets. Thousands had been killed by a Nigerian military, often criticised for being too close or too inefficient, and in return the jihadis came again and again in mass kidnappings and bombings of police stations, churches, schools, government offices, prisons and missionary hospitals.

And, now, they were coming for us, or for me I wondered, in a deliberate raid.

For a few second, our captain pushed his motor to the limit, but it would never have bought us nearer to safety and would only enrage our pursuers. The engine was switched off and we wallowed in the waves. Ahmed dived under the canvas cover and reappeared, crouching, holding two 9 mm machine pistols, one of which he slid across the boat planks to me. I pushed BuBu to the floor and away from immediate harm.

'Where did these weapons come from?' I demanded.

'Nianankoro arranged them for me, Uncle. I have had them since Timbuktu. He was worried that word of your cargo would reach the extremists. He became even more worried because he thought Attou had overheard what was going on. She is not sane when she does not get her own way. With you and I disappearing, he was desperate, not knowing what she might do. I have been trying to keep her sweet on the phone.'

'Not sweet enough. This doesn't look random. This looks well organised. We will have to take them early.'

The leading boat bumped alongside making us stagger as we raised our arms above our heads. Two men stepped lightly over the gunwales into our pinasse, firing single shots in the air as they came. I knew the AK-47 well, a stalwart of the Tuareg rebellions, but not of the Western-supplied Nigerien and Nigerian forces. The only reason this gas-operated workhorse would stop firing was when it ran out of ammunition. Thirty 39 mm bullets would deal easily with the limited cover on our boat. There was nowhere to hide, not even the water.

The spokesman was a small bearded man sporting a Benfica T-shirt whose red eyes seemed half-crazed on drugs. He shouted, 'Amkssa'. That was all the confirmation I needed. Immediately, one of the crew pointed at me and as a thank-you all three were sliced, unwanted, to the deck by our visitors.

'Now, Ahmed,' I said quietly, reached down for my gun, pressed the trigger while our two visitors had their weapons pointed at their victims and we were partly shielded from the other craft. It took me a half-second to realise the safety catch was still on, but I caught both men in one short sweep and they fell. Ahmed blazed wildly at the boats, not used to the kick of a machine-pistol. I dropped to my knees and fired over the gunwale where the terrorists were unsuspecting sitting targets. Despite their surprise at our ferocity, they quickly returned fire and, out of the corner of my eye, I saw Ahmed drop. I had aimed in small bursts, but my gun was empty and I had no spare magazine.

We were done for. I decided to try for the canvas where I hoped there might be other magazines when I heard two short, trained bursts from my side. It was a sight I would never forget, the true horror of it. BuBu, each holding an AK-47 from the fallen men, methodically killed every *Boko Haram* member left in the stationary boats. They stood in plain sight and did the job like the professional soldiers they were. I saw the shock on the faces of the dying men as they were executed by children. I also saw the cold hatred on BuBu's faces. They continued pumping single rounds into the lifeless bodies and kept their fingers tensed even afterwards. I went over, took their guns and put my arms around them, but their eyes were elsewhere, their bodies not in the pinasse, but in some distant Bozo village. I wondered if they would ever come back.

Ahmed was dying, stitched from his abdomen to his chest. I cradled him in my arms and started to cry. This young man had become my friend and confidante in a very few weeks. I did not want him to leave me. I wanted to say that I was sorry. I felt all of the blame and all of the loss.

He was coughing and blood trickled from his mouth. 'Don't cry, Uncle. It was a good fight. I always wanted to be a soldier.' He paused. 'Tell Nianankoro that I have avenged his daughter, Inshallah. Now you must look after BuBu and complete your mission. You are a good man whatever they say about you.'

'Tell me the last part, Ahmed, the bit about Attou.'

'I will tell you, but only you. It is a matter of great shame. Before you came to Timbuktu, I succumbed to her. She is a beautiful woman. I told her it was over, not to be repeated, but she said nobody would ever again leave her like her daughter and husband. If I didn't come when she called she would tell my wife and it was my marriage that would be over. I would never see my children again. Would you tell …'

Then Ahmed died and a rush of water surrounded my ankles. The pinasse was sinking. I looked over the side and two of the pirogues had already gone, the bodies of the jihadis floating slowly on the grey tide towards the distant dam and its turbines. A small inflatable, partly deflated through bullet-damage, was our only hope. I placed unresisting BuBu inside one by one, fetched our baggage which I placed on their knees and shoved one loaded AK-47 down the side. There was no room for me so I slipped into the water, grabbed a rope and kicked for the shore.

All these circumstances crowded in and I confess that my spirits began to fail. I was certain we would all die. I felt I had no alternative, but to let go and sink down to Mungo Park and Old Boussa. I was dreaming about my own dead children when strong arms picked at my trousers and I was lifted into a cutter. It was the marine police who had heard the shooting and finally got their boat started and had come to see what was going on. The boys, the goods and the AK-47 followed me onto the deck.

When I came to, I was dazed and lying on grass. The extreme beauty of a small green moss caught my eye. The whole plant was no bigger than the top of my finger. I looked at it with admiration. It began to rain heavily and I was carried inside. Being looked after by the Nigerian police after a gunfight was not something I would have sought. I wondered if my freedom was at an end? Was my head now firmly above the parapet?

'You've been asleep. Good thing, too. You missed a massive thunderstorm. How do you feel?'

'*M na-eche ezi.*'

'Good. Thanks be for a quick recovery. And, also, you know I am an Igbo. I am Inspector Okonkwo.'

'I'll never forget the accent. How are the boys?'

My interrogator was a man, perhaps thirty, English-educated, in an officer's uniform, clean cut, with a warm, open expression and twinkly eyes; a man who liked the ladies, I guessed.

'They're good physically, but their eyes are dull. It must have been a dreadful experience for them to see that happen. They haven't talked about it and they won't give us their names. They are staying with the wife of one of my sailors who is a Bozo. You, for that matter, are an Englishman in my bed in the marine barracks in New Bussa.'

'Thank you, *daalu*. I am their guardian. They have no living relatives. You may tell the lady '*daalu*' also and to call them 'BuBu' as they see themselves as linked. It's a joke, really. Their real names are Tabu and Kabu. I expect they will want to see me soon.'

'Why don't you take your time, Mr Azebry-Rose; such an unusual name. All the bags from your dinghy are over there. Have a shower, get dressed and come into the office in the next building for a bite and a chat and, if we can sort things out, you can be on your way. There is just one thing immediately that would help me a lot. How many bodies are we looking for?'

'Three crew, twelve terrorists and my good friend Ahmed, a hero, a Bambara from Timbuktu, who died doing most of the damage protecting BuBu.'

'*Daalu.* We shall treat his body with respect. See you later when you can tell me your story.'

So many thoughts. Okonkwo must have been through my bag to find my passport with its Nigerian entry stamps. That probably meant that he had seen several passports and that could mean I was in trouble, something his demeanour didn't suggest. He didn't know that BuBu had done much of the killing and I badly wanted to keep it that way. And, he also hinted that I could soon be on my way. That sounded very good.

Within the hour, I presented myself at the office and a sergeant with razor-creased trousers took me to the officers' mess where Okonkwo was waiting lunch. Two other junior officers broke their meal to come over and shake my hand, congratulating me on my escape and my success. Okonkwo was relaxed and freely told me that the bodies had been recovered, but the boats had gone to the bottom. From papers found, it was clear that the men were from *Boko Haram*, that they had been instructed to stop our boat and kill everyone except an 'Amkssa' who was to be taken with his baggage back to their camp.

Lightning from the storm had put out two masts and the police had only been able to report brief details to their command by a patchy satellite link. Part of the road and two bridges had been washed away. Okonkwo was ordered to travel by boat to Port Harcourt to report the full story in person as soon as possible.

'Politically, this is very important,' he explained. 'My government has been embarrassed at its continuing failure for which, of course, they blame the police and the army. We have been looking for these particular bastards for almost a year. They are devout and committed. They gladly wield the "unsheathed sword against wrong-headed people who arrogantly refuse to accept the plain truth after it has become clear".'

'I see that you know your *Qur'an*,' I countered. '"Fight until there is no more disbelief and all worship is devoted to God."'[6]

'Now you have done our job for us. They are believed to be part of the same group who killed six of our soldiers a few months ago. My superintendent has taken most of our men to find the jihadi camp and to see if we can add to your tally. These terrorists were of the worst kind so please do not reproach yourself for what you did.

'You may not have heard, but the British are coming to help us all with three of their Chinooks to add to the three they already have in Gao,' he continued. 'We think the French are getting tired of the war in Mali.

Macron and the Americans have been asking for men and now we have 250 cavalrymen to act as the point of our bedraggled UN spear.

'Now they have been kicked out of Iraq, all these militants are coming to the Sahel. Five thousand people were killed there last year – Mali, Burkina Faso, Niger, Chad, Mauritania. The fight is complex, a game of cat and mouse in a vast territory with a highly mobile enemy able to vanish into the landscape. They are here, but hidden. We search for them, but we cannot find them. This is why we are grateful to you for what you did today.'

Okonkwo paused and assessed me. After a full minute of looking me in the eye, he made a decision. 'I will trust you, *enyi m*,' he said, 'and life will be easy for you if you first answer some simple questions.'

I told him that I trusted him in return and would tell him as much as he wanted to know. I explained that I was travelling with BuBu to Lagos where I hoped to place them in a kind home with good education. They had had a bad life. I had flown in the Biafran War in 1969, had seen combat and had delivered supplies to the famous Uli road-strip.[7] At that time, I had other names. The name Azebry came from a grandmother of a long time ago who had married a colonial officer. There was just a chance that the one descendant I knew, a distant cousin, Aisha Azebry, might be alive, early sixties and willing to help me. Also, I wanted to see if I could track down Okigbo Biggar, who had been a close friend in the air force. I called him 'Chuck' because he was a cousin by marriage of Chukwuemeka Odumegwu-Ojukwu, the ex-president of the secessionist Biafran province. I could not help him with the identity of 'Amkssa' or any more of my past life.

'You conjure up some impressive names, Mr Azebry. OK, here is the deal. I leave with a cutter from below the Kainji Dam in two hours. I am going to Port Harcourt to make my report. My report will say that my superintendent, through a combination of carefully-garnered intelligence and bold initiative, laid a trap for the terrorists and lured them in. There was a gunfight on the lake and all twelve were killed outright. We had no casualties and are currently conducting follow-up operations. There will be no mention of you or your party. You were not there. You do not exist and therefore have no alternative story to tell. My superintendent, and his fellow officers, will get the credit for this courageous enterprise. Our political leaders will be very happy. I would not be surprised if one or two of them had already announced their participation as observers.

'Do you have any problem so far?'

I shook my head.

'In return Mr Azebry, you and, err, BuBu, will accompany me to Port Harcourt. I will make arrangements for you to travel to Lagos, your papers suitably stamped, where you will be free to make your own arrangements. Also, you will have your baggage on the cutter with you, unopened and uninspected. There will be no awkward questions about Amkssa and why the attack happened.

'Do you have any problems now?'

'Just one, inspector.' Okonkwo's eyes narrowed.

'It is a small request. Ahmed and the three crew were all devout Muslims. If possible, they should be buried in suitable graves this afternoon as is their custom. I would like to say a few words over them.' I smiled. 'As they were not here, there should be no need to wait for any paperwork?'

'I will make arrangements immediately. Just before I do, I have two other matters which might cement our bargain. First, I believe and appreciate what you did for my country fifty years ago. Here is my card. Call me if you find yourself in difficulties. I will see if I can find Chuck. Second, I can already help you with your namesake, Aisha Azebry. You will find her in Lagos. She is the head of one of Nigeria's most famous fashion houses.'

'She always did like clothes,' I offered. 'This is excellent news. *Daalu, enyi m.*' We shook hands. I ate a good lunch.

An hour later, Bubu, animists, and I, an atheist, the Christian Inspector Okonkwo and a small detachment of sweating police-gravediggers stood around four newly-dug mounds each correctly aligned with stones placed to show passers-by that devout Muslims lay below who were deserving of respect. BuBu clung to my trousers as I read,

When that Judgement Day comes, no soul will speak except by His permission, and some of them will be wretched and some happy. The wretched ones will be in the Fire, sighing and groaning, there to remain for as long as the heavens and the earth endure, unless your Lord wills otherwise: Your Lord carries out whatever He wills. As for those who have been blessed, they will be in Paradise, there to remain as long as the heavens and earth endure, unless your Lord wills otherwise – an unceasing gift.[8]

'Nicely said,' offered Okonkwo after he snapped a salute. 'That's the first time that I have heard the *Qur'an* in English. Thank you for sharing it.'

'There is not a lot of difference to the Bible,' I offered. 'Ahmed was a good man and a good friend.' What I didn't share was that many years ago in London, Aisha Azebry was my first wife, married for convenience, money and an untraceable passport. There had also been a week's holiday afterwards in Paris that we jokingly called a honeymoon.[9]

As soon as I could, I would send a sizable sum of money to Nianankoro to give to Ahmed's widow. I took the boys' hands and led them to the Chinese off-roader and then to the cutter and their new life.

---

1 *Qur'an*, 4:74–75.
2 Landers, *Niger Journal*.
3 Hallett, 'Introduction', *Niger Journal*.
4 Crone, *God's Rule*.
5 *Qur'an*: 3:83, 13:15, 41:11.
6 *Qur'an*: 8:39.
7 Heal, *Disappearing*.
8 *Qur'an*, 11:105-108.
9 Heal, *Disappearing*.

8. LOST FRIENDS

The Negroes lead a beastly kind of life, being utterly destitute of the use of reason, of dexterity of wit, and of all arts, yea they so behave themselves, as if they had continually lived in a forest among wild beasts. They have great swarms of harlots among them; whereupon a man may easily conjecture their manner of living; except their conversation perhaps be somewhat more tolerable, who dwell in the principal towns and cities: for it is like that they are somewhat more addicted to civility.

Africanus, *Geographical History of Africa* (trans. Pory), 1600

'Perhaps four nights,' declared Inspector Okonkwo, 'if we push it through daylight and there's no more rain. All a waste of time, really.' He had just emerged from the main cabin where he had written his report.

'Why do you say that?' I asked.

'Well, the report was easy. No witnesses so I just made it up for my hero superintendent. I anticipate my trip will prove unnecessary as the radio will soon be fixed. I fully expect that all the details will have been invented before we get to Port Harcourt. I'll have to rewrite my report so that everything tallies. But,' he smiled, 'I'll enjoy a short break in civilisation before I have to come back to the dry season with withered grass and dust devils.'

BuBu shouted from the bow in excitement. This was a rare sight even for these experienced river boys. Two West African manatee, fifteen feet, each weighing nearly 800 pounds, popped up for a look.

'That is unusual,' mused Okonkwo. 'They are on the extinction list. They usually prefer salt-water, but being herbivores they sometimes come up above the oil pollution and get trapped closer to the dam.'

Below the dam, the Niger is easily navigable all the year round and runs through a monotonous broad and shallow valley between five and ten miles wide. It was late and we stopped at a river police station near the bend at Jessao, an unseen town. The men went ashore to the small barracks while we and Okonkwo slept on the boat. I was sitting on my bunk, beginning to undress, having finally got BuBu to sleep, when there was a fearful scream from the shore. I sensed it was a snake for I had been dreaming about them since we reached the Kainji, mainly psychedelic flash-backs of vipers either among sand dunes like the gold-flash that had bitten my brother or the sultry, grey horned variety that had, unseen, killed my friend, Asso, in the Sahara.[1] Bathed in the light from above the barrack door, this was no viper, but almost four metres of African rock python, entwined around a slumped member of our crew. Blood wept from every facial cavity of the squeezed body. With every gasp, the snake tightened its grip.

'He went for a pee,' shouted one of the guards. 'We told him not to go off the veranda. We told him there was a python's nest there.' The man was hysterical. 'He stood right on it.' The evidence was on the ground, a long scrape in the earth, about thirty elongated eggs, several broken into a khaki mess.

The python's skin was covered in thick blotches of olive and chestnut. Its head, dark brown, lined with yellow, shaped like a spear, was beginning to disarticulate as it sized up its meal. It looked like it had coiled the man's leg as he stood, urinating and unsuspecting, and kept on climbing. As I stepped forward, Okonkwo fumbled his pistol out of its holster, but was unsure where to fire.

It was a long time since I had got up close and personal. Pythons carry no venom, have no bite, their sharp, inner teeth curved backwards to ease the swallow. I faced the animal, inches away, and gazed into the hypnotic eyes. Within seconds, its grip loosened, steadily relinquishing its prey. Its eyes never left mine and the head swayed to keep contact. As the python moved to the undergrowth, Okonkwo lined his gun, but I pushed it down softly.

'Bad luck,' I advised.

'I can see that it could be awkward to get on your wrong side. You have some surprising skills. In Hausa, they call it, 'Bòòríí, spiritual power.'

He quoted from the *Qur'an*:

From the evil of the slinking whisperer
who whispers in the breast of mankind
of djinn and men.

As I looked up, I saw BuBu standing open-mouthed on the cutter's deck. The man jerked, moaned and died, I suspected of heart failure.

'Damn. He was not the best policeman, but at least he did what he was told.'

Next day, we chased the river at breakneck speed. About seventy miles from Jebba, with its hydroelectric power station, the Niger is joined by the Kaduna, Hausa for 'crocodile', where we smashed onwards, oblivious. It was little different a few hours later at Lokoja where the Niger forms a 'Y' with its principal tributary, the Benue, as we cut through an inland salt lake full of islets and shoals. The river then began its descent from a 2,000-foot-high plateau, due south to the sea 340 miles away. We tore, crew laughing, through a restricted valley, enclosed by hills. The landscape flattened at Onitsha, the largest town on the Niger's banks in Nigeria and the third largest after Bamako and Niamey. We emerged from sandstone cliffs into rainforest at Aboh where the delta began and its hundreds of capillaries leaked river water into the Gulf of Guinea.

The Niger delta is the second largest in the world after the Ganges. It is so vast that Europeans who traded there for centuries never realised that it was all part of the same river. It is also the largest mangrove swamp in the world, but no one has yet discovered what mangrove is good for besides breeding malaria. The delta is a hothouse soured with the rank smell of rotting leaves. Its backwaters are narrow with branches laced overhead to form dark vaults. At one police post, the smell from dying vegetation was nauseous. The sergeant told me to stay close as white people were not respected. That night we could hear crabs bubbling through the mud.

The delta has its relics, the rotted hulks of the small-masted trading ships that changed West Africa. The second half of the nineteenth century was the fabulous era of the 'palm oil ruffians'. The slave trade was abolished, but the growing use of soap and the need for lubricants for the first locomotives in England created a demand for palm oil. The delta slave centres or 'counters', like Bonny, Brass and Calabar, became palm oil depots. Oil was collected in the interior and brought down the channels in puncheons to be burned in copper urns. Living conditions for Europeans improved with the use of the river hulks. Ships ready for the breaker's yard were sunk close to shore, roofed with thatch, and served as office and home for the company agent and as storehouses for the oil. The hulks cut the ships' loading time, but not the mortality rate among agents.

Today, large amounts of palm oil are still needed for food additives, cheap and multi-purposed, but the delta's real wealth is now a different oil, petroleum. The slave counters turned palm oil depots now made a final conversion. Teams of English and American technicians, living in air-conditioned trailers, dredged the channels, built the pipelines and dug underwater wells at a 'million dollars a bung'. The 'crude oil ruffians' were the direct descendants of the 'palm oil ruffians'.

Oil was the true cause of the Biafran war, but it was strongly flavoured by religious and tribal animosity. Everywhere, channels were dotted with the metal towers of the wells that pumped up Nigeria's main source of revenue. Oil refineries and gleaming steel cylinders were closed off by high metal fences. Sunken modern yachts and speedboats, war casualties, dotted the inner channels. Giant tankers lay offshore.

We witnessed the slow poisoning of the waters of this country and the destruction of vegetation and agricultural land by oil spills ... Since the inception of the industry more than twenty-five years ago, there has been no concerted effort on the part of the government, let alone the oil operators, to control environmental problems.[2]

At our last overnight stop, Okonkwo and I were invited by a bedraggled delegation to a small village. It was a pathetic visit. The evidence of oil pollution was everywhere, stained into the vegetation and even the palm leaves on the roofs. The villagers were hungry and explained that there were no longer enough fish coming upstream from the sea. The river fish had almost all died and those remaining were their only sustenance. They fed us well enough, embarrassingly more than they could afford, and then asked a favour. They had heard that I had a strong spirit with power over animals and hoped that this extended to fish. The news of my encounter with the python had leapt several hundred miles and many isolated villages in a few days, as fast as our boat, itself a magic feat. I was asked to cast a spell to bring back the fish so that their children would not starve. Okonkwo went outside while I led a short ceremony. We didn't speak on the way back to the cutter but, early next morning, I saw him and two men carry the remainder of the boat's food supplies to the village boundary.

As we left the steamy shade of the mangrove forest, the broadening river abruptly turned blindingly bright and salt spray filled the air. Directly ahead, surf pounded a spit of yellow sand crowned by giant cottonwoods. At Port Harcourt, the flanged roots of mangrove marked the high-tide level. Scattered among the mangroves were white lilies, banana trees with pale green leaves and wild palms. We pulled into a deserted police dock. There was no reception suitable for heroes.

Okonkwo went off to report and BuBu and I kicked our heels outside the guardhouse. We had quickly developed a composite language. From their fishing near Timbuktu, Bubu had a little French and, then, as soldiers, developed a simple knowledge of Hausa and pigeon English, which they had kept hidden. With my creaky recall of Igbo, we chatted away with sign language until, when we found a word we shared or liked, whatever the language, it joined our vocabulary.

Okonkwo came back displaying a large ironic grin. 'Option 3,' he explained. 'It seems that my report is unlikely to match that reported in parliament two days ago. I am ordered to Lagos to make the necessary adjustments. If you would like to come with me aboard a military helicopter, no passports, I can also give you a lift into town and we can say our farewells.'

I said that would suit the three of us very well. BuBu burst with excitement, followed by rising apprehension, when they realised they were going to fly.

'Give me a moment while I look after my men and then we'll get going.'

Two hours later, I was leaning on a balcony of a small suite on the tenth floor of the plush Eko Hotel, large gin and tonic in hand, all courtesy of the country's military police. The Atlantic rolled in a long line of steady surf onto Lagos's Victoria Island Kuramo beach. Inside, BuBu battered each other with plump down pillows. A Huey helicopter from the 97 Special Operations Group had picked us up quayside at Port Harcourt for the hour to Murtala Muhammed airport. Three Chinese 4x4s, complete with sirens, took our party straight to the hotel. All I saw of Okonkwo was a languid hand flapping from the leading vehicle as the convoy left almost without stopping. The receptionist was surprised at what the convoy disgorged, but impressed that our room was pre-paid for two nights.

Friday evening at the hotel was a themed all-you-can-eat American buffet designed to challenge the stomach of any passing Bubu. While we waited to begin our assault on the tables, I collected some naira from the ATM, about 450 to the pound, which made for some interesting high denomination notes. Close by was the excellent *Bookworm* bookshop. I admit I was drawn in by a small display of *Disappearing* in the window with the claim that 'Convict's EU murder story tops charts'.

If you want to buy a novel in any Muslim country, it is best to stick to the big cities. Muslims don't warm to novels, particularly books that are unread but declared dangerous like *The Satanic Verses*.[3] Today, there are many novels in Arabic, Persian and Turkish, but they are still scarce in other Muslim languages like Hausa. The novel is indeed a Western importation to the Islamic world. I picked up back-shelf copies of Patricia Crone's *God's Rule* and Bernard Lewis's *Islam in History* and, almost in a fit of nostalgia, decided to try Joyce's *Finnegans Wake* after my multi-year humiliation as a young man trying to read *Ulysses*.

I bought three other items, not knowing how long we would need to stay in the city: a local tourist guide, a copy of *The Guardian*, Nigeria's biggest-selling newspaper and, from a near-by stall, a 'pre-used' burner mobile phone with some of its previous contacts and texts unscrubbed. I took ten minutes to text Nianankoro that I was in Lagos and to report Ahmed's bravery, his death and his proper burial.

I took a deep, deep breath and moved on.

The Guardian solved an immediate dilemma. There, large on the cultural page, was an interview with my erstwhile sham wife, Aisha, looking fabulous, slinky dress, sultry body, dismissive, authoritative, mistress of her domain. I learnt that Nigeria has the third-biggest film industry on the planet after American and India, dubbed 'Nollywood'. Forty-five videos are produced each week in Lagos's Surelere heartland because Western cinemas, although gaining ground in the richer suburbs, are still a rarity in this country of dubious electricity supply. Aisha was named the 'Queen of Surelere'. No production aspiring for critical applause could proceed without the leading actresses being adorned in the produce of her fashion houses. The spin-off clothing, heavily marketed, that filled the department stores at affordable prices had made Aisha one of Africa's richest women. Tomorrow I would make contact.

One of the affirming pleasures of my two charges was their open-mouthed and innocent enjoyment of their discoveries. Last night's four generous burgers each might have slowed them down, but the impatience with which they set to work on the breakfast tables reminded me of brown bears getting ready for hibernation. They were abetted by the waiters whose infectious grins acclaimed Bubu as record breakers. We then walked down to the beach for their first real view of the ocean, the extent of which had been obscured by the thumping and spray of the police cutter. Their different personalities were evident: Tabu just wanted to dive in, Kabu sat on the sand, went quiet, then asked if there was a waterfall on the other side. We talked for a while and I began to explain that the world was round, but my poor language skills and the boy's disdain for my silly joke reminded me that I had to find a new life for Bubu which they would accept. I needed to move quickly for their sake and because I had commitments in Edinburgh and Paris.

After half an hour of frustrated phone calls where everyone refused to put me through to Aisha, I finally found that she was watching a shoot near her home or, rather, watching her costumes with a team of seamstresses nearby to make any last-minute corrections. I couldn't get her home address, but I did find the location.

'They won't let you through, man,' I was told.

Lagos was another wonderworld to Bubu as we squeezed into the back of a motorcycle taxi. For me, it was a horror show of traffic jams and kamikaze drivers, chaotic road crossings, blaring music from competing speakers, crumbling dirt pavements crammed with street sellers and endless people, albeit mostly with a ready smile. This was a town lanced by raised expressways hanging over throbbing streets. Garbage was ever-present and slums sat cheek-by-jowl with the richest addresses in Africa. For Bubu, for all the same reasons, it was a place full of astonishment. After twenty minutes, I gave up clutching the metal guardrails and gasping at near accidents and concentrated instead on their babbling and shifting expressions of sheer joy. It was a world away from the desert quiet of fishing nets on sluggish water after the moon cooled the sun's excess. One might have thought this blaze of conflicting colours and dreadful cacophony would drive them into bewilderment and fear, but it was the opposite. Their faces were lit with excitement and identification. This was their natural home.

Along Western Avenue, we pulled off near the main entrance to the ragged National Stadium, mostly used for football matches and now a set for Aisha's current movie. 'Falling down now,' said the taxi driver. 'Watch your step. And watch for those *area boys* as well. If they surround you, just pay up if you don't want no knifing.' The hotel receptionist had also warned against these *Agberos*, gangs of children and teenagers who roam the streets extorting money from passers-by and traders.

I saw the security muscle strutting around the shabby entrance and also spotted two separate groups of dishevelled groups of sauntering youths sizing up targets. In the background, armed and tense military sat in their Chinese Cherokee jeeps. I grasped my walking stick against any sudden attack. An enterprising outlet had set up a stall proclaiming 'Aisha's creations: See them in the Movies' where I steered Bubu and covered their arms in dresses, hardly bothering to negotiate with the excited vendor. We marched straight to the guards. 'Urgent costumes for Miss Aisha.' And we were through.

Inside was seemingly bedlam with a dozen cameras, some hand-held, were all pointing to a stage where a large band was supporting a musical performance. At least, I think it should have been because there was a heated row underway with a lot of bruised egos and weeping males and females. BuBu had been transfixed by the 55-inch television in our hotel room. I explained as best I could that this was how the movies they had seen were made. I stopped a passing flunky and learned that the video was a long-awaited tribute to Fela Kuti, now dead for over twenty years, called 'Afrobeat and the Kalkuta Republic'. From what I knew of Kuti, if this was a full-life tribute, then the watchful attendance of the military was guaranteed. Kuti had been a large itch in the side of the Nigerian government and his self-proclaimed republic, a free-love commune dedicated to exposing government hypocrisy and corruption, was attacked in 1977 by over 1,000 soldiers. Fela was severely beaten, his studio, master tapes and instruments destroyed and his mother thrown to her death from a window.

Without pause, Kuti's prominent hits were blasting over the speakers: drums, shekeres with their dancing cowries, West-African and bass guitars playing the riffs and melodies, while horns and two baritone saxophones blared the tunes. I knew that Kuti's songs were all long, often with an instrumental introduction lasting over fifteen minutes, but this all seemed endless.

Amid the bickering, I heard a voice of unarguable command launch itself through a microphone. It was her, Aisha, more lovely than an old man's dreams, a reminder of what youth throws away, of the ghastly waste of expediency. And Aisha was pointing at me. No, she wasn't, that was just my first hope. Did I see a flicker, some recognition that reached towards a stopped figure with a walking stick, some recall of London and Paris over fifty years ago?

No, it wasn't me at all, it was BuBu. They were dancing with Aisha's dresses across their shoulders, in their raised arms, forming rainbows in the air. They had quickly recognised the pigeon English lyrics. Oblivious. Entranced. Committed. Dancing with a *duende*, a spirit that took me back to the heart of the flamenco.[4] BuBu had fallen in love with the sound of Fela Kuti. They embodied the music.

Sometimes, just occasionally, during a dance, people can only stop and watch; there is completeness, nothing to be said. I could not say what BuBu were dancing except that I felt that it was from their home, from the villages of the Bozo, something they had learnt at their parents' knee, something of the crocodile and the hippo, the violent storms, the scalding sand, of belonging and hope. The auditorium quietened behind the music, the bickering drained away. Aisha came down from the dais to the boys, the hangers-on parting before her, and took them by the hand and drew them to the platform. I followed unnoticed, I thought. I had responsibilities; after all, I was the nearest they had to a parent.

'Kuti reached across generations,' Aisha announced. 'He was a call to the youth of our land. These boys represent the young ones. They dance from the soul for those Nigerians who were reached by Kuti. They are his promise. They are Africa's promise.'

A murmur of agreement developed into rhythmic hand clapping and then wild applause. I admired Aisha's panache and poise: the combination of crowd control, the way she had seized the argument and found a solution, an answer, it must be said, that was modelling her lucrative creations for the ordinary people.

I realised that I was wrong about one thing. Aisha had noticed me, knew that I was important to the boys who had clasped their eyes on me for guidance. Then her eyes widened and she knew, her memory whirling back to her youth and to Europe.

'I just want them to dance for me, for us,' she said. 'Do you look after them?'

'I do.' I turned to them. 'Boys are you happy to dance for Aisha?'

Tabu looked to Kabu who nodded to me and both looked at this goddess for instruction, their faces shining with adulation.

'What are their names?'

'BuBu,' I replied and her face lit with possibilities as my answer translated into advertising riches. 'I am their guardian. They speak Bozo and pigeon.' And, with a smile, 'I will stay close by to look after their interests.'

'Trust me,' she said. I looked at her for several seconds, beautiful, and nodded. She turned to the director, told him where to place BuBu, adjusted their clothing and asked them to dance as before. The actor playing Kuti came to the fore, the music re-started and magic happened.

Two hours later, I decided enough was enough. BuBu were flagging amid the retakes despite frequent drink breaks. Someone discovered they liked burgers and little piles of greasy plastic wrapping dotted the stage front. Even though I had found a chair, I was beginning to lean on my stick. The noise, sorry, the music was deafening. Aisha had her own chair placed close to mine, was constantly jumping up to issue instructions, make adjustments, to congratulate and guide BuBu. We spoke little, snatches about the boys, nothing of personal consequence. But, from time to time, she stroked the back of my hand, which, sadly, took me back to an adobe-yellow room in Timbuktu.

My phone buzzed. It was the hotel texting me a message. Inspector Okonkwo had done me a great service. 'I don't recognise your name, but if you used to fly the DC-3 very badly, please call this number. We can meet and I will give you a big hug.' Okonkwo had found Chuck, Okigbo Biggar, my one-time best friend at flying school in the 1960s, and, later, comrade-in-arms during the Biafran war. I had expected him dead and the shock of contact with him, and with Aisha, brought a stream of tears. My distress was sufficient for BuBu to jump from the stage and cover me with small hugs of their own and, of course, that made it all the worse so that Aisha joined in. I was happier than I could remember in, oh, so long a time.

Aisha insisted that we three stayed at her mansion just outside Surulere. I called Chuck and he agreed to meet us there. Excited as he was to see me again, I thought the prospect of meeting Aisha Azebry might be top of his mind. Like the president of Nigeria, we travelled in Aisha's black armoured Mercedes Benz. BuBu disappeared to the pool to see if it held any fishes, a driver was despatched to the hotel to collect our few belongings, a maid to the market to buy boys' clothes, another to prepare our rooms, and the cook to the kitchen to prepare the evening meal.

Two cold Guinness were brought to the veranda. At last, the old married couple were alone and we embraced leisurely letting our hands run from buttocks to nape.

She looked directly at me. 'You just seem the same, but perhaps fifty years older,' she said. 'It wouldn't be true to say that I have thought of you every day, but I do think of you often. After all, it was your money that set me up in business. My parents died soon after I got home from London. I invested in a small clothes shop, worked hard, very hard, until, in the last twenty years I became successful with more money than I know what to do with. And all alone. Lots of men over the years, but no one permanent.

'From your eyes, I think you have changed a lot. There is a lot of pain in there. Sit down and share your story. But, before you start you have to pay your way. Tell me about BuBu.'

It was a great relief to open the doors without reservation. And it was no hardship to talk to her; every so often I found myself stopping just to soak her up. I went back to the slave market in Niamey, through the attack by Boko Haram, and the river trip of gratitude in the police cutter. I told her nothing of the efficient work of my boy soldiers.

Just then, there was a roar of a large diesel engine from the front of the house followed by a larger bellow demanding, 'Chris, I am here. Where are you, you excuse for a pilot?'

Chuck was ushered in, a fit, muscled giant in T-shirt, smart, but dishevelled jacket, jeans and a large grin. All my six feet was enveloped, kissed, squeezed, stroked, hugged some more. His eyes shone with happiness. 'I was told you had been captured and executed,' he said. 'And, look what I have for you.' He reached into his inside pocket and pulled out a small box which I opened. It was the Biafran Presidential Medal for Valour. 'Not worth a bean, old bean,' he said, 'but fun to have. More than I got from my mingy uncle. He just left me his haulage company which explains my truck outside. My car is in for repair.'[5]

Looking at the medal, I felt memories crowding around and thought of Stan, my flight engineer, long dead with drink and memories. I turned to Chuck and saw him on one knee, instantly smitten. His jaw lowered like a krill-scooping basking shark.

'Will you marry me?' he managed.

I expected an instant put-down, but there was something in Aisha's eyes.

'I'll think about it,' she said. 'I suppose you'll want dinner as well?' Her phone buzzed and she reluctantly looked away from her sudden suitor. 'Let's get BuBu in. The video rushes from today are ready.'

I helped Chuck up and led him towards the children. 'Have you gone mad, Casanova?'

'Perhaps I have, but sometimes the heart takes over. What a wonderful woman!'

We got to the poolside and I pushed him in. Silly, I know, but she was my wife. Well, sort of. Once.

My petulance brought another unexpected event. Chuck surfaced with a walrus roar and was leapt upon by BuBu. Small bodies were thrown, bottoms bit and Aisha dived fully clothed into the mêlée to save her boys. It was ten minutes before everyone was landed and wrapped into towel gowns brought out by a bemused staff who clearly had never seen their mistress drop her soberness like this. Still trying to attack Chuck, Bubu eventually quietened in front of a cinema screen and saw themselves dancing to Kuti's music. They were dumbstruck. I had seen it live and I was dumbstruck a second time.

'A star is bu-born,' said Aisha.

Chuck wanted to know who the two ugly boys were spoiling the movie. This brought about another fight which Aisha joined in with cushions.

I suddenly felt quite old and out of place, but I did know the one way to bring order. I instructed the staff to bring in some food. BuBu quickly slid to the table.

Over a crisp Sancerre, I told parts of my story. I explained that it would not be good for my friends for me to stay long in their company. Despite all the gaiety, I was under some threat for I would probably be traced to Lagos. I needed to leave soon for London and, seizing my opportunity, could not take BuBu with me. In any event, I needed to see them settled. I was no parent, no long-term role model. They needed love and education.

BuBu were prepared to let me go on my journey providing they could stay with Auntie Aisha and Uncle Chuck. I saw looks pass. Aisha was already preparing the boys' movie career, but was wary of looking too commercial; Chuck wanted Aisha and recognised that with the boys included a deal could be struck. No one, apart from me, recognised how quickly all this domestic bliss could become deadly. By midnight, over brandy and with the boys in bed, the debate quickly became life changing.

Aisha looked at me. 'Can I have custody of Bubu? They will not want for love or security.'

'Yes. If they agree, I agree.'

Aisha looked at Chuck. 'You asked me a question when you first came in. Did you mean it?'

'Yes. Even more so now I have seen you in the pool.'

'Then my answer is "Yes", but only if your pilot friend, Chris whatever-his-name-is, agrees for reasons only he and I understand.'[6]

'I'm not so sure ...' I began. The two of them rose from their seats. '... but, after some thought, I think you deserve each other. You realise that this is madness. You have only known each other for a few hours.'

'I've known Chuck for ...' said Aisha and her voice tailed off as she placed her hands in her lap and dropped her head.

Sometimes in life, rarely, but enough to savour the moment, stars fall into a new alignment. Before, confusion, worries, problems obscured any obvious future. Then, planets that had never met suddenly conjoined and shifted their orbits as if a heavenly hand had reached out and pronounced a new order of contentment and commitment. There were a few moments of reflection around the room as each of us realised the enormity and simplicity of what had been decided. We were glad for each other.

Breaking the spell, I told Aisha and Chuck that while I needed to leave soon for Europe, there was one more thing I would like to do. I wanted to go back to Uli. When the fledging secessionist state of Biafra hovered on the point of death in 1969 as the Federal noose tightened, the rain poured down and thousands starved to death, three major towns – Aba, Owerri and Okigwi – fell. One airport – Obilagu, was overrun, and another – the vital Uli – came within Federal shelling range, closed temporarily, reopened and, finally, after a desperate struggle, was made secure. Uli, part of the road from Owerri to Ihiala, turned into a busy international runway. Uli was never used during the day. Its disguise was simple, but effective. The widened road verges, loading bays and airport buildings were camouflaged with palm fronds while the main runway was left uncovered. It was where Chuck and I had fought our war some fifty years ago.

Chuck pondered, then announced, 'I won't be needed here or in the office tomorrow. It seems that, if you insist on visiting Uli, I should take you. It's about seven hours' drive. We can stay overnight and have plenty of time to talk. Come back the next day and you can take the late-night flight. Do you agree Aisha?'

She nodded. We all knew where the power would lie.

'You'd better stay here the night,' she said, 'and I'll lend you a 4x4 for the journey.'

I asked Aisha to buy me a ticket to London and gave her the name I would be using. She didn't turn a hair. I also left a message for Inspector Okonkwo and asked him to call me on my burner as soon as he was able.

As it turned out, after a simple goodbye at breakfast, I never saw Aisha or BuBu again although we spoke in excellent English many times by phone, less so when the boys became superstars.

---

1 Heal, *Disappearing*.
2 Greenpeace International, *Shell Shocked*. The World Bank planned a $500 million credit to fund sustainable increases in water resource productivity in the Niger in 2009 with the first credit of $185 million shared between Nigeria, Guinea, Benin, Mali and Niger.
3 Crone, *God's Rule*.
4 Heal, *Disappearing*.
5 Heal, *Disappearing*.
6 Heal, *Disappearing*.

9. FOR OLD TIMES' SAKE

Through the greatness of my power I held both east and west.
We were summoned to the true way by a rightly guided man,
But we did not obey and called out: 'Is there no refuge?'
Then came a cry out of the far horizon;
We were cut down as though we were a harvest field.
Shut in our graves, we wait for Judgement Day.

Mahdi, *Thousand and One Nights*, Vol. 1

Chuck and I were drinking cans of beer as he drove from godless Lagos through Benin City on our way to the old republic of Biafra.

'The thing that I remember most, apart from the starvation and misery, was the togetherness of the people even in those awful conditions,' I offered. 'Everybody seemed prepared to share with the thousands of refugees even when they had nothing.'

'Remember that we were, are, a tribe,' said Chuck. 'It was always us against the Hausa, always Christian against Muslim. This was the choice of the Northerners in both cases. They always were feckless, venal and lazy and hated our commercial success.'

'I see you've softened your opinion after fifty years,' I chided.

We had been talking about the central thesis of the *Muqaddima*. In the harsh conditions of desert life, tribal groups developed a group solidarity which Ibn Khaldun called *'asabiyya*, a word he used over five hundred times.

I quoted from memory a much-discussed argument among the Berbers on desert nights. 'The root verb *'asaba* means "he twisted (a thing)" and *'usbah* means "a party of men who league together to defend one another. *'Asabiyya* was defined in medieval Arabic dictionaries as a "strong attachment of several persons closely united by the same interest or opinion".'[1]

I told Chuck of the old joke that every Arabic verbal root has a camel-related verb or noun that derives from it. It is not much of a joke, but *'usub*, derived from the same root as *'asabiyya* means 'she-camel that will not yield her milk copiously unless her thigh be bound with a cord'.

'It takes me back to Lagos,' I explained. 'With the gradual decline of the nomads, people who moved with their animals, there came a new unstable breed, the parasitical city dweller, traditionless, utterly matter of fact, religion-less, clever, unfruitful and deeply contemptuous of the countryman. In London, they mostly live in Islington and Richmond.'

'You've captured Lagos, all right,' said Chuck. 'I guess that it's inevitable when people suddenly have no need of the old certainties they become arrogant yet yearn to go back to being primitive in a comfortable way.' He opened the window and threw out a beer can. 'This is one of those countries where that's not littering. Some peasant will pick it up and put it to good use.'

'That's not my original thought. That was Spengler,' I explained.[2] 'He wrote after the German defeat in the First World War. He predicted a doom-laden future for a Faustian Europe and that the triumph of European materialism would in turn bring violence. In one way, he foresaw the next world war and the violence that would spring up around religious and tribal communities like in Ireland and the Basques and the old Yugoslavia.'

'And now with the revenge deaths over Brexit,' added Chuck.[3]

'Spirituality has exhausted its religious possibilities and is in decline,' I continued. 'When a priest was elevated above the rest of mankind, he was a haven through which even the poorest wretch could grasp God. Now, no religion, no God; no God, no religion. Luther said life was a desperate battle against the devil which everyone had to fight.[4] It's too late for old people like you and me, but, nowadays, if you do fight, you fight alone.

'Like Ibn Khaldun, Spengler was hostile to urban culture and thought the 'world city' was full of rootless parasites that constituted the last phase of a civilisation. It was the dying phase of a culture, an inability to reform, a failure to live through inner strength. Artists can now only be successful if what they produce is free from form and proportion. Everyone relies on materialism; just like Lagos which has gone in the blink of an eye from a primitive barter-centre to an oil world-city where it feeds off its own vigour. Spengler reckoned that in the old days any city state would self-destruct in a thousand years. Lagos will beat that easily.'

Chuck mused for a few minutes. 'These days,' he offered, 'any good man is too far ahead of his time to have much influence. He is a solitary traveller.[5]

'This doesn't augur well for BuBu because Aisha and I will be long gone. It will be their challenge. Lagos is one of the most populous cities in Africa. Parts of it are already prohibitively expensive, even for visiting Europeans. One can see the trend. Already we have great specialisations of labour. A sedentary culture leads to diversification, luxury, immorality, corruption and a disdain for other lives. Because the services of workers, craftsmen and professional people have been much in demand in Lagos, they themselves have already become arrogant.'[6]

'I have been reading the *Qur'an*,' I put in. 'The prophet often got it right. Truth doesn't always have to be clothed in religion. He said that the "final hour will not come until people compete with each other in the height of their buildings".'[7]

'Change of subject,' said Chuck. It was mid-afternoon, a time to be thankful for air-conditioning. The traffic was the usual mix of blaring, diesel-belching Chinese trucks and plodding animal carts piled high with desiccated fodder. 'We are coming into Uli. And that black 4x4 has been following us at a careful distance for at least thirty minutes.'

What immediately struck me was that the doors of the native huts were decorated with bits of metal. It took me a while to work it out: the metal was plane fuselage.

We went first to a small church near Ihiala, which was doubly significant for aircrew supporting the Biafran republic. The church's two tall spires were engraved on the eyeballs of pilots as a positioning point for landing aircraft. There were 7,350 relief flights into Biafra in the three years of war, perhaps seven flights a day taking in almost a million tonnes of supplies and, towards the end, only into the beleaguered and hidden Uli airstrip.

The pilots were an extraordinary bunch of people, most of whom worked for passenger or cargo airlines. They felt they were 'doing something useful' when they spent their annual holidays on the airlift. Many stayed on, arranging leave of absence, some quitting their regular jobs. Most of them had never flown in a war zone before. They also broke the international rules, limiting aircrew to a legal maximum of 120 flying hours within any twenty-eight-day period. Some pilots achieved more by having themselves rostered under false names, sometimes with the name of a captain who had long left the airlift. It became quite normal for pilots to average 180 and, sometimes, over 200 hours a month. Chuck had been one of these pilots although he flew for his country and his planes were as often filled with armaments as with food and the wounded.

Fifteen relief aircraft had been lost and thirty-five aircrew, twenty of them Biafran, had died and were buried in the small cemetery close to the church. The graves were bulldozed by the Nigerian Army the day after the war ended. The local field commander explained in the press that he wanted the crews to be 'eternally forgotten'. 'We don't want their families poking around here looking for their remains.' He hadn't been entirely successful. Broken tombstones had been dug up and arranged with taste alongside the southern cemetery wall. After fifty years, there were still some recent floral tributes. Most prominent, was a propeller with two snapped blades sticking upright in the dirt.

'Looks like it was from a DC-4,' offered Chuck. I thought it was from a DC-3, my old plane, which set me thinking. I could imagine the Igbos crammed into their enclave, hunkering down and waiting for the massacres. They never came, but there were vengeful acts. Hausa soldiers ran exuberantly down the Uli runway firing into the air.

As we drove away heading for the old landing strip, the 4x4 which had been waiting patiently, pulled out and took up position. I could make out two men inside.

'How dangerous is what you are wrapped up in, old man?' asked Chuck. 'Only I've got something to look forward to now and I've suddenly got some little responsibilities as well.'

'Life and death,' I said. 'Lots of upset people, some pretty powerful.'

'We'll have to ask them for some identity.'

We parked on the main road at Uli where much had changed. Swathes of jungle that used to shelter transport planes during the day from Nigerian Mig-17s had been cut to provide arable fields. The clearances meant less rain and some years new and old crops withered. Around the fields, there were peasant huts, a few wells and clear poverty.

'You know what we were talking about before,' offered Chuck, 'about long-term enjoyment of material comfort bringing about the ruin of economies and empires, that still has some currency, even here. Despite this country having some of the greatest oil reserves, these people in these fields have been left behind by corruption. In this last election, Muhammadu Buhari took the helm. The top team are all admirers of your Jeremy Corbyn, who is himself a devotee of Venezuela's late Hugo Chavez. What do Nigeria and Venezuela have in common? Both have recklessly alienated international capital and utterly failed to harness their oil wealth.[8] Our brightest and our best, about a tenth of our wealthier citizens have left in recent years – doctors, nurses, engineers, accountants, entrepreneurs, lawyers, and so on. Success and wealth are routinely demonised by the Buhari regime.

'Don't believe me? I shall put Tacitus to the test. He said, "Prosperity is the measure or touchstone of virtue, for it is less difficult to bear misfortune than to remain uncorrupted by pleasure".'[9]

Three men walked up, tired after a day's work in the heat, soiled T-shirts and torn shorts, honest but unrewarded sweat. 'Who did you vote for in the election for president?' asked Chuck.

'We don't know,' answered the eldest. 'We sold our votes to the soldiers when they visited. We bought two spades and some okra seeds with the money.'

Traffic was light and I walked out to the middle of the road. All the tyre marks from the large airliners had gone, now completely covered by the Chinese tarmac team that must have passed through a few years ago.

I remembered.

From the air, where I stood was a long, boring stretch of open highway only twenty-one metres compared with a normal runway more than twice as wide.[10] *The last leg into Uli was flown at night. The pilot took an extended, twisty route, doubling the flight time, but avoiding Nigerian fighters and flak. About an hour before landing, the cabin and navigation lights snapped off without warning. It took a lot of judgement to fly like this with no reference to a visual horizon and I felt a serious drain in confidence. There was no radar, no instrument landing system; pilots depended on radio beacons, some of them mobile, and a primitive radio. A neat pattern of tiny landing lights appeared below for less than thirty seconds: Uli, briefly each night the busiest runway in the world.*

Landing at night was dangerous enough, but it was made worse by the steady, closely stacked line of aged relief and supply planes that waited out of sight. The skills and experience of their crews were variable. Timing was crucial. A Russian bomber or a converted DC-4 or DC-3 tauntingly broadcast warnings. When the tell-tale lights came on, the mercenary pilot attempted to join the queue of incoming planes, dropping bombs onto the runway and firing at the momentarily highlighted laden freighters. Early most mornings, Russian-supplied MiG jet fighters, flown by Egyptians and Brits, rocketed and machine-gunned any planes visible on the ground. If fighting was nearby, Nigerian shells came from British-donated guns and armoured vehicles.

The pilot spiralled tightly downwards as on a helter-skelter funfair ride. We could see lights, palm trees and two church spires flashing past through gusts of rain and blotches of heavy cloud.

'Put your heads down and hold your knees.' That instruction was seldom good news.

The pilot circled once more to get his bearings and, I thought, overshot, but gently made contact, hit a badly filled crater, lurched, lifted a little, and ran smoothly in. I settled further into my seat and eyed the ammunition as the dowager 'Queen of the Atlantic' pulled sharply off the road into the trees. I was impressed and shaking. The door opened. Someone screamed into the fuselage, 'Out, out'. In charge of unloading was a legend, a priest whom everyone called Glade. He was about fifty, walked with a limp, and shook hands with his left, guarding his badly injured right. He claimed, and proved time and again, that any plane could be unloaded in twenty minutes. I was in the way.

'Are any of the plane wrecks left from the war?' I asked as I handed over some large denomination notes?

'Most of them have been used for the huts,' I was told, 'but, over there,' and the man pointed several hundred yards up the road, 'there are still some bits of one or two. We don't go there because of the snakes.'

We drove closer and watched out of the corner of an eye as the 4x4 stopped by the field labourers and questioned them without anyone bothering to get out of the vehicle.

In the shade of the hard woods, the temperature and humidity climbed so that our shirts dripped. In the waistband of our trousers, 9 mm semi-automatic pistols were clearly outlined. Dead leaves were inches deep, the protected bottom layer slimy and shifting under foot. All unseen, there were slithers and scuttlings. And, just a few yards within, there it was, the creeper-covered but unmistakable carcass of a DC-3, badly pierced and ripped by the strafing fire of a MiG-17. It was not my plane, but the other of a pair of ridiculous gunships that had combined to shoot down a modern Russian jet fighter.[11] We searched some more, but did not find my aircraft, just some discarded engines.

We both stood still for several minutes, re-living an almost forgotten life. Then there was a larger scuff and we unfroze. I moved inside the fuselage where the snakes undoubtedly lived and Chuck crouched and moved at pace behind the sound. I waited, as behind a tree at 'They hear not' on the road to Kabara only a month before. There were two shots from two different guns and then a third more muffled. A man ran headlong straight in front of my position. I shouted, 'Stop', and fired into the air. He turned, took wild aim and squeezed his trigger. My second bullet hit him in the shoulder and he fell to the ground screaming and writhing. I moved quickly to his side, stood on the wrist of his injured arm and took away what looked like a cheap, homemade revolver. What surprised me was its capacity of fifteen rounds, most likely attractive to a criminal with very little understanding or training. I pressed my gun to the man's forehead and suggested he lay where he was.

Then, I found the safety of a large tree trunk, made myself small and waited. In the clearing, my target moaned and tossed, perhaps hoping to be a Judas goat, but making no attempt to get up and run. The jungle had gone quiet, but slowly came back to life when I heard someone approaching steadily. The man stopped and Chuck shouted, 'Coming in, Chris.'

'All clear. Come on in. Follow the moans.'

Chuck appeared. He had walked around a tree and almost fallen on the two men who were stalking us. One fired a shot, nicking Chuck's arm. His return took the man in the chest while the second man took off. Enraged, Chuck went to the man on the floor who was gurgling his last blood and shot him in the head.

'I need to sit down,' he said. 'I thought I was fit for my age.'

I checked his arm. It was the slightest of cuts, his blood already congealing. I tore a piece from my shirt and bound the wound. 'We'll need to get it cleaned. This is not the healthiest of places.'

'What about him?'

We both went over. The man had recovered a little composure, but was dropping into shock. The shoulder was badly damaged, but he would live. He wasn't an impressive specimen, in his fifties, overweight, rat's-tail hair, but with a good suit. I went through his pockets and handed my pickings to Chuck.

'Hausa,' he spat. 'From Lagos. Nice wad of cash. Looks like he's been paid. Gun for hire, I would say. Petty criminal. Not someone with a loving family waiting for him. More likely some poor drugged girl in a brothel. Well, we need information.' He trod on the man's wounded shoulder and got a scream in return.

I dropped to my knees so that I could look him in the eye. His deep black face had gone almost white with the pain. 'Your friend is already dead,' I told him. 'Shot in the stomach. Died slowly and in agony.'

'No friend. Boss man.'

'You have one chance,' I said, raising my pistol to his other shoulder. 'Why are you following us?'

He didn't put up a fight. He didn't know why, he spluttered, 'but we were following you not your big friend'. He didn't know who I was, but his boss had orders to see who I contacted and then to kill me. He didn't know the client who had been spoken to on the phone. They had been told to wait on the road out of Lagos to Biafra and had picked us up by chance. The boss had not reported in other than to say they were following us. He wanted to finish the job first.

I believed him. I couldn't see any more information that would help so I shot him in the forehead. We had BuBu and Aisha to protect.

We took the bodies into the plane wreck, checked their pockets, found the car keys, then covered them a foot deep in rotting vegetation. I took the 4x4, Chuck his own vehicle and we drove for an hour to Onitsha and the Dolly Hills hotel, arriving after dark.

'When you are in the haulage business, you have contacts and places to stay everywhere,' explained Chuck. 'This hotel is about the best in town and they serve some good Indian dishes.' I drove the 4x4 to the Onitsha Recreational Club where tennis balls were being banged about under floodlights, took out the overnight bags, and left it locked and tidy. On the way back to the hotel with Chuck, the bags went into a dumpster from where they were immediately taken out and inspected by a family of beggars; the key went into a drain. We stopped at a veranda bar overlooking the Niger for some pre-dinner drinks and to let the river breeze blow away some of the pollution.

'You know,' I started, 'just three days ago, I was aboard a police cutter with BuBu and we tore through this place on the way to Port Harcourt. I didn't even notice this town.'

I told Chuck all that I knew of BuBu's story including the part that was a state secret. He was deeply shocked, not with the deaths, after all we had just killed two people, but with BuBu's living trauma. However, he had a right to know. He would be dealing with the aftermath, hopefully for many years to come.

I piled it on. 'There's a lot more I could tell you about who could be after me, but I won't,' I said. 'There are several possibilities. Some are mad and others are very bad. The important thing is that, from what the assassin said, whoever they worked for doesn't know about you and that means they probably don't know about BuBu or Aisha. We should work to keep it that way.'

Chuck nodded slowly and my phone rang. It was Okonkwo returning my call. I moved away from the table and asked the inspector my big, final favour. He knew there was much I wasn't telling him, but after five minutes he agreed to my request on my assurance that BuBu were well settled and on my promise that I would stay away from Nigeria for several years. When I finished the call, I also sent a text to Nianankoro, 'Watch your close friend. Contact cut. Going north. Uncle.'

'OK, it's all arranged,' I told Chuck. 'Again, you're going to have to trust me. Here's how it goes. You are going to stay at this hotel on your own. Run me to another hotel in a few minutes and pick me up at the main gate at 0800. This evening, call Aisha and tell her to get my plane ticket to the reception at the Eko Hotel tomorrow morning. You can drop me with my bag about ten minutes' walk from the Eko and that's us done. Tell her that I'm sorry, but that it is much safer for everyone if I don't say goodbye. I will telephone in a week or two if it is safe. Nobody is to refer to me by name again. With the boys just call me "Uncle". Give them a big hug from me.'

And then I wept like a baby. I found it so hard to be with real, deep, old friends and my two boys, to rediscover, to make a family, to embrace happiness and then to have to walk away. What on earth was I doing with the residue of my life? What nonsense had I created? Suddenly, Chuck had his arms around me and our tears mingled.

We had the second and third drinks that we needed. Chuck told me of the irony of visiting Uli because the international airport at Enugu, once a main conduit into Biafra, had recently been closed. The lack of Government investment meant the buildings were in danger of collapse, the runway was potholed and large aircraft were in serious danger during take-off and landing.

'I told you that the middle classes are leaving the country,' he said. 'The figures show that migration from the developing world peaks when the national income gets to around £5,000. Nigerian GDP is only £2,450 so that mass of the population is not going anywhere soon. Yet, at the same time, there is going to be mass migration into the country from the sub-Sahara. Nigeria's crime-ridden towns are going to explode. Our population is going to more than double over the next thirty years, reaching a scarcely credible 750 million by 2100. We are getting larger and poorer by the day and Buhari is making it even worse.'

'Oil might still help Nigeria make it through,' I suggested.

'We've driven out the investors,' Chuck countered. 'I've read some research by some economists on what is needed to establish a new middle class.[12] They came up with three preconditions. First, a minimum literacy rate of seventy per cent; China got there in 1995; India in 2015. We are way off because of our religious and ethnic divisions. Then, we need a minimum investment rate of twenty-five per cent of GDP and also an electricity consumption that reaches an average of 300 kilowatt hours per person, enough to power a TV and three low energy light bulbs. Our investment is half of what is required. We don't even manage the light bulbs.

'What I'm getting at,' he continued, 'is that we may need to get ourselves out of the country for the boys' sake. Aisha and I are not going to live for many more years. We need to have the boys financed and settled elsewhere.'

'Perhaps we can find you when we do,' he finished.

'I doubt you'll end up where I am going,' I said as we made for the car.

The drive next morning to Lagos was uneventful on roads that had become crowded, but we had time. Chuck dropped me at the *Yellow Chilli* restaurant with a short squeeze of the arm, wished me luck, and drove off quickly. I had dinner and then made my way to the Eko where I collected my ticket and took a seat in the lounge and waited for Okonkwo. In good time, his convoy swept into the hotel forecourt. A door opened in the middle vehicle. I got in and found myself alone apart from the driver who sat tight-lipped. At the airport, we passed through two security gates and, clutching my cabin bag with Nianankoro's parcels, my collection of passports, and a few clothes, I got out at the steps leading to the British Airways flight. The window of the lead car slid down and I went over.

'You been promoted,' I exclaimed. 'Thoroughly deserved.'

'You should see my medal,' said Okonkwo. 'Thoroughly undeserved.' He paused, then added, 'We might have been friends in another time. I am grateful for what you did for my people all that time ago.'

I reached into my pocket and pulled out my Biafran Presidential Medal for Valour. Okonkwo broke into a broad smile.

'I'm glad that I made the right decision. I enjoyed our talks on the cutter, but matters end here. I'm not going to stay to see you off. If your passport or ticket are not in order, don't call. I trust you that BuBu are safely cared for. Remember our deal. You will stay away from Nigeria for some time. Senior politicians would become nervous if the truth of what happened on the lake became known. The repercussions could be personal.'

We shook hands and, as I mounted the first step, the convoy sped away. Because of my promises, details of Okonkwo and what happened between us have been adjusted so as to protect his identity.

One of the delights of having rich and influential friends is that they buy you first class tickets and convenience. There was no passport check on the plane. To be truthful, I couldn't even remember what name I had suggested. I sank into the leather seats and sipped champagne. I had an hour's wait until the other passengers arrived so I decided to get started on *Finnegans Wake*. I had no idea what was coming in the pages; it was a decided surprise. After twenty minutes, I was asleep.

As we touched down in the blackness before dawn, my main concern was that my chosen passport would cause me trouble. This was the most dangerous moment. If I was searched, the game would end and I would likely be quickly interrogated by EU police. Also, if my name were to be cross-matched with incoming flights, it would not appear on any manifest. There were several flights from Australia and the Far East landing at the same time. I opted to be French, went for the electronic gate, confident that the visual identification software would recognise me, and expecting there to be no alert flagging me to officials.

If there had been a heartbeat monitor, I would have been stopped immediately. There wasn't and I was through and away. I caught the Heathrow Express to Paddington where I bought two burner mobiles from a street stall and said goodbye to my Nigerian phone. I settled down in an internet café and sent requests to three of my 'undercover' credit card holders where funds were running low. Two immediately agreed to continue, happy to anticipate another £10,000 management fee, and using the 'all OK' code. I sent encrypted signals to one of my UK Hawala bankers instructing them to deposit £100,000 in cash in both accounts by courier that day. Just as I finished, the third card holder – a member of parliament nearing retirement – came through indicating the account may no longer be safe. I pondered whether this was wet feet, a con or a serious alarm. I decided to cut ties immediately and binned the card; the money loss was inconsequential. On the way to Kings Cross, I bought a flat cap and scarf, some cheap glasses, bloated my cheeks with cotton wool, and took out maximum cash while squatting at different heights in front of the ATM cameras at five different machines.

On the train to Scotland, I had another go at *Finnegans Wake*,

A way a lone a last a loved a long the riverrun, past Eve and Adam's, from swerve of shore to bend of bay, brings us by a commodius vicus of recirculation back to Howth Castle and Environs ... For a nod to the nabir is better than wink to the wabsanti. Otherways wesways like that provost scoffing bedoueen the jebel and the jypsian sea Cropherb the crunch-bracken shall decide. Then we'll know if the feast is a flyday.[13]

I soon set to remembering a Scottish lady called Morag who rescued me from Belgium after Juncker and Selmayr were assassinated in Brussels.[14] We had lived and laughed and loved and left each other in Paris. It was the sight of Morag who, seemingly arguing with the police in the Prado in Madrid, had spooked me badly and driven me to flee to Morocco. I felt kindly towards her and hoped she had not suffered under the baleful influence of the EU. If I had 'recirculated' with Aisha and Chuck, why not Morag? I guess I felt lonely after leaving all behind in Lagos. Why not a phone call before I got to Edinburgh? Human warmth. Untraceable. Safe.

The siren called, 'It will be you who will make the mistake. For some reason, you will pop your head above the parapet and we will see the movement. Then we will have you.'

I fell to wondering how to open my campaign to sell Gordon Laing's long-lost diary. I was confident that Nianankoro didn't care where it actually ended up, was not even bothered if he never heard of the document again. He had given me some names of academic contacts in Scotland, but I felt that negotiations were in my hands and, in this time of Brexit, an auction between French and Scottish interests might be productive, even the English if it came to it. I knew how much money Nianankoro was hoping for. If the amount was met and received in Timbuktu, its only purpose was to provide for the future protection of Nianankoro's precious library.

Somewhere near York, I found Morag's number and made the call. It was answered after a couple of rings by her elderly and helpful mother.

'No, Morag doesn't live at home any more. She's left being a tour guide because of the long hours.' Out of the blue, she had an offer to 'work in security for those people in Brussels'.

Shaken, I thanked her and cut the call. I slipped the SIM card from the burner, twisted it and dropped it out of the window. The wiped phone went down the back of the seat. A few hours later, I checked into the old George Hotel in Edinburgh New Town with *Finnegans Wake* and went to bed with a malt.

Next morning, with all my smugness knocked out of me, I decided I had to work quickly. I called the two university professors, one in Edinburgh and one in Glasgow, and told them what I had. I was surprised at their immediate attention. I took some copies of the first page of the diary along with my letter of authority from Nianankoro to conduct negotiations and set off for urgent meetings each side of lunch. By mid-afternoon, I had a meeting scheduled early the next morning in Edinburgh with the two men and representatives of the departments of the School of Geographical and Earth Sciences and of Historical Geography and, through them, various royal societies.

After coffee and croissants (this was Edinburgh), the discussion was at first aggressive, then understanding, and finally looking for a solution. I said that I had interest from other parties. I would fly the following afternoon for London and waved my plane ticket for effect. I explained Nianankoro's motives and it helped greatly that he was known and respected in the room. It was an absolute requirement that his name, mine, and the amount of money were kept secret. I gave them details of the financial arrangements I had made to aid their confidence. After the deal was done and the money held inextricably in legal escrow, I would hand over the full diary. There would be two hours for verification while I was in the room. If they were not satisfied, I would release the money immediately by phone and take back the diary. I placed the last diary page on the table for inspection as further bait.

The problem, of course, was the amount Nianankoro wanted, which I had doubled on instinct. Most university professors struggle to get money for minor purchases and travelling expenses. Two ideas were forthcoming for funders. One was the Explorers Club in New York, headquartered between Park and Madison Avenues on the Upper East Side of Manhattan. The other was a nebulous department in the bowels of the Scottish government that reportedly had nationalism in its soul. Its lady representative, I didn't catch her name, sat quiet throughout the discussions, but paid particular attention to my descriptions of French duplicity and their possible involvement in the murder of Laing.

The full details are unimportant. Indeed, I do not know how the money was gathered although several phones were in almost constant use. It was clear that the diary was of greater importance than I initially suspected. I wondered if, even at twice the requested asking price, I had gone too low. Again, I have changed some of the names of the participants, omitted others. I never saw any publicity for the acquisition.

I declined a celebratory lunch, I think to their relief, and decided to walk to Waverley Station. As I left, the lady from the government shook hands and I felt the small piece of paper left behind in my claw. I have always loved New Town, the trip through Rose Street and across Princes Street and the descent through the glacial scour to the railway line. I bought two tickets, the first openly to Glasgow and the second, covertly, to North Berwick. There, I sat on a bench and called the number on the paper. She answered immediately.

'Am I right that neither you nor your principal in Timbuktu has much interest in whether Laing's diary becomes public,' she asked?

'That is correct,' I said.

'Am I also correct that there is a copy of the document?'

'There are two copies,' I said. 'One I have with me. The other is in a vault in Timbuktu which is not available to anyone but its owner.'

'Would you both be interested if I doubled the amount of money that has been paid?'

'We would.'

'The copy you hold would need to be handed in at your nearest police station with Gordon Laing's name on the envelope with my phone number. I would need your assurance that the copy in the vault will stay there for at least the next five years.'

'You will need to give me a reason, in confidence, why this control is so important to you.'

She paused for the first time. 'The French government has asked us to ensure secrecy. We believe we have an excellent chance of winning the next referendum on Scottish independence. After that, French goodwill will be very important to our future political direction.'

'I understand. Make it four times the amount previously paid and I guarantee that it will be done.'

'Almost excellent. I expected you to ask for a five-fold increase. I will trust you also. I see you left from Waverley. Where and when might I expect your package?'

'I'll tell you in ten minutes,' I replied, unsurprised that I had been watched.

'We have a deal. I wonder who you really are.'

'That is something I've recently taken to wondering myself.'

I took a taxi along West Bay to the North Berwick police station in High Street where I deposited my package and, bribing my driver to radio silence, was driven the thirty minutes to Dunbar where I caught trains to Newcastle and Hull. Hull was a last 'recirculation'. I used the phone twice more, first to alert my unknown lady contact, the second to send a text to Nianankoro. I told him I was heading east. I also told him the amount he should be receiving and the conditions. By return, he said that the blessings of Allah would shower upon me.

I hoped so. If I could find my old contact at the marina, I could be across the North Sea quietly and in quick time.[15]

Blessings were with me. I tailgated through security and recognised the timber-built North Sea trawler yacht. A stocky man in his fifties, short white beard and hair, an untipped cigarette stuck to his bottom lip, sat in a canvas chair on the deck, pink gin in hand.

'Hello, again,' he said. 'I was thinking about you only last week. The boat's keel needs a good scrub. Now, here you are.'

'Any trouble after my last visit,' I asked? 'Any visitors? Any ripples?'

'Not a dickey,' he replied. 'Want to go again?'

I smiled. 'Yes, I do. Same price, same deal?

'OK. I'll need to call my son to crew. When do you want to go?

'This afternoon would be good.'

Thirty-six hours later, I was in Paris.

---

1 Irwin, *Ibn Khaldun*.
2 Spengler, *Decline of the West*. Penman, *Biohistory*.
3 Heal, *Disappearing*.
4 Charles, *Chronicles of the Schoenberg Cotta Family* (1864); often Lutcher.
5 Burke, *Vico*.
6 Khaldun, *Muqaddima*, Vol. 2.
7 *Qur'an*: 17:6.
8 Warner, *Daily Telegraph*, 6/3/2019.
9 Tacitus, *Dialogus de Oratoribus*.
10 Heal, *Disappearing*.
11 Heal, *Disappearing*.
12 Mary Jean Bowman, further developed by Charles Robertson, *Renaissance Capital*.
13 Joyce, *Finnegans Wake*.
14 Heal, *Disappearing*.
15 Heal, *Disappearing*.

10. REVENGE FOR A MURDERED DAUGHTER

Neither speak ill of others,
Nor well of yourself.
The moment you open
Your mouth to speak,
The autumn wind stirs
And chills your lips.

Yosa Buson, *Portrait of Bashō, Deep North*

Some academics fail to recognise hard realities amid the excitement of scholarship. We were discussing an original document of unimpeachable provenance written by the renowned master, Ahmed Baba al-Musufi, al-Tinbukti, at the end of the sixteenth century. Baba was known today in all universities that conducted serious Arabic studies for his brilliant mind and unparalled output. The previously unsuspected Baba treatise that lay on the table in full sight assailed all corrupted interpretations of the *Qur'an* which sought to justify the degradation of females. Baba stood firm on the independent rights of women to education, marriage and fulfilment and against the forced wearing of the burka, the practice of genital mutilation, the blaming of women for men's sexual arousal and the assumption of their primary guilt in adultery. Women were not property to be passed and sold among men.

I had explained to the worthies staring at the document that Nianankoro wanted a productive revenge on those adherents of *Ansar Dine* who had raped and murdered his daughter in Timbuktu. He wanted a fearless standard bearer who would take his discovery into the evil heart of the medievalists and unclothe their narrow, self-serving arguments. Where in this elegant salon in the centre of Paris, its air musty with the tang of aged vellum and parchment, the walls filled with treasures in locked, glass cases, was this champion?

And what was the intelligentsia discussing? One, with goatee beard, mutton chops and waistcoat, lectured on the appropriateness of Baba's document coming to light in the French capital. The first Arabic text of *Muqaddima* was printed in Paris in 1858. The first complete translation into a European language was the French version of Baron William MacGuckin de Slane, who published in the 1860s. The French had a leading role in the provision of Islamic history for European sources through an Orientalist called Jean Sauvaget then Claude Cahen and his son, Michel.

I drum rolled a loud devil's tattoo.

A man well into his eighties, with evidence of his breakfast on his tie, argued that different types of state or society necessarily gave rise to different types of law. When society changed, the law must also change unless, of course, you believe like some Islamic fundamentalists that law is set for all time and trapped in the fourteenth century.[1]

'Do a writer's words contain one literal interpretation which must be accepted rather than interpreted leading to narrow mindedness?' he asked the room. 'Certain ideas are screened out or suppressed because they are subversive or fail to fit the mental agility of readers of the period.' In printing Baba's revelations, the academic community would be dealing with fanatics for whom the written word was not allowed to be the springboard for other interpretations. All was to be trapped in an original meaning that was deduced and, most probably, anachronistic.

I heaved a deep and lingering sigh, but failed to gain any attention.

The only woman present came nearer to the point. She leant forward earnestly, glasses precarious on the tip of her nose, long hair reaching the table top, and explained that females were still subject to polygamy and concubinage. Some interpretations of Islamic law today recognised three categories of legal inferiors: slaves, women and unbelievers. Human nature, in defiance of Islamic law and morality, created other categories of inferiors, both social and racial, like the peasantry, the voiceless classes of Islamic society.[2] In some places, women had the right to own and dispose of property, and to found 'wages', a pious endowment of income-producing property. This was perhaps the only area in a traditional Muslim society in which they approached equality with men.

The question of personal danger to those present returned. Arguments slithered around the table:

Salman Rushdie's *fatwa* was brandished. The medieval Muslim, little different from many in the streets of Europe, was profoundly convinced of the finality, completeness, and essential self-sufficiency of their religion. Islam was the one true faith, beyond which there were only infidels (the *kuffār* or *kafir*), the Muslim equivalent of the Greek term 'barbarians'. The Muslim collective was the one divinely ordained order beyond which there was only tyranny, anarchy and wickedness.

What of the possibility of threats from abroad? The auguries for self-emancipation were poor. There had been states with a majority Muslim population where formal Islam did not have a central place in the constitution and in secular legislation. The paradox was that liberal laws, such as equal rights for women, had been espoused and enforced only by autocratic rulers like Kemal Ataturk in Turkey and Mohammed Reza Shah in Iran. These moves were now under strong attack. They were part of the many grievances of Recep Tayyip Erdoğan and Ayatollah Sayyid Khomeini. Khomeini, for instance, expressed the sentiments of the conservative merchant and artisan classes and the devout poor by condemning the extension of political rights to women and non-Muslims.

In the eyes of many Muslims, Western-inspired political change brought tyranny, economic change brought poverty, and social change brought immorality and corruption. Khomeini and his disciples were profoundly convinced that the experiment in modernisation in Iran had failed and that the only salvation for Muslims was to return to the divine origins of their faith. All that was worth taking from the West were its devices and its appliances and these could be bought. Its so-called culture was contaminated, dangerous and doomed, along with all those who were foolish enough to join it.

From near the large window and a face half-hidden by the glare of the winter sun came the argument that Islam had nothing to do with politics.

Then came the counter-argument from across the table. Khomeini observed that the *Qur'an* contained a hundred times more verses concerning social problems than on devotional subjects. Out of fifty books of Muslim tradition, there were perhaps three or four which dealt with prayer or with man's duties to God, a few on morality and all the rest had to do with society, economics, law, politics and the state.

Islam 'is political or it is nothing and a significant and growing number of Muslims in many countries agree'.

I stood up. 'Madame, messieurs,' I interrupted rudely, far above the discussion. 'If no one here understands or accepts Nianankoro's purpose, then I will remove the treatise.'

There were shouts of disagreement, outrage even. Did I not understand that the document had to be studied, thought about, put into context, explained, before it was placed before the public? The effect on Islamic sensitivities needed to be considered.

'I need you all to recognise, difficult as it may be,' I said firmly, 'that female genital mutilation is taking place all over the world right now, today. Stopping this disgusting practice is not a matter of academic priorities.'

It was a shock to the room that scholarship might hold less sway than social action. I scooped up the document and left. Howls followed me down the corridor.

I decided to forego several worthy organisations based in Paris like the *Institut des Cultures d'Islam*, overseen by the City Council, and the Arab World Institute that sought to build bridges based on tolerance, art and understanding. Rightly or wrongly, I felt none of these would pursue Nianankoro's message with suitable vigour. I caught a taxi driven by a taciturn Moroccan from Marrakech to the Saint-Ambroise neighbourhood of the eleventh arrondissement where we found the rue Nicolas-Appert. We swopped a few words in Arabic and reminisced about the *djemaa el fna*. I got out in front of a nondescript white-walled office building, showing cracks and signs of age. My driver looked around, wagged his finger at me, and said, '*antabah ahdhur khuda balka*', 'Be careful'.

A plaque by the side of the front door above two wheelie bins with blue and yellow lids gave the names of the eleven employees and visitors to *Charlie Hebdo*, 'Charlie Weekly', the French satirical weekly newspaper, shot to death in early January four years before. Two brothers, identifying with al-Qaeda's Yemen branch, broke into the building and opened up with rifles, sub-machine guns, pistols and shotguns. Altogether, twelve were killed and eleven injured. There were several related attacks and, in one of them, four Jews were murdered in a kosher supermarket.[3]

The brothers, Chérif and Saïd Kouachi, left shouting, 'We have avenged the Prophet Muhammad. We have killed *Charlie Hebdo*.'

A few hundred metres away on the corner of rue Moufle, a police officer was wounded then executed at close range. From their getaway car, the gunmen hijacked another vehicle, ran over a pedestrian and shot at police officers. Two days later, they were tracked to a signage company in Dammartin-en-Goële where they had taken hostages. After a siege lasting about eight hours, both men were shot dead when they rushed from the building firing weapons.

It seemed back then that the world divided into two camps. Some in the Muslim diaspora believed that attack on *Charlie Hebdo* was justified, including eighty per cent of pupils at a Saint-Denis primary school who declared for the killers and threatened to shoot teachers. Vladimir Putin used the murders to direct anger against the West. Printing the cartoons in Russia was criminalised. The Chinese called for a limit to freedom of speech. *Charlie Hebdo* was always irreverent, stridently non-conformist and strongly secularist, anti-religious and left-wing. The suicide bombings by ISIL in Paris that winter that killed 130 people in a spill over from the Syrian civil war were also directly linked. *Charlie Hebdo* repeatedly enraged the sensitivities of traditional Islamists by publishing satirical cartoons of the prophet, particularly re-publishing the twelve notorious lampoons by the Dutch newspaper *Jyllands-Posten* of 2005. The magazine was dragged through the French courts by various French Muslim organisations; in 2011 its offices were fire bombed. Muslims who believed emphatically in an Islamic concept of *Gheerah* found an uneasiness in their hearts which moved them to guard their family from indecency. Zealots felt they were required to protect Muhammad from blasphemy. Extremists wished to punish the perpetrators by death:

We must respond and punish them so as to deter them from their kufr, *'denial of the truth of Islamic teaching', and enmity. If we leave the* kuffar, *'a highly derogatory term referring to non-Muslims', and atheists to say whatever they want without denouncing it or punishing them, great mischief will result, which is something that these* kuffar *love ... The Muslim has to have a sense of protective jealousy and get angry for the sake of Allah and His Messenger (peace and blessings of Allah be upon him). Whoever hears the Prophet ... being insulted and does not feel any protective jealousy or get angry is not a true believer.*[4]

Director of Publication of *Charlie Hebdo*, Stéphane Charbonnier, claimed, 'We have to carry on until Islam has been rendered as banal as Catholicism.' In 2013, he was placed on a chilling hit list, along with Rushdie and nine others, in *Inspire*, the al-Qaeda recruitment magazine, and was among those murdered at rue Nicolas-Appert.

Rushdie responded to the slaughter, 'Religion, a medieval form of unreason, when combined with modern weaponry, becomes a real threat to our freedoms. This religious totalitarianism has caused a deadly mutation in the heart of Islam and we see the consequences in Paris. I stand with *Charlie Hebdo*, as we all must, to defend the art of satire, which has always been a force for liberty and against tyranny, dishonesty and stupidity.'[5]

Crone had previously identified the theme in medieval Islam. 'A Muslim was someone who surrendered to God and lived as his servant in a society based on his law. Infidels were rebels against God whose societies could never be more than robbers' nests. Since they did not live by God's law, nothing they did had any moral basis. Relationships established by them were not legally valid, compacts made with them did not have to be honoured, they could be freely killed "like wild animals before the arrows and the spears", their property could be taken as booty and "all their wives and children were free spoil for slavery". Bereft of holy guidance, infidels were not truly human. Some infidels became closer to true humanity than others. Unlike pagans and idolaters, the Jews and the Christians had received revelations from God and therefore were *ahl al-kitab*, "People of the Book". But they were still infidels for they denied that Muhammad had brought a new revelation from God and they had perverted their scriptures and their original faith. Those of them not brought to Muslim sovereignty were outlaws on a par with infidels.'[6]

English philosopher Roger Scruton explained that the difference is that 'Western societies are governed by politics; the Rest are ruled by power'.[7] A state founded on a social contract is 'maximally respectful of the autonomy, freedom and dignity of the individual'. Elsewhere, it is the interpretation of the word of God by those in control which holds sway; legal order is founded in divine command; human rights for non-believers is often an alien concept.

After impressive security with state-of-the-art scanning devices, I climbed the stairs to the editorial offices where the shootings had taken place. I was received warily after being searched a second time by a man in his thirties with inky fingers sitting at a drawing board of cartoon ideas.

'How can I help?' he began as he greeted me and transferred sticky daubs of colour to my hands.

'I have something for you, for Charlie.' I said. 'I think it will interest you greatly. I want to ask you a few questions first. It will only take five minutes or so. If I am satisfied and you accept my conditions, you can have I what I have brought for free. I will leave and you will never see me again. Agreed?'

'OK. I'm intrigued. Agreed. Ask away for five minutes.'

'You have a lot of security. Do you feel that it is still needed?'

'More than ever,' he replied. 'The income from every other copy we sell goes to pay for it, about one and half million euros a year. Do you think that it is normal in a democratic country? That's how much it costs to take on Islamist fanatics.'

I nodded. 'There was a great outpouring of support for *Charlie Hebdo* after the murders,' I continued. 'I recall that soon afterwards about two million people, including more than forty world leaders, met in the city for a rally of national unity. There were demonstrations across all France attended by double that number decrying the atrocity and calling for the defence of freedom of speech, even against Arab outrage. You sold a lot of copies.'

'We did. Our first issue reached eight million in six languages. Till then, we were running at about 60,000 and only in French. We received cash donations from many places, including the *Guardian* newspaper in England. The slogan *Je suis Charlie*, 'I am Charlie', became international. In the week after the attack, there were fifty-four anti-Muslim incidents in France: shootings, grenades, IEDs, and plain threats and insults, all called right-wing terrorism by the authorities, so that means it cannot have had anything to do with us.

You have to remember that in this country around 1800, so long ago, the Republic was emancipated from the Catholic Church and blasphemy laws ceased in France. The principle of *laïcité* came out of this separation. We stand against the influence of religion, all religion, in the state. This is very important to us. It still is. We are not going to stop. Nor do we think that the militants will stop trying to kill us.'

'So, at heart, you believe this is an issue of freedom of speech and action. You stand against any repression based on religion by anyone.'

'Exactly.'

'A last question, please. I do not read *Charlie Hebdo*. I understand that some of the humour is difficult to understand. Your circulation has fallen to below where it was before the attack. I have heard some heartfelt criticism of some of your stances. You lampooned those killed when a Russian airliner was downed over Egypt, poked fun at a Syrian migrant boy found dead on a Turkish beach and joked about the victims of an Italian earthquake.'

'You are right; our circulation has fallen to below what it was before. Sometimes, perhaps, we have got it wrong. Also, we are not angels. I think that's more than your five minutes.'

I slid Nianankoro's French translation of Ahmed Baba's treatise across the table towards him. 'The original was written in about 1650.'

He picked it up, determined, I thought, not to be impressed. His dismissive face did not last long. He sat bolt upright and read with hunger, I could even say revenge, in his eyes. He read it twice.

'Provenance?' he asked.

'Here is the name and phone number of the scholar in *Tombouctou* who found the document in his private library. He is unimpeachable. You can contact him. He speaks French and English well. You do not negotiate with him. However, one of the conditions, for his safety, is that he is not personally named in any story you run nor do you keep his contact details in your office files.'

I paused. 'Also, there is this. It is a top quality machine copy of the original in Arabic. It was written, as you see, by Ahmed Baba al-Musufi, al-Tinbukti. You have freedom to place pictures of the manuscript in *Charlie Hebdo*. You are also free to share it with whoever you like under your own conditions.'

'I know Baba and his reputation. This is dynamite. Are there other conditions?'

'Only three,' I said. 'One, as explained, is that you will never identify the document's source in *Tombouctou* without permission. The second is easy: you never make any attempt to identify me or to describe me to anyone. When I leave, I disappear. The third may be a little troublesome for you. I want wider publicity for the content of this treatise than you are likely to get yourself just from *Charlie Hebdo*. I want it to be a clarion call for women's rights against oppressive religion. You must find a journalistic partner with worldwide reach. You must with them establish a community that will carry this message into the heart of Muslim fanatics. You can take the lead and the credit for this discovery, but I want your enthusiasm for its dissemination.'

'Can you give me an hour?' he said. 'I need to talk to some people.'

'If you give me the name of a good local restaurant for lunch, I'll leave you for a while. I trust you with the documents.'

Ten minutes later, I settled down with a plate of Concarneau oysters followed by veal kidneys in a mustard sauce and a very decent Bordeaux, all paid for, I was assured. I pulled out my copy of *Finnegans Wake* and bided my time.

Back at the office, I faced a court of five staffers, the management team, I assumed. I was asked to confirm briefly my offer and my conditions. There were a few nods around the table. There was no discussion.

'We have a deal, Mr X. We have spoken to your principal in *Tombouctou* and are convinced by the provenance.' He slid back the paper with Nianankoro's phone number. 'We do not need this any more so you can both be sure that no link can be found.'

I nodded.

'We are very grateful to you. We are individually and collectively in complete agreement with your motives. Do you want anything in writing?'

I smiled. 'No, that's all right. I know where to find you. And I know your security arrangements.'

As I left, I put my copy of *Finnegans Wake* on the table.

'A gift,' I said. 'I just can't get on with it.'

Outside, I sent a text to Nianankoro letting him know what I had done and that my task was concluded. His daughter was avenged. I forgot to bin my burner and made for the Metro. I felt I deserved the rest of the day at the Musée de l'Orangerie in the Tuileries Gardens. It was almost devoid of people and permanent home to Monet's eight large murals of water lilies in two oval rooms. The flowers were reproductions from his garden in Giverny. Displayed in the intended diffused light, Monet presented these works to the nation as a solace after the Great War and this effect continues to this day.

They worked their magic. Is it possible to have too much Monet?

The next morning my train trundled out of the Gare St Lazare and gathered pace through dreary graffiti and dim, cold suburban stations, raindrops from lazy showers part-obscuring the view, the mist from condensation gradually completing my seclusion. I had a morning newspaper, but no book to read. Three more British members of parliament had been murdered for their attempts to overturn the three-year-old referendum to leave the EU. One person arrested last week for previous assassinations had been released; two more had been arrested. French commentators vacillated between unashamed glee and horror at this contagion near the heart of Europe. Was open civil war a possibility in Britain? What had failed? Why were the English not more like the French?

The killer of Juncker and Selmayr was still free, but, as ever, close to arrest. In Brussels, advanced plans for the deconstruction of NATO and its replacement by a European Army to be led by a German general were announced.

Across metropolitan Britain, especially in the major university centres, there were serious concerns about a decline in mental health among those who abhorred Brexit. There were prominent and distressing examples of illness in Westminster. The debate, if it can be called that, was increasingly vitriolic with all opponents of EU membership lambasted as 'far right' or fascists. The mental distress turned first into chronic migraines, according to research from Warwick University.[8] Those in the laager saw walls where none existed, sought friendships exclusively among the Remainer community, automatically objected if a close relative consorted with a Brexiteer.

A US psychologist, Jonathan Haidt, showed that progressives, particularly, struggled to comprehend the motives of conservatives. When asked to think as their opponents did, conservatives answered moral questions as the liberal might, but socialists were unable to do the reverse. This tendency to mischaracterise perhaps explained liberals' heightened fear of ending on the losing side since their opponents must have the worst of intentions. Many of the progressive movements possessed a quasi-religious quality with an Islamic strength of feeling taking precedence over argument.

'It is true because I feel it is true to the depth of my being, not because I can actually prove it.'

For the first time in many months, I realised I, an aspirant nomad, was back in control with no guide to hold my hand, no company, no objective but to try to throw off an immoral, confused, controlled and divided society.

My lack of success to date was breathtaking.

The forgotten burner buzzed twice. It was a lengthy text from Nianankoro split into three and I repeat it here. I have nothing to add to its message:

May the blessings of Allah be doubly showered upon you. You have more than fulfilled your promises. I thank you and release you. Two payments have arrived from the north as you reported. My library is safe.

Aisha is dead. She had gone mad with what she had done. Her body was found in a stagnant pool in the canal, pockets weighted with stones and a red rose embroidered into her hair. She knew that she could never climb the steep sides if she changed her mind at the last.

Yesterday, we had a confrontation, mostly about you. I accused her, Allah forgive me, of having a hand in Ahmed's death. She finally admitted she had tried four times to have you killed, but would not, could not, explain the source of her rage. I told her what you were doing for me, for us. She went quiet and she withdrew from the world.

Our daughter is avenged. My life is now my old and dusty books. For them, I have lost by beloved nephew and my friend of fifty years. There is no blame with you.

Ahmed is secure in heaven, I am sure. But will the prophet take Aisha to his bosom?

I took the SIM card from the burner, twisted it several ways and flushed it down the carriage toilet, a quiet room where I had gone to cry. The carcass, I wiped and forced down the back of the seat while I gazed out of a now fully misted window which showed only my reflection.

---

1 Burke, *Vico.*
2 Crone, *God's Rule.*
3 Lançon, *Disturbance, Surviving Charlie Hebdo.*
4 *Islamqa Fatwa 14305*, Salafi scholar Muhammad Saalih Al-Munajjid, 17/4/2004.
5 *The Age*, Lucy Cormack, 8/1/2015.
6 Crone, *God's Rule.*
7 Scruton, *West and the Rest.*
8 Grant, *Daily Telegraph*, 7/8/19.

11. FINDING FATHER

Meine Ruh ist hin,
Mein Herz ist schwer,
Ich finde sie nimmer
und nimmermehr.

Goethe, *Faust*, 'Gretchen am Spinnrad', words used in a *lied* by Schubert:
My peace is gone … My heart is sore … I will find it never … and
nevermore.

A long, long time ago when I was a teenager, I sat in the back of a car driven
by my father. Turning to tell me off, he ran into the back of a lorry carrying
over-hanging scaffolding poles. His last words were that I was a 'complete
and absolute failure'. My father and mother died almost instantly. I told the
story in my last book, *Disappearing*.

I remember that I sat for a while, then got out and walked to the side of the
road. I might as well have not been there. For a full minute, nobody realised
the seriousness of the accident. A woman began screaming. I walked over
a bridge and hitchhiked home. After a dinner of four lamb chops, I forced
a locked wooden bureau that contained my father's papers. Alongside
my passport, unused since my brother's death, were an undated French
newspaper cutting and an adoption certificate. The one-paragraph story told
that a woman had been killed in another car crash, this time in Rouen in
France. There were a few skimpy details, just her name and that she was in
her early twenties, French, and unmarried. Her name was also on my adoption
certificate as deceased and so she had been my natural mother.

The gap between my birth date – at least what I had been told was my birth
date – and my adoption was only a few weeks. The woman I had thought
was my mother came, I knew, from a Huguenot family and she had taught
me to speak fluent French. I wondered if there was some family connection
between my two mothers. That might have been a further reason why I was
brought up in England.

Reading between the lines with my papers in my lap, I realised I might have been a convenient replacement for a child who had died in childbirth. I decided that I was pleased to be adopted, that my father wasn't my father. None of this had been a bombshell, more a harmless unexploded device that set me free of encumberments. I decided to keep the information secret.

The train entered a long tunnel minutes before reaching the old station at Rouen on the Seine's right bank. Since I returned to France, I was dogged by an unexpected restlessness. In Paris, it surfaced as a newfound and morbid preoccupation with my roots. The subject had hardly surfaced over the last fifty years. Yet, here I was, free to take what I hoped was a final leap into the unknown, to leave Europe again and forever, but I had delayed to visit a town I thought I had never been to.

From my research into *Sound of Hunger*, I knew Rouen only for its role as a prisoner of war camp for German troops during the Great War. In this, it was no different from almost every other town with one exception: it was a place of bad reputation as French guards, embittered by their own war experiences, maltreated their captives, some to the point of death. I also knew that the skyline was dominated by the spires of Cathédrale Notre-Dame, much-painted by Claude Monet. This was all I knew of the river port where my birth mother had died.

As the train pulled up, I grasped the truth of it, probably obvious to any trained observer, but not to me till then. I had so hated my supposed father that when I realised he was not my blood relative I let him slip easily away. I did not believe that I felt the loss. For almost all my life, I had been a man without a father, pleased only that the real and emotional scars were no longer mine to carry. My mother's short life held some interest, but, in truth, I saw her as a route to my actual father who was completely unknown to me. Discovering him might give me some salvation in my last few years, some inner belonging when I was finally fully alone. I wondered whether he was a pleasant man for he had not married my mother.

At the side of the train, I was taken aback by an unusual work of art. One of the old platforms, unused and redolent of a different age, had been brought to an hallucinatory new life by the use of subtle and time-bridging lighting. I should have recognised that the dramatic omens implied by throwing new light on old identities and emotions, no matter how thoughtfully disguised, might be a two-way process. If I had known the can of emotional worms that I was about to prise open, I might have caught the train straight back to Paris.

It was Monet that led me naturally to the Hôtel De La Cathédrale in the cobblestoned town centre where a medieval half-timbered house provided a simple bedroom. I dumped my bag, a carefree tourist, and spent the afternoon at the Musée des Beaux-Arts. I didn't move around much, happy to be among the impressionists and, particularly, with Alfred Sisley. This Englishman turned French captured the village of Marly-le-Roi, close to Paris, in great contrasts of colour, of stability and movement, when the Seine flooded its banks almost 150 years ago.

In the morning, I took a pleasant half an hour stroll across the river to the regional archives in the splendidly modern building that also houses the Simone de Beauvoir library. I explained to the charming Daphné that I had seen a cutting from a Rouen newspaper almost sixty years ago concerning a road accident and I wanted to see if I could trace it. Daphne's eyebrows leapt above her half-moon glasses and her shoulders shrugged delightfully. She wore a cashmere sweater of the palest blue which matched her eyes and accentuated her shapeliness. I was about to be written off when I added that the woman who had died in the car crash was my mother whom I had never known nor, indeed, had I seen a photograph of her, and knew nothing of her family. The blue eyes sparkled with concern. I had a committed archival friend. I gave Daphné the name which I had never spoken out loud.

She led me to a computer terminal and paused to assess whether someone of such age would be capable of an online search. She decided not and, swishing her pleated grey skirt, sat down, her legs sheathed in thick black tights. Daphné motioned me to bring a swivel chair alongside. Despite my concentration on my mission, I drank in her subtle perfume. After a few moments of punching the keyboard, she gave a little hiss of triumph.

'*Journal de Rouen*,' she exclaimed. '12 June 1947.' It had been digitised recently in a major project. 'Was this the cutting?' It was.

'Just as I remember it,' I said. 'I am so grateful,' with what I hoped was an alluring smile. 'The same typeface, but, unfortunately, the story that I remember was, I see now, complete.'

I paused. 'I wonder if there might be more information in other cuttings in this newspaper, or in other newspapers?'

'There are three other mentions in the *Journal de Rouen*,' she said. 'You can see them highlighted here. Are you able to follow these? We are limited in the amount of time we can give to each researcher. But, of course, yours is a special case.'

I said I could manage.

As she got up, she said she would see if she could find any other references. I breathed deeply. She seemed to me, an old man with few dreams beyond today, to be too young to have any real sense of time, of what the future might hold and how the past might reappear. I called up the other stories, devoured their contents and then sent them for printing. At the collection point, I asked a serious young man with a close crewcut where I might find death certificates. He looked suspicious as if I would misuse such valuable information.

'You are British?'

'No. It is the death certificate of my mother,' I explained, realising that I had no need of explanation. I pulled out carefully one of my two French passports and showed him that my surname matched that of my mother. 'And, is it possible, there was an inquiry, an inquest, into the death and there is a public record?'

He looked delighted to be able to block me. 'For the death certificate you must go to the office in the Place du Général de Gaulle.' He refused to accept my Frenchness. 'The French do not hold inquests like the British. If there are any papers, and as you are a family member, you will need to employ a lawyer. Only they can get access.' Which, of course, was out of the question.

The *Acte de Décès* arrived, followed shortly afterwards by Daphné with the smile of success broad across her face. She handed me a small sheaf of copies of cuttings. 'These are from *Paris Normandie* and *Ouest France*.'

'Thank you. I think that I shall retire to read for a bit. Is there a good local restaurant for lunch nearby?'

'We have a small cafeteria in the building otherwise I recommend the Bistrot des Abattoirs just across the road.'

'I don't suppose … I would be very happy …'

She declined with a drop of her lovely head. They were short staffed. 'Désolée …' But she suggested that I call in afterwards to see if she had managed to find any additional material. I smiled, bowed slightly, picked up my papers and left.

Over a leisurely and welcome magret de canard and crème brûlée on the lively garden terrasse caught in a late burst of winter sun, I read all the documents and mulled my findings, more excited and surprised than I cared to admit.

My mother, Annette, had died, aged twenty, unmarried, on my birth date in May; her surname I shall keep to myself so as not to prejudice one of my passports. She was in full term and was being driven at speed to a midwife when a Jeep went out of control in a village street just outside Rouen and hit a tree. The crash brought on the birth and the baby arrived at the roadside assisted by ladies from nearby houses. My mother died as I was placed in her arms. The driver was uninjured. There were no other passengers.

Annette's father, Gabriel, a widower, was a prominent Huguenot pastor in the old town who lived at rue de l'Écureuil. His house was in a row with the home of a previous pastor, Henri Basnages de Franquenay. There was much detail about the ancestry of this renowned family from the sixteenth century: Norman parliamentarians, jurists, international men of letters, involvement in the St Bartholomew's Day massacre, and connections in exile with the Walloon Churches in Threadneedle Street in London and Norwich. The reason for the information was an inferred relationship between the Basnages dynasty and Annette, the dead woman.

The driver of the vehicle was Enseigne de vaisseau second class Gaston Albert, aged twenty-nine, who was serving aboard *La Moqueuse*, a sloop-minesweeper, of the French Navy, based in Lorient. The ship was an occasional visitor to Rouen in its engagement to clear Atlantic tidal rivers like the Seine of German mines from World War Two.[1]

Over a second coffee, I thought about my mother who had died giving birth to me. Perhaps that was too melodramatic. Annette was killed as a result of a car crash for which I was hardly to blame although I had been a contributory factor. She had probably never seen my face. It was possible I would never see hers. She came from a strict religious background and for some reason had not married her lover. Could there be any doubt that her lover and my father was Enseigne de vaisseau Albert who had driven her to her death? Why had they not married? They were still involved after nine months of pregnancy. Was there something of family and religion in the explanation? My move to England and my adoptive parents had been almost immediate, even indecently so. Was I not wanted, an embarrassment, or was there some practicality involved?

I started my laptop using a TOR browser to evade detection. *La Moqueuse* was not a famous ship, but there was sufficient information about its history to answer one of my questions. The ship had been sent to Lorient at the end of 1946 to prepare for service in Indochina. The French sought to re-establish themselves in Vietnam and Laos after the end of the dubious administrative co-operation between the Vichy French and the Japanese invaders. *La Moqueuse* left Lorient on 11 May 1947, calling at Toulon and Piraeus and reached Saigon on 30 June. If Gaston Albert was indeed my father, his ship sailed within a few days of Annette's death and my birth. What turmoil and heartbreak there must have been.

Daphné waved at me from her desk when I re-entered the archive.

'Have you found what you wanted to know?' she asked, bubbling with interest.

'A lot of it,' I replied, 'but every answer seems to bring other questions. I am not sure how much further to go.' I looked at her and caught her excitement. 'You know something more,' I guessed. 'You've discovered another piece of the jigsaw?'

'I've gone further than I should, perhaps. I hope you won't be angry?'

'Too late now. Tell all.'

'Well, your surname, is a local one, but it is quite rare. One reads it occasionally in histories, but I have never met anyone who has it. I wondered whether there were many people of that name still living in Rouen, perhaps even relatives. I checked the population register for the town, a lot of the records go back to the *Révolution française*, you know, and then I cross-checked against the electoral register and the telephone directory.' She paused for breath and looked apprehensive knowing she had overstepped a librarian's mark.

'I forgive you in advance,' I said. 'How far did you go?'

'I made a telephone call to the only person with your name in Rouen, a lady who lives in a small house around the corner from rue de l'Écureuil. Her name is Babette, she is very charming, lively in her mind. She is eighty-five according to the registers.'

'And …'

'She confirmed that she is the niece of Pastor Gabriel, but that she never knew him as he died soon after she was born. It means that she is your mother's cousin. I did not mention you or your mother. Babette thinks I called about possible research into Rouen's Huguenot history. She is very curious and happy to be involved. She is waiting for my call back.'

I smiled and said, 'Thank you', and watched the tension flow out of her. I didn't know how big a professional crime she had committed, but I was grateful. However, I realised her interference had placed me on the threshold of a place I maybe should not go to. The consequences might be life changing. I was also a wanted man and had no right to bring political and police scrutiny into the last days of Babette's life for my own selfish reasons.

'What do you want me to do?' she asked, holding my gaze. It was one of those few moments when I deeply regretted my age, all the losses in my life, my second wife and our children, all the other women with whom I had shared love and departure. For the first time, I thought about dying alone and unremarked.

'What I would like you to do, Daphné, is to make that call. Explain that you are acting for a third party to protect her privacy; that I am in Rouen on a visit and would like to meet her to discuss family history. All I seek is information. I am at her disposal.'

Daphné nodded agreement and went into an office. I could see her have an animated conversation through the window. She was back inside five minutes.

'Babette is more than happy to see you. In fact, she can hardly wait. She proposes six o'clock this evening at her house. I have accepted on your behalf. Babette then said something unexpected and strange. She said that she knows who you are, but that she doesn't know your name, and that she has been waiting a long time for you to make contact.'

'There's one more thing,' said Daphné. 'It is a great impertinence, but I would like to come with you. I am fascinated by your story.'

'You realise that means that I have to buy you dinner afterwards. I will have to talk through all that I learn.'

She gave me a radiant smile. 'A pleasure, monsieur.'

The house was timbered, akin to its neighbours in rue de l'Écureuil, small, even squeezed into the terrace, full of memories and impeccably kept with the solid furniture shining with regular beeswax. Babette was a delight, half my size, a confident mistress of her environment, and welcoming. Her grey hair was tight in a bun, her spectacles hanging to her waist on a silver chord, her cardigan long, loose and open. First, we admired her small collection of hard-paste Sèvres biscuit porcelain figures. Two ruler-high translucent beauties caught my eye and I said so: *La Mélancolie* and *La Méditation*, based on Falconet's sculptures.

'Are these originals?' I wondered. '1770 or 1780? They must be worth 20,000 Euros.' Babette was delighted and our friendship cemented.

Coffee was ready. I was offered *une verre* as an opened bottle was placed on the table. For a glass of Margaux, I hesitated, but thought it best to hold back. Daphné was welcomed like a favourite granddaughter. By our previous agreement, she sat slightly apart and took out a pad to make notes. Babette and I talked for almost two hours. Towards the end, I did reach confidently for the bottle. We parted with a heartfelt, but delicate clasp. Babette said she hoped to see me again, but she sensed, with great sadness, that my history would take me away. I would always be a most welcome guest and cousin.

Daphné and I walked arm-in-arm for perhaps half an hour towards and around the old town until we began to feel the cold. I said little while I mulled matters over. Finally, she guided me to *La Marmite* to meet a friend, Frédérique, Rouen's renowned woman chef. The room was friendly, warm, with just enough space for a private conversation. At the table, while I savoured the *foie gras*, with an eyebrow-raising glass of iced vodka, Daphné squirrelled into a large bag, produced her notebook and began to read.

Here's what I had learned:

There were three sisters, born into a family of ten children in and around the Great War. One of these, Bernadette, became the wife of Gabriel and died young leaving only one daughter, my mother, Annette. Annette led an unhappy, lonely life made worse by the religious extremism of her father. She fell for a sailor, my father, Gaston. For a reason no one understood, Gabriel took implacably against Gaston from their first meeting and the young people's relationship became clandestine. When Annette became pregnant, she was thrown out of her home without debate. Her father was able to refuse permission for a marriage because she was under age. Annette took refuge with friends in the Rouen countryside where her lover visited her whenever he was in port. Twice, he missed sailings and was on a final warning of imprisonment from his commanding officer.

I was born in the circumstances I already knew. Gaston's ship was sailing for Indochina within the week. He had a baby son whose grandfather refused to acknowledge him and banned any of his family in Rouen from providing any assistance. Doors were shut in his face although Annette's youngest aunt did slip him a small bundle of banknotes. Gaston had lost the love of his life. He saw one thin ray of hope. Annette's other aunt, who lived in England, had just had a stillbirth. He telegrammed with his story and asked if they would take in his boy until he returned and was able to make better provision. A positive answer came quickly and he left without much thought for London with a female child nurse. The arrangements took almost all the money that had been put aside against the eventual marriage.

As Gaston met my adoptive parents for the swap to take place, cold and transactional in a run-down, shabby post-war hotel in Charing Cross, he received the devastating ultimatum. The baby would only be taken if it was for ever. Any future contact would be rejected. I would replace the stillborn child as if it had never existed. The truth would be denied and attempts to regain custody would be ruinously expensive and fought in English courts against an unsuitable foreigner.

Gaston had no choice. It was thought at this time, speculation only, that he suffered a breakdown. After several hours that evening in a succession of London pubs and a night on park benches, woken and moved on by the police, he returned to France. Two days later, he arrived at Lorient to find La Moqueuse had left an hour earlier. Time no longer of importance, he used the last of his money to take the train back to Paris where he had distant family and stayed the night. He then took a slow cheap train to Toulon where he was spotted by the naval police, drunk and in a filthy torn uniform. He spent the next few *days in a cell, left to dry out with little food, waiting for his ship to arrive when he would be guaranteed further confinement.*

Babette knew all this from her mother who was the youngest sister and the one who had passed over the secret money before shutting the door firmly in Gaston's face in fear of Gabriel's anger. Babette's mother lived with shame and regret for her action all her life. Gaston wrote to her from prison in Toulon and told her what had happened. There were to be no more letters; Gaston was never heard from again.

Babette's mother's own letters to her sister in London pleading for fairness went unanswered and the family broke apart. Now, all were dead, except Babette, whose wealth had accumulated as the legacies drifted in like dried leaves.

The *filet d'agneau* was excellent as was the bottle of Saumur recommended by Frédérique. I drank a little too much. Daphné moved to tear the pages out of her notebook, but I stopped her.

'It's all imprinted,' I said, 'and there is nobody to share it all with anyway.' I took Daphné's hands in mine, kissed them, and thanked her for what she had done. It was that time of the evening.

'I want to thank you,' she said, 'for sharing with me. It was an eye-opening experience.'

She pulled out her mobile and explained, 'I need to call my boyfriend who's waiting nearby in his car to drive me home.' We stood, she smiled, and she kissed me full on the lips. 'Perhaps in another time,' she said.

With a swish of her grey skirt, I was alone. I admit to a tear. Frédérique's husband, Jean-Luc, who ran the front-of-house, arrived unbid with a cognac in hand.

'She's a wonderful girl,' he said. 'You are lucky to have met her. We all love Daphné to bits. Will you need a taxi?'

The next morning, I took the train back to Paris. The platforms at Rouen were unlit, the magic gone. Rouen was a town of lost opportunity and heartlessness. I admired Daphné's enterprise and her sure-footedness. My old man's schoolboy crush would fade with time, but I knew I would never forget her.

I now knew all that I really wanted to know about my own background.

Most of the small missing pieces, I could guess. What a man my grandfather Gabriel must have been, so confident in his righteousness, so damning to his only daughter, so dismissive of his only grandchild. If I had come to find some slither of love for my remaining days, I had found only rejection. I had two remaining, personal questions that gnawed away.

What had happened to my father on board *La Moqueuse?* I knew from the computer records that the ship took part in coastal bombardments of the idyllic island of Phu Quoc in the Mekong Delta and, in the Baï-Doc estuary, destroyed four junks, and defended the railway line between Tourane and Hué. After a refit in Toulon in 1949, *La Moqueuse* returned to Indochina where, in 1951, it supported an attack on Kikuik Bay, north of the minor port of Quảng Ngãi on the Vietnamese coast (later known for the My Lai massacre in the US Vietnamese war). The ship ended its days at Toulon attached to a gunnery school. It was condemned in 1965 and sold for demolition three years later. But of Gaston Albert, I knew nothing more.

And what was the reason for Gabriel's abrupt dismissal or his daughter's love, seemingly on first meeting? Was something said that had instantly poisoned the old fanatic's heart?

I had put aside one thing in the excitement of my meeting with Babette. Towards the end, while I was reaching for the Margaux, she excused herself and was gone for five minutes. She returned triumphant brandishing a letter. It was the letter, the one that my father had written to her mother from his Toulon jail. It was a special thing; all that I had of him. But, in content, I thought, it was but the source of part of the story that Babette had told me and, therefore, of no investigative value. Babette had given the letter to me, complete in its original envelope, as its rightful owner and, perhaps, to assuage her mother's guilt. Daphné and I had read it together and put it aside, or rather in my pocket. I reread it, and was tapping it against my leg, while I thought that it meant the end of my personal journey when I noticed the back of the envelope. There was written the sender's address. I had assumed the letter was all written in Toulon, but my father had started it at his relative's address in Paris.

Could it be that more than seventy years later, someone of my father's family still lived there or nearby? This was a leaping heart moment, a frantic fingertip scratching for purchase of the downward slope of a hopeless case.

I arrived at Gare St Lazare in the late morning and took a taxi to the rue Mouffetard in the fifth arrondissement, once the home of a vibrant food market that I had known well during working trips to Paris almost thirty years before. The square had been the workplace and casual shop of aspiring street painters. It had often seemed to me that this was the world's most painted townscape. I had bought a work there myself but left it behind when I quit my home in Hampshire for the last time. There were still restaurants and bars a plenty, but the cosy village atmosphere was long gone. It did not seem a safe place and I saw many tell-tale signs of a vibrant drugs trade. I remembered happy hours reading in the evening sun in the *Jardin des Plantes*; now I don't think I would go there alone.

The address on the back of the envelope was in a row of terraced houses, unkempt, with a concreted front garden just large enough for a small car and two dustbins. The car was missing, the windows half-covered with heavily cobwebbed lace. Only a couple of the buildings had seen recent paintwork. The whole looked more like workers' cottages that had never been gentrified. The street was empty as I rang the bell and heard a sad tune deep within. No one came. Half a block down there was a brown café that smelled of yesterday's deep-fried fat. I ordered powdered coffee that came with a splash of cigarette ash and took a seat in the window among the stub ends. After an hour, as the light began to drop, an Arab woman, head sheathed in a hijab, walked slowly to the door, her arms extended by two crowded, string shopping bags. She pushed the bell three times and was let in. Success looked a long way away.

The door opened to my triple ring and the woman in the hijab looked at me in surprise. We spoke in French, but there was no flash of recognition in her eyes to my father's name. In the dark background of the hall, I could make out the shape of another woman, much older and heavily shrouded. She had been home when I first called, but, driven by convention, had not responded to a visit by an unknown man. I tried once more to get through the brief and guttural responses when a battered Fiat crawled into the parking space. A middle-aged man dressed in jeans and green pullover got out and eyed me.

'What do you want here?' he demanded. 'You have no right to bother these women when there are no men at home.'

'Information, only,' I replied. 'I am searching for information about my father whose family lived in this house a long time ago, about seventy years. His name was Gaston Albert. He was a sailor in the French navy.'

'We know no one of that name.'

However, I did notice a reaction from the hazy figure in the dim background. I sensed some quickening of interest.

'How long has your family lived here?' I asked, as pleasantly as I could.

'I've told you we know nobody of that name.'

I decided to take the risk. I spoke in Arabic directly to the old woman and she nodded briefly and came even closer.

'How dare you speak directly to my mother,' shouted the man and moved to within striking, or knife blade, distance.

'I mean no disrespect to your mother or to you as her protector,' I said, still in Arabic. 'I think it is possible that she may know something of my father. Of course, I am prepared to pay for any help I can get.'

There was a short, private conversation I did not grasp. The Arabic had helped. The offer of money helped even more. The atmosphere subsided and I was invited into a kitchen filled with aged and grimy fittings and decorations from the last century. The only light was from the dimming window. I placed fifty Euros on the table as an initial contribution.

Ever since the advent of European rule of foreign countries, the writing of history has been controlled by the colonialists and their native disciples. These historians had a dual purpose: to justify the establishment and to facilitate the maintenance of colonial domination. This they did by blackening the pre-colonial era, which they depicted as an age of barbarism and backwardness, and whitewashing the colonial regime, which they presented as an instrument of enlightenment and progress. This invented history was taught to both rulers and ruled and served the double purpose of demoralising the latter and nerving the former for the sometimes disagreeable duties they had to perform. After tea was properly prepared and poured, we drank though sugar lumps and our cups were refilled.

The family was Algerian, long enough away from their homeland to enquire about my Moroccan accent, tinted with Malian. The younger woman was the man's wife, the old lady his mother and only she knew of Gaston Albert, but I directed all my questions through her son. We spoke in French because his grasp of Arabic was limited having spent most of his life in Paris. It took a while for me to grasp, but the mother's family was related through a second marriage to a cousin of my father. It was this cousin who had once lived in the house and who had provided shelter to my father in the 1940s.

'So, we are not related,' said my host. 'I would like to tell you more to be worthy of a further payment, but what is there to say?'

'Not family in blood,' interjected the old lady, 'but family in the sight of Allah.'

This was one of those moments when you don't see what is coming, and don't realise what it means till the truth has rushed past and you are left, mouth open and brain whirling.

'I knew Gaston had a son who was lost to him,' she explained. 'My mother used to visit your grandmother when she was a child, a friend of the family. Your grandmother was Algerian and a good Muslim, but she broke with her own father when she decided to marry your grandfather who was a Frenchman in the Foreign Legion. There was a great scandal. They were never again accepted by either faith. Their families were torn apart by Algerian politics. It was brother against brother, sister against sister. Your grandfather died fighting somewhere, in some battle.

'Your own father joined the Legion after he lost his son in England and served in Algeria and French Indochina where some said he died, some that he was captured, and others that he just never came home.

'Where was home for him? His mother, your grandmother, was killed by a street bomb in Algiers. I have no more details. You are alone in the world.'

Another tea followed and we all sat quiet. Seeing the man was restless, I pushed another fifty Euros across the table.

'*Inshallah*,' I offered. '*Aškorak 'alā ehtemāmak*.'[2]

We sat awkwardly. 'I suppose you have nothing of my father's?'

'There is nothing here of value,' said the man, waving his arm as if to display their lowly standard of living. The two women nodded in agreement.

I thanked them again and began to stand to leave.

'Unless you would like the letters,' said the old lady. 'I had forgotten them. I suppose they are rightfully yours.' She spoke quietly to her daughter-in-law, giving her instructions so that she left the room.

I managed a strangled, 'What letters?'

'These are the letters my mother gave me. I have never really looked at them as they were private and personal. When your grandmother was killed, she was living in poor circumstances, relying on charity from the mosque. Her family never forgave her for marrying a Frenchman. His family was unknown; he was a Legionnaire.' She shrugged. 'All of your grandmother's sticks of furniture and her clothes, rags mostly, were burned. The letters nearly followed them, but as they were her most precious possession, it was decided that the thing to do before Allah was to send them to Paris to my mother. Thinking about it now, I suppose they were for you if you ever appeared, *Inshallah*.'

The daughter came back into the room and handed me a small cardboard box wrapped in a military ribbon.

'There you are,' said the old lady. 'These are the letters your father wrote to his mother while he was in the Legion.'

I slid a small handful of notes across the table. The amount caused a sharp intake of breath. I teased the ribbon. There were about thirty letters in their envelopes, some stained with mud and, I thought, blood. They seemed folded with love, but then, within the shock, I was feeling sentimental. The letters were all in Arabic, deciphered, I found, by a friend at the local primary school for a mother who could neither read nor write in any language and who had to wait impatiently till the early evening to receive news of her only son who was a soldier, a devout son of Allah and always fighting for France.

Here was reason enough for my Huguenot grandfather to shut the door on his daughter's proposed marriage to a boy who was an unforgivable mix of Roman Catholic and Muslim.

1 Sub-lieutenant.
2 A formal 'thank you' for consideration.

12. A SAILOR'S STORY

[It is] useless to ask a wandering man
Advice on the construction of a house.
The work will never come to completion.

Shih-ching, *Book of Odes*

The letters often nudged a tear down my cheek. They held the rawness of a young man who had seen and done terrible things, but also descriptions of enlightenment and enjoyment; they showed a deep respect and care for a mother only to be seen a few times again.

It was a strange matter to feel attached to a man never truly met, who had only held me in his arms for less than a week. There was little written about me, but I felt that he burned with the injustice and bad luck of my loss. It made him an angry man, always calculating, never carefree. I sensed that he was casual about violent death, never expected to fall in love again and, certainly, never to be truly content. Happiness was a fleeting bedfellow.

I could understand a lot of what turned out to be twenty-eight letters, from the extremes of Algeria when my father had no chance of permission to visit his mother in the capital, from Vietnam and Egypt where he survived the national embarrassments of Dien Bien Phu and Suez, from France when in hiding, and from the country where he eventually went to ground.

Arabic is neat and complicated, like the laying of mosaics of which I was so fond. Vowels were sprinkled here and there, long ones that you must take the trouble to write and short ones that are indicated by little flicks, stops and flying commas, and by the addition of certain consonants, so that the various parts of speech are formed. However, much subtlety was lost to me amongst the dialect, the family's sometimes childish abbreviations and the casual flecks where it was assumed that the meaning would be understood.

I needed help and took my little package to the Algerian embassy in Paris in the rue de Lisbonne where, after a long wait on a hard chair, among dull portraits of my father's recent adversaries, my first contact was with a short man with a goatee beard and the haughty and dismissive manner of a junior bureaucrat. I asked where I could buy the services of a translator, preferably one that had grown up in Algiers. He waved his hands at the silliness of the request. However, my twenty Euro note disappeared into a ready, sweaty paw.

After another fifteen minutes, an efficient young man, another Ahmed, asked me to repeat my story. He inspected the letters and led me to a small side office. After a short discussion as to the way forward, I offered to translate the pages to him in French as best I could while he sat by my side and corrected and explained while I spoke. No letter was more than four sides of paper. As I took no notes, we spent less than three hours including automatic interruptions for tea. He asked for fifty an hour which I happily doubled and gave him when we shook hands on the steps afterwards.

'It is an amazing story,' Ahmed said. 'So much of my own family's history. Such anger and sorrow. Thank Allah, it is all over. I wish you well on your journey.'

And, so, for this chapter about his time in the French Navy, and for the next, I think it best for my father's letters to tell their own story. What I have done is to leave out much of the small news, the titbits that a mother loves to hear of her child's casual doings. I have also combined some of the letters so that they fit into a cohesive history and, from time to time, to make sense of the references, added background which I gleaned from books that I bought and from Wikipedia. Some of these additions would never have escaped the censor of the day, but I have the advantage of hindsight. Other than that, I leave it to each reader to react and, perhaps, to take sides.

Each letter began with a place, sometimes vague as 'In France', or 'At Sea', a date and 'My dearest Mother, how are you today?' أمي العزيزة, كيف حالك اليوم?. It was a phrase I had never used myself.

September 1940: I am at sea! All around me is a great grey ocean with little splashes of white. I cannot tell you where I am as I don't even know myself. As you know, I was to be in training in Oran for eighteen months. I was in Alexandra when a ship arrived flying the flag of the Free French in the Mediterranean. I was ordered with ten others to join her because some of the crew were suspect following what happened at Mers. I can tell you my ship is called La Moqueuse *and it is a sloop minesweeper.*[1] *Our captain is Lieutenant Commander Louis Ploix, from Brittany, and I see him from time to time, but I have not spoken to him yet. At the moment, I have just general duties, nothing special, but I hope to work on one of the big guns.*

Looking at the sea reminds me of you at the street window of our three rooms. I remember the striped shade of the carefully closed shutters when the heat outside was baking and when, in the half-light, there always seemed to be two energetic flies buzzing around like aeroplanes as they searched for a way out.[2]

Are you sitting by the window with the red and yellow blinds or on the little balcony with its peeling iron rail if it is not too hot, Mother? Are you hunched forward in that old uncomfortable chair, with your small grey blouse set off by a white collar, with a white handkerchief clasped in your hands, your eyes with that soft look they always had? Are you watching the traffic and the pedestrians? Can you see the haberdasher's shop across the street, the curtain of multi-coloured beads masking the entrance to the tobacconist's, and Jean's café all empty except for the cat lying on the sill between the sawdust-covered floor and the dusty sidewalk, and sleeping as if it were dead.

Are you thinking of me?

I salute you for all the hard days you endured working in the service of others, washing floors on your knees among the greasy leavings and dirty linen of other people's lives, the long days of labour.

Does my money reach you to add to your tiny war widow's pension? When I come home ...

Notes from my research: After the defeat of the Allies in northern France, Marshal Pétain's cabinet agreed to end the war and signed an armistice with Germany on 22 June 1940. The French had autonomy in a southern free zone, headquartered at Vichy. On 3 July, the British attacked the French fleet at the Mers-el-Kébir naval base near Oran in Algeria to prevent the French handing over these vessels to the Vichy Government and then, possibly, to the Axis powers. Almost 1,300 French servicemen were killed. Vichy severed diplomatic relations with Great Britain on 8

July. Two days later, the Third Republic was dissolved and Pétain was granted full powers by the National Assembly. In retaliation for Mers-el-Kébir, French aircraft raided Gibraltar on 18 July.

La Moqueuse was launched in January 1940 and seized in Portsmouth by the Royal Navy that July, along with other French ships in Plymouth. Two British naval officers and a French sailor were killed during resistance. *La Moqueuse,* pledged to General de Gaulle with patriotic fervour, was almost immediately handed over to the Free French Navy and based in the southern Mediterranean in a confused situation where Moroccan ports remained loyal to Vichy France and fought American attempts to land troops.

... November 1942: We have been at sea for ever it seems since we last left Alexandria. Most of the time we have been fighting Italian air attacks as we look after merchant ships going to and from Malta; on one trip, we ran out of anti-aircraft shells. I landed at Valetta once to help with some unloading, but we only stayed for a few hours. It was too dangerous. Much of the town, especially round the docks had been bombed many times. They are very short of food and we were pleased to get out of the trap and have a decent meal on board. As soon as we got back to Alexandria, we all worked to refuel and take on supplies and ammunition and then off we went again.

I remember when we children would play in the black cellars dug into the earth beneath our homes, sweating with humidity, reached by four steps covered in green mould, where everything that was not wanted was piled. There were no doors and no locks because what the poor did not want, nobody wanted. Jean and Joseph were the two sons of the Spanish barber, then there were Pierre and Max, and, of course, Albert Camus, the cleverest, who went on to university in Algiers. Sometimes we get Paris newspapers and I see that Albert become a journalist on the Paris Soir. *He also writes plays that people pay to watch. We would take torn sacks, get rid of the grey cockroaches, and then make evil smelling tents. The best days were in the summer when we would walk to the experimental gardens and then dodge the guards and head towards the eastern part through rows of enormous mangroves, passed the big rubber trees where the dropping branches mingled with their roots, and then to the big palms that bore at their tops tightly packed bunches of round orange fruits, sweet and rich, that we called cocoses which we would knock down with catapults and steal away to eat before rushing to the beach to wash off the juice. Our favourite place was near the ruins of a bungalow where we left our clothes. The sea was always gentle and warm …*

Notes: There were thirty-five Allied large supply operations to Malta from 1940 to 1942, eight of them were turned back or suffered severe losses. There were long periods when no convoys were attempted and only a trickle of supplies reached the island by submarine or fast warship. The worst period was from December 1941 to October 1942, when Axis forces had air and naval supremacy in the central Mediterranean. From June 1940 to December 1943, about 1,600 civilians and 700 soldiers were killed on Malta. The RAF lost about 900 men killed, 547 aircraft on operations and 160 on the ground and Royal Navy losses were 1,700 submariners and 2,200 sailors; about 200 merchant navy men died. Of 110 convoys by merchant ships to Malta, seventy-nine arrived, three to be sunk soon after reaching the island. The Mediterranean Fleet lost a battleship, two aircraft carriers, four cruisers, a fast minelayer, twenty destroyers and minesweepers and forty submarines.

… February 1944: Well, your son is finally back in Egypt. Our ship is being refitted at Port Said. Moqueuse *became very tired in the last year. All of her hard work had begun to show. I am now in charge of one of the 72 mm guns and its small crew and sometimes we had a real job to keep firing. After the Malta convoys and the best half of the French fleet being lost at Toulon, we had another great disappointment. We were sent to the Greek Dodecanese Islands near the Turkish coast. We all hoped that with the Italians out of the war we could take control of the Aegean Sea. But then the Germans counter-attacked and threw the British troops on Kos and Leros into the sea. The Allies lost a lot of ships and, apart from fighting off aircraft, we picked a lot of men out of the water, including a small leaking boat full of Jewish families, so that our*

little ship got very crowded. At least we don't see so many u-boats these days. We are hoping for better things this year.

Being in another port reminded me of why I joined the navy. I used to run errands for an export firm during the summer holidays. Do you remember? I thought the merchant ships lining the docks in Algiers were so romantic with their promise of freedom! I used to stare at the longshoremen walking up and down the gangplanks into the bellies of the ships. The men had bare bronzed torsos and were dressed in blue trousers rolled to mid-calf. They had a cloth that covered their shoulders on which they loaded their sacks. I thought it was all so exotic!

I know better now ...

Notes: When the Allies invaded North Africa, the Germans were provoked into assimilating Vichy France whose Secretary of the Navy, Admiral François Darlan, defected to the Allies. His replacement, Admiral Gabriel Auphan, guessed that the Germans aimed to seize the large inactive French fleet at Toulon and on 27 November 1942 ordered them all scuttled, destroying seventy-seven ships, including three battleships and seven cruisers.

The Allied invasion of the Dodecanese islands following Italy's surrender in September 1943 was a disaster due partly to a last-minute withdrawal of American air support. Only seven islands were taken; 7,500 Germans beat the British to the punch on Rhodes and, within two months, the combined British and Italian forces of almost 60,000 men were almost entirely captured, killed or thrown out. The British lost almost 5,000 men, 113 aircraft and over thirty ships sunk or damaged.

The failure cost the lives of eighty per cent of the Jews who lived on Rhodes with just some 160 surviving the death camps. On the other islands, 1,200 out of 6,000 Jews survived by fleeing to Turkey.

... September 1944: What a glorious time! Last month, our French soldiers under General de Tassigny landed with the Americans on the Côte d'Azur, and your son was there! In truth, we had very little to do. I have never seen so many warships at once. We spent three days scurrying around between Oran and Toulon shepherding the supply

ships. It was a great victory and the Germans were soon fleeing to
the Vosges mountains, murdering civilians in atrocities as they went.
Meanwhile, Paris has fallen to General de Gaulle . . .

Notes: Operation Dragoon, the Allied invasion of Southern France on
15 August 1944, was charged with securing the French Mediterranean
ports. The Allies had almost complete air superiority. The invasion
force of over half a million men, about half of whom were French, was
joined before and after the landings by 75,000 fighters from the French
resistance. It was this latter which sparked vicious German reprisals
during their retreat including the murder of 642 civilians at Oradour-
sur-Glane. Marseille and Toulon were captured within ten days. The
Allied advance was hindered through lack of fuel because they had failed
to anticipate the speed of their own advance.

In Paris, the French resistance led an uprising upon the approach
of General George Paton's Third Army and General Philippe Leclerc's
2nd Armoured Division. The next morning, on 25 August, Dietrich von
Choltitz, commander of the German garrison and the military governor
of Paris, surrendered to the French at the Hôtel Meurice. General Charles
de Gaulle arrived to assume control of the city as head of the Provisional
Government of the French Republic.

December 1944: I am in Paris! I am staying with your relatives near the
rue Mouffetard. They have been very kind and they send you their love
in Allah. It is very cold and dark and there is little food or heat unless
you are an officer or know an American. Generally, people are kind to
me because I wear my uniform all the time.

I promised you, Mother, that if I ever got here, I would do what you
had wished to do for so long. You never spoke much of this man and so I
could picture nothing of what I was going to see. I took lifts on military
vehicles to Saconin-Breuil, south of Soissons. It took me six hours to
get there. The caretaker showed me to a square plot enclosed by small
markers of grey stone connected by a heavy chain painted black. The
plots were all the same, plain rectangles set in soldierly rows. Each was
decorated by a small bouquet of fresh flowers, the work of the French

Remembrance. I read the dates, '1885–1918', and automatically did the arithmetic: thirty-three years. My whole body shook. The man buried under that slab, my father, was younger than me. I could not muster a filial devotion that I did not feel. I said prayers, one Catholic for him and, for you, said words from the Qur'an.

The day after I read this letter, over seventy years after it was written, I made my way to Soissons. For me, a grandfather I never knew was again alive, a strange silent life, but I knew I was going to forsake him, to leave him to haunt more empty nights. The blue sky resounded with an explosion as an invisible aeroplane broke the sound barrier. I stood for thirty minutes, but, when I was hassled by the taxi driver, I easily turned my back on the grave. I abandoned my grandfather as his own son, my own father, had done.

I looked back on my life, a life that had been foolish, courageous, cowardly, wilful, and always straining towards a goal I could not describe. That life had all gone by without my trying to imagine who was this man who had given my father his life and then immediately gone off to die in a strange land on the other side of the sea.[3] There is a terrible emptiness in me, and an indifference that hurts …

Notes: In November 1915, the remnants of the Foreign Legion's 1st (which had lost two-thirds of its strength in one attack at Artois in May) and 2nd regiments were combined into the RMLE, a part of the Moroccan Division which was now the Legion's only representation on the Western Front.[4] RMLE became the most decorated regiment in the French army for a butcher's bill of 139 officers, 349 sous-officiers and 3,628 legionnaires, not counting the wounded. In the final German offensive in the spring of 1918, the allied front gave way. At the beginning of April, the Legion was sent hurriedly to the Amiens sector. They counter-attacked at Hangard Wood. The slaughter was so great that, at one time, a battalion was commanded by a private soldier. In May, the Germans attacked again and reached the Marne near Chateau Thierry. The Legion was sent to Saconin-Breuil, south of Soissons, which had fallen. The regiment clung to its positions knowing that if they broke, the road to Paris lay open. This was where my grandfather finally died. The German General Erich

Ludendorff recalled in his memoirs how much the defence of Saconin had contributed to the failure of his grand and futile plan.

... June 1945: I feel eaten by shame. I know there was a great wrong to right at Sétif, but what have we fought the war for? We were ordered from Toulon with two other sloops and the cruiser Duguay-Trouin. *Lying off the Gulf of Béjaïa, the big ship fired salvo after salvo towards our own country. We all knew it was at the limit of its range and there could be no accuracy. And what was* La Moqueuse *there for? To guard* Duguay-Trouin *against an attack by bows and arrows? How many innocent people did we kill that day?*

I had hoped to see an Algerian federation in which the Arab and European peoples would be equally represented. That seems to be impossible now. Everyone will have to decide. It will be very difficult for families like us with black feet who live on neither side of the divide.

I expect to be in Algiers on leave soon. I have passed my exams to become an Enseigne de vaisseau. I will make every effort to visit you ...

Notes: While a haggard France was celebrating the end of the war on 8 May, the United Nations charter was about to be signed in San Francisco amid pious declarations of self-determination for subject peoples. In Cairo, the Arab League was born. In Sétif in Algeria, the Muslim population mobilised. More than one hundred Europeans were murdered, plus another hundred wounded, many were *petits fonctionnaires*, symbols of the *présence française*. Over the following few days, much like the Mau Mau uprising in Kenya, settlers were attacked by 'faithful' servants and the women appallingly mutilated. In retribution, more than forty of the less accessible *mechtas*, Muslim villages, were attacked by Douglas dive-bombers. The *Duguay-Trouin* bombarded the environs of the town of Kherrata killing, official reports said, perhaps 600 people. Cairo Radio claimed 45,000 dead; the official Tubert Report said a little over one thousand. Later, all agreed that it was 'an event which marked every Algerian alive at the time ... every Algerian nationalist traces his revolutionary determination back to May 1945 ... some sort of armed uprising would sooner or later become necessary'.[5]

... February 1946–July 1947: I am so pleased I was able to spend time with you. You don't look a day older that when I left six years ago to join the navy. How do you like your son in his junior officer's uniform, a poor boy from the back streets made good! I was also pleased to see Albert on his brief visit. He has become a famous man of letters, but like me he is very unhappy with the state of Algeria. Like me, he was horrified to find children fighting with dogs for the content of rubbish bins.

Our small yard looks much the same, covered on three sides by the walls of houses. On the fourth side, the big orange tree still stretches its branches over the garden wall, with its seasonal scent filling the air, an Arab household nearby roasting coffee in the evening, the sound of chickens scratching on the straw of the high roof.

After I left you, there was a bomb in a street near our barracks. The people were fleeing and the road emptied. 'That filthy race,' said a worker in a stained shirt, looking at an Arab standing as if glued to a shop doorway. 'I didn't do anything,' said the Arab. 'You're all in it together, you lousy traitors.' Other men held him back. I took the Arab by the hand and led him into a café while outside frightened men shouted for a hanging ...

... I have found a girl that I am very close to. Her name is Annette. She lives in Rouen which we visit from time to time to clear river mines. I hope it goes well and that you will meet her, but there is some trouble with her father ...

... Everything is going badly wrong. I think I am going mad ...

1 Mockingbird.
2 Camus, *First Man*; the unfinished manuscript was found in the wreckage of the car accident that killed Camus in 1960, aged forty-six.
3 Camus, *The First Man*.
4 *Régiment de Marche de la Légion Étrangère. Young, Foreign Légion.*
5 Behr, *Algerian Problem*.

13. A SOLDIER'S STORY

Deep is autumn,
And in its deep air
I sometimes wondered
Who my neighbour is.

Bashō, *Deep North*

There was a gap of three years until early in 1950 before the next run of letters in my mother's much-loved, much-handled pile. The solitary letter of 1948 confirmed what I had already been told in Paris. There was no opportunity to check the details other than they fitted the public record. My father had joined the Foreign Legion of the damned, the most ruthless fighting force in the world where its soldiers had 'forgotten how to love and how to pity'.[1] He described a 'mixture of anger with his life and a disgust that no one wanted to fight Communism'.

While being transferred from his cell to his waiting *La Moqueuse*, he found a chance through sympathetic sailors to slip away to the closest recruiting office at Bas-Fort Saint-Nicolas in Marseilles. The medieval fortress with small barred windows stood on a commanding rock overlooking the old port. At that time, the place also functioned as a prison and torture house.[2] The majority of the Legion's recruits at the end of the war were Germans anxious to escape their past yet keen to re-embrace the security of a masculine and military background where duty and performance were expected and rewarded.[3]

My father changed his name and spent a week of idling and sleeping on a straw palliasse in a draughty stone passage. After a further two weeks of unremitting and repetitive questions from the Legion's security officers, and vetting by the 2ème Bureau to weed out murderers, major criminals, hopeless perverts and, above all, Communists, he was accepted. One signature committed him to be a soldier subject to martial discipline. He renounced his French Algerian passport and any right to appeal to a court or consul. No one could buy him out. The penalties for desertion were severe.

As far as the captain of *La Moqueuse* was concerned, Gaston Albert had disappeared and was reported first as absent without leave and, later, as a deserter. Perhaps, in the maelstrom of post-war France, he was identified, but the authorities no doubt thought that five years in the Legion was punishment enough and no apparent effort was expended to take him back, especially in the midst of mass demobilisation.

My father spent most of his first year and a half in the deep Algeria countryside and often straddling the Tunisian border. He was certainly based for a time at the Legion's headquarters at Sidi Bel Abbès, 'Bella Bess' to the legionnaires, some 50 miles south of Oran, and set in a wide plain of vineyards. The barracks was not the romantic stuccoed Legion fortress with crenellated walls overlooking a palm-shaded oasis; it was nothing more than a French-African version of a British garrison town like Aldershot or Colchester. There was even an out-of-place bandstand in the middle of the square fronting the main gate. Albert was a regular at the Legion's infantry training centre at Mascara, east of 'Bella Bess', at the foot of the Atlas Mountains. At Mascara, cranes still built their nests in the eaves of the old barrack buildings, standing on the roofs on one thin red leg with the other tucked away in grey-white plumage and their long necks curving against the sky. Here, each day after a twenty-mile route-march into the hills, he was 'educated in the art of butchery: how to gouge a man's eyes out with his thumbs, how to use a bayonet with the greatest effect and least effort, how to cut a man's throat so that he died without making a sound, how to shoot a man in the stomach so that he died slowly and mad with pain'.[4]

Most of the NCOs he met were ex-Nazis who formed the backbone of the regiment. Many were psychotic, unsurprising considering their recent employment. Nearly all the equipment, from machine-guns to field dressings, was German war booty, too. On the return in the late-afternoon sun, my father sang *Der Horst Wessel, Panzer Rollen in Afrika Vor* and *Heute Wollen Wir Ein Liedlein Singen*, the rhythmic marching songs of Rommel's Afrika Korps, three years after the capitulation of Germany to the Allies. I think he must have been part insane with confusion and regret.

After six months confined to camp, my father was able to make rare visits to his mother. In his single letter from this time, he drew a parallel between playing football in thick-soled boots, first as a child that his poor family hoped would last forever, and then with his fellow legionnaires. Both times, his soles were studded with large, protective cone-shaped nails, making them hopeless for ball control and balance.

The Legion took him to many parts of the country that were new to him and he joked about how his mother was unable to fathom the names of his various desert camps. He told her that Camus had told him that if so distinguished an arabist as T E Lawrence should admit defeat over the endless variation in the spelling of proper names what did it matter as long as the Legion knew where it had put its soldiers. His experiences stretched his political convictions. He saw that full-scale war was coming. He was convinced that the only honourable outcome was that Algeria should remain allied to France. The settlers had earned that right for all the effort and ingenuity they had put into industrial and agricultural development. When the first Europeans came, he wrote to his mother, they died at the rate of ten a day in the heat and the brutal rain and the lack of hygiene. Then they had an idea. You had to dance to stir up the blood. Every night after work, the settlers would dance beside the fire between the burial mounds to the sound of a violin and the mosquitoes and insects buzzing. All around, sentinels watched for cattle rustlers, Arab bands and black-maned lions. It was 'not such a bad idea with the heat, these people sweated out everything and the epidemics stopped'. Even today, quinine is sold as a drink in the cafés.

But it was the old story of the Europeans with their superior techniques, resources and aggressive vigour progressively assimilating the best lands while, at the same time, the more numerous and increasingly oppressed indigènes were pushed to the periphery. My father could never bring himself to join his fellow soldiers in stealing from Arab adobe huts, built of camel dung, straw and mud, with the occasional treasure hidden against a rainy day. 'The Arabs who have often only a camel, a goat or two, and a barren plot of ground are a great deal closer to poverty than any of us.'

My father often saw action, mostly futile, chasing shadows. The most important engagement his battalion fought during this time was easy to identify from his story. The men were driven from the railway line at Métlaoui in Tunisia into the foothills near the Selja Gorges far above the treeline. 'We marched up for over an hour towards the clouds and the cold in a single file on a narrow stone path which ran alongside a stream.' The patrol was ambushed by the *fellagha*, a pejorative 'bandits' in Arabic, who took up armed struggle against French colonialism in North Africa. My father told his mother of a snowflake settling on the black muzzle of his rifle. As he squirmed into a clump of four-foot-high esparto needle grass, he felt a sudden cold wriggle under his chest that made him roll onto his side. There was a sharp hiss and a jolt on his boot. An upset viper struck several times at the black leather. He killed the snake with the butt of his gun, all the while kneeling and presenting a clear target. The enemy were encircled, surprised, and after an exchange of mortars, surrendered. No prisoners were taken as it was a long walk home. The Legion's bayonet training was put to work.

Perhaps because of this fight, and the murder that followed, perhaps because of his age and experience, my father was promoted *sergent* and moved to a camp at Kahmisis, south of *Bella Bess*, to join the 350 men in the Legion's first airborne unit in North Africa, the 1er Battalion Étranger de Parachutist, '1er BEP'. For three weeks south of the port of Philippeville, now called Skikda, they learned to jump. The transfer changed his life as it did all the men of 1er BEP. The unit was destined for the Indochinese War in today's Vietnam, Cambodia and Laos, where it was twice annihilated in action, at Cao Bang in 1950 and at Dien Bien Phu in 1954.

My father's Asian war was one of a hopeless colonial reconquest as France sought to regain its vast eastern domains lost in World War Two to the Japanese and, to a lesser extent, Japan's ally, the Thais who wished to create a land for all the Thai people. The result was a confused and multi-factional struggle between colonial and independence forces and became a story of greed and innocence suitable for a Greek tragedy.

Bernard Fall, a respected French student, journalist and American academic, who reported on and eventually died in the front line, described the battles over almost ten years against the Viet-Minh, always nationalists seeking independence until they were rejected too many times by the French and slipped into committed communism. The dropping of the atomic bombs on Hiroshima and Nagasaki and the surrender of the Japanese created a power vacuum in Vietnam allowing its people to rise before the Free French returned. The US identified with liberation from French colonialism. On the same day as the Japanese surrendered, great crowds gathered in Hanoi to see Ho Chi Minh, 'The Most Enlightened One'. Uncle Ho addressed the people using Thomas Jefferson's 'Declaration of Independence'. The CIA stood nearby on the rostrum.

The French forces were well equipped for a modern war, but the 'very plenitude of heavy equipment, proved a handicap'. It tied the French to the 'few roads there were' and led their units, time and again, into easily contrived ambushes. 'The French contended with the jungle while the Viet-Minh made use of it.'[5]

To the West, Vietnam was just a piece on the global chessboard. It was the time of Cuba, the Bay of Pigs, the Berlin Wall and communist insurrections all around. Mao Zedong's conquest of the Chinese mainland and subsequent attack on Korea meant the red armies were on the Vietnamese and Lao borders by 1949 and these became a sanctuary for Viet-Minh training and rearmament. With the Korean ceasefire in 1953, the whole Asian Communist war effort was available to the Indochinese theatre.

At first, the French failed to hold the fortress barrier they had constructed in North Vietnam because it was surrounded by a jungle which the Viet-Minh controlled and used for free movement and for surprise. Then, the French attempted to match the Viet-Minh's mobility on foot with mechanical mobility. 'Even when the French took to the roads on offensive, the initiative remained with the Viet-Minh who would choose their targets, attack at will from the jungle and then retire when convenient back whence they came.' These strategies were equally doomed when, after the French capitulated in 1954, they were immediately repeated by the Americans through the next twenty years until 1975. The Americans followed the French in using their technology to compensate for 'the woeful lack of support and political savvy' of the corrupt regimes they tried to prop up.

Eight hundred men of 1er BEP landed at the port city of Hai Phong in November 1948. The task of all the French troops was to keep the roads and rivers open, the rubber plantations and factories working and to build new posts in Viet-Minh-held areas. The communists spent their time mining roads, attacking convoys, ambushing patrols and attacking small posts at night. A favourite pastime was to ring the rubber trees, cutting an inch-deep band of bark around the lower part of the trunk, letting the trees bleed dry. The war was often called the 'Michelin war' as the company's vast estates profited both its owners and the slow regeneration of the French economy. The Viet-Minh broadcast from their loudspeakers during attacks on lonely outposts, 'Why do you men from North Africa want to die for a French tyre company?'

Three days after landing, the battalion suffered its first losses. Three legionnaires were killed when a train ferrying them the one hundred miles to Hanoi was hit by an improvised explosive device. The unit was split to mount guards of military convoys using two *routes coloniales*, RC4 and RC6, vital supply arteries.

For the next several months, there was a steady dribble of casualties. In December, the Viet-Minh attacked the road close to Yen Trinh, west of Hanoi, and two men were killed; in January, two more guarding a convoy in the Cao Bang region in the north; in March, several more as they fought their way along RC4 to relieve legionnaires trapped at That Khe. In April 1949, my father took part in his first airborne operation over Cha Vai outpost, west of Hanoi, under heavy attack. Later that month, men were wounded at Loung Phai, again, a jump near Phu Loc when fifty rebels were captured; 170 rebels killed next month at Phu Tho; six unit legionnaires dead at Dinh Bang in July; two more in July in Banc Ninh, including a German *Fallschirmjäger*, a paratrooper, who participated in the World War Two invasion of Crete; August, five more dead; and at Lung Vai when fourteen men were seriously injured on landing.

'We have just had a bad month,' my father wrote to his mother. 'I have been lucky, but I lost two good friends.'

And so on without more than a few days respite between skirmishes and full-scale battles until September and October 1950 and the Battle of Dong Khe, and later of Cao Bang, when my father's battalion was annihilated, losing 481 men, and was reduced to twenty-three survivors. The unit had returned to the same sector where it began its planned two-year tour in Vietnam and was within a few weeks of finishing its posting. 1er BEP fought up RC4 to meet and enable the escape of a heavily embattled infantry regiment coming down towards them. The Viet-Minh attacked in a suicidal 'human sea' on the long march taking immense losses, 'the reds will not count the cost'; French casualties were over 6,000, their greatest colonial defeat since General Montcalm died fighting the British at Quebec in 1759. Abandoned equipment in lost outposts, or *herissons*, hedgehogs, close to the Chinese border and along the main roads, supposedly placed to threaten communist supply lines, was enough to equip an additional Viet-Minh division.[6]

The 'lucky' legionnaires licked their wounds and relived the horror at Bach Mai airfield, near Hanoi, repatriation forgotten because of the overall desperate situation. 'We few are all very tired. I am sick of the fighting. The French are justly and universally unpopular and nearly every native is willing to pass onto the Viets the slightest piece of information, no matter how unimportant. The Viets know the weaknesses of the majority of officers and NCOs, be it drink, women, opium, boys or gambling.'[7] Many of the survivors were promoted, my father to *sergent-chef*, the Legion equivalent of a British sergeant-major, trained new arrivals from Algeria, and added to his handful of *Croix de Guerre*, plus a *Médaille Militaire* and a minor *Légion d'honneur*, 'a desultory and soulless ceremony made worse by the heavy rain'.

It was March 1951 before the rebuilt unit was ready for action. Little learned, the fighting was much as in the early days with several pursuits around Hanoi, which sometimes developed into major engagements and over the end of the year into the Battle of Hoa Binh and, through the year, further large scale engagements in the Red River Delta and at Noi Thon and Na San. Hoa Binh was the capital of the Muong tribe, probably the oldest survivors of the original Vietnamese people and fiercely loyal to the French, supplying two battalions. The ten-day battle at Na San at the end of 1952 was of particular importance as a forerunner of Dien Bien Phu, also a stronghold in a valley with an airstrip, a large 'hedgehog'. At Na San, eleven battalions of French troops lured nine Viet-Minh regiments into an attack in which they lost 3,000 men.

During this time, the two generals who led the French forces were Jean de Lattre de Tassigny and Raoul Salan, both veterans of the invasion of Southern France and the latter later having great personal influence on my father. De Lattre re-galvanised the French troops, but was already dying. Salan, commander of the French forces in Vietnam from 1945, and all French land forces in East Asia from 1948, replaced de Lattre as commander-in-chief in Indochina on his death in 1952. Salan was a solitary man through choice, especially in the dark, sleepless nights of drug recovery. At any moment, he could expound, citing Baudelaire, Celine or Queneau. His curiosity and accumulated knowledge were remarkable including learning the Lao language. He was, at the last, a forgiven sinner and revered man, the most decorated soldier in the French army.

It must have been during this time that Salan and my father met, both were at Na San, and began a bond, at least of respect among professional soldiers with similar ideologies. Early in 1953, Salan ordered my father from operations in Vietnam and loosely based him and a platoon of paratroopers in Vientiane, the Lao capital.

The French first landed at Da Nang in 1858 to bring civilisation to an inferior people and to steal their natural resources. Their presence in Laos dated back to their acquisition of Cambodia in 1863 and their trade expeditions up the Mekong River. A consulate at Luang Prabang was secured after a contrived colonial war against the Siamese in 1893 and later forced concessions which brought further territory.

There was just one photograph included in my father's letters and it came from this period showing him (although I cannot recognise him) in May as part of an escort party for Salan's meetings with Lao Prince Sisavang Vatthana in Luang Prabang, the religious capital and home of the Lao royal family. My father wrote of the 'open shock' in the capital because, as the prince had been sent to France for his education, aged ten, he could no longer speak Lao when he returned a decade later. With the natural support of the French, the prince became king on the death of his father in 1959 and was in reducing power until his forced abdication by the Red Pathet Lao in 1975.

My father began a close association with the Hmong guerrillas, the Lao of the mountain tops, who had been armed by the French as a secret militia to fight the Japanese during the collaboration and to ease their way back into the country after the Japanese surrender and, again, to resist communist incursions from the north. His time was spent mostly deep in the hills north-east of the city close to the Plaine des Jarres preparing for small-scale airborne exercises.[8] In one letter of this time, he explained to his mother that he lived a simple life. He enjoyed the comparison between the Berber people of North Africa who spread across much of the southern Mediterranean. The Berber's Greek-given name signified barbarians, people whose chatter could not be understood. The Hmong among the single vast mountain range stretching from southern China into northern Laos and Thailand were also thought a barbarian people and their pejorative *miao* in Chinese implied slavery and contempt.[9] The last recorded king of the Hmong and his entourage were tricked into a peace accord by the Chinese who then cut them into small pieces.

The Hmong, naturally, took a contrary view as 'free people' who 'must have independence'. My father wrote that his Hmong hosts were tolerant, reasonable and peaceful who had spread from the Yellow River region of China to within 300 kilometres of Bangkok after the 1830s. He told his mother that he smelled of the rich, red earth, black pigs and *lao khoa*, the local rice wine.

The French commander of this small mountain special forces group to be called the Meo Maquis was Captain Jean Sassi. Importantly, the commando included a Hmong second lieutenant Vang Pao, already impressing his leaders as a natural soldier. My father's few months in this wilderness freed him of some of the constraints of his background and his wars, but, I suspect, they also trapped him within those of another.

In Vietnam, the French lost outpost after outpost as they fell into the plan of the Viet-Minh military commander General Vo Nguyen Giap.

The enemy will pass slowly from the offensive to the defensive. The blitzkrieg will transform itself into a war of long duration. Thus, the enemy will be caught in a dilemma: he has to drag out the war in order to win it and does not possess, on the other hand, the psychological and political means to fight a long, drawn-out war.[10]

And then came France's greatest defeat in 'one of the truly decisive battles of the twentieth century' in a small town in the north-eastern corner of Vietnam with the unlikely name of the 'Seat of the Border County Prefecture', or, in Vietnamese, Dien Bien Phu.[11] Two years before, this outpost, only 125 miles from Luang Prabang, had been a Viet-Minh stronghold.

Salan had been recalled to Paris, and France's seventh local military leader, General Henri Navarre, desperate for victory despite orders from Paris to avoid a major battle while peace talks were hovering, decided to threaten the early Ho Chi Minh Trail while offering Giap a target so tempting that he would accept a set-piece battle in which France's natural superiority in fighting men and equipment would prevail. Many French citizens were horrified by 100,000 losses over seven years, stories of French brutality and the use of napalm. Returning troops at Marseilles were pelted with rocks for participating in *La Sale Guerre*, 'the dirty war'.

In November 1953, without telling his superiors, Navarre ordered an initial 4,000 troops, including 1er BEP on the second day of the operation, to parachute into the valley. By the time the siege proper started in March, the French had some 11,000 troops on the ground, one-third of them Vietnamese, and 1er BEP had already lost ninety paratroopers killed and wounded out of its 653 strength. Fifty-six days later, the unit had been wiped out almost to a man.

I do not know exactly the part my father played in the battle; he never described it in his letters, but it is straightforward to reconstruct at the broadest level. In the first of two offensive sorties, 1er BEP and others reached the abandoned village of Ban Tau, where they were ambushed and lost over fifty men. In the second the following month, they were fought to a standstill trying to take the strategic Hill 633. It was the failure of these two missions that persuaded the French high command that their grand mission had failed. In a later book, Navarre blamed the French political system, intellectuals, politicians, journalists, and communists.[12] He also warned of the possible necessity for an army coup to replace the Fourth Republic.

By a monumental effort thought impossible to the French staff, over 50,000 Viet-Minh troops of which two-thirds were combatants, had Dien Bien Phu surrounded and achieved another spectacular feat in dragging 200 well-supplied artillery and anti-aircraft weapons up dense jungle slopes into camouflaged positions within easy range of the camp. It was one of the greatest logistical feats in history. The grand plan to resupply unmolested from the air proved a chimera. French ammunition quickly diminished, supply drops were largely lost to the enemy, medical support was unable to cope, over 200 aircraft were lost or damaged, and the airstrip was hardly in action. The French assumptions of superiority in men, equipment and leadership were proved to be hubris, 'outrageous overestimations of one's own worth'.[13] The high command had their pitched battle and it was a salutary fight to the death.

Over the last few weeks until the capitulation, 1er BEP was stitched and sliced as it lost its operational core and its men were flung to all parts of the shrinking battlefield, reminiscent of World War One trenches, as hopeless reinforcements. The unit ceased to exist. Navarre begged President Eisenhower to act directly and, too late, the US sent covert, painted-over supply planes whose parachutes, dropped from too high, were mostly gathered by the Viet-Minh. By this time, seventy-eight per cent of the cost of France's war was met by the American taxpayer. Britain refused assistance, but Prime Minister Harold Wilson and Foreign Secretary Michael Stewart found themselves under attack for duplicity in their support for the United States as they had been in Biafra and Rhodesia, the Israeli-Arab war, Rhodesia again, and Vietnam again and again'.[14]

At the last, my father found himself with a small group of Thai Hmong and, rather than face captivity, they slipped into the jungle and headed to the Lao border. It was a rare, but, with hindsight, sensible decision. The French occupation lasted 209 days, the siege fifty-five. Over 3,000 of the French force were killed during the battle, but a further 10,000 died on the ensuing death marches to and in the Viet-Minh concentration camps. Only some 3,000 men were repatriated. The Viet-Minh lost over 20,000 men, dead and wounded, never really counted.

All a solitary letter said was that my father lost half of his comrades in skirmishes at Lao river crossings until they found sanctuary in a high, isolated Hmong village that I sensed he knew from before the battle. In a rare flash of humour, he said that local people taught him what he could eat from the ground. For meat, they would fish rivers or try to catch snakes or squirrels. I asked, he wrote, 'What about tigers?'

'Tiger meat is tough,' he was told by a deadpan face devoid of irony.

For one reason or another, it was another six months before he reached Vientiane. In August, the war ended and, in February 1955, the rump of the battalion left a Vietnam divided at the 17th parallel, for Algeria. My father was flown to Saigon, missed the boat for a second time in his military career, and spent the next month in a foul German freighter seized ten years before in war reparations. He left behind him the dead from his unit, fifty-two officers, 110 NCOs and 877 legionnaires. He suffered badly from the heat and the cramped conditions through the Indian Ocean, calling at Pondicherry and Port Said without being allowed off.

The French army left Saigon completely after a two-day street battle with an international crime syndicate.

At Zerelda, 20 kilometres west of Algiers, there was no glorious homecoming for the defeated soldiers. The one respite was 30 April, the annual traditional fete of the Foreign Legion, a three-day, anything-goes bacchanal to celebrate a company of legionnaires massacred in the village of Camerone in Mexico in 1862. It took a few months for the remnants of 1er BEP to assimilate the flood of recruits and to settle down to the new order. Denied the outlet of indiscriminate Viet-hunting, looting and easy sex, the old hands turned to the local bars and massage parlours to let off steam.

Throughout the next year, there was no respite from the patrols and the ambushes. The early days of the war for the liberation of Algeria spread with increasing intensity and moved into Tunisia and Libya. My father's few letters were sparse as he was able as a senior NCO to take time to visit his aging mother. He wrote lovingly of the weeping fig and soldierly palm trees, but longingly of other remembered palm trees, forest canopies, rooting pigs and Hmong children. After the first military operations in May in the Aures Mountains, the unit was moved from the other end of Algeria back to the Tunisian border. After the mass executions of settlers by the fellagha and of Muslim prisoners at Philippeville, there was no hope of reconciliation among the die-hards. In 1956, the reconstituted 1er BEP, had re-earned its spurs and was re-designated a regiment, the 1st Foreign Parachute Regiment, the 1er REP. The unit's count of rebels killed mounted steadily. By the time of Operation Timgad late in the year, and Casbah, the next May, their tally had reached seventy. In the latter, with thousands of other troops, they scoured and looted the old centre of Algiers, arresting some 400 suspects.

Then, 1er REP was snatched from one war and thrust into another. They were the front unit in the Anglo-French force, which, together with Israel, invaded Egypt by way of Cyprus to secure the Suez Canal for international traffic. The invasion itself was a rout. 1er REP quickly seized Port Fouad on the Sinai side of the canal at its mouth into the Mediterranean. The crisis was provoked by an American and British decision not to finance Egypt's construction of the Aswan High Dam, as they had promised, because of Egypt's growing ties with Czechoslovakia and the Soviet Union. In response, Egyptian President Garnal Abdel Nasser nationalised and seized the canal and announced he would pay for the dam with raised transit fees. Britain and France said they feared that Nasser might close the canal and cut off oil shipments through the Persian Gulf. The French were also angered by Nasar's open supply of the Algerian rebels. As ten Israeli brigades swept across the Sinai, British and French forces landed claiming they were enforcing a cease-fire. The ruse fooled no one and the allies were forced to withdraw when the USA, fearful of Russian intervention, brought crushing financial pressure to bear on Britain through the United Nations.

By the end of the year, the UN had evacuated the French and British, the British in perpetual humiliation, the French seething at their partner's duplicity and weakness. One can guess at my father's feelings about a career that was mired in failure: the capitulation of the Vichy government, the loss of influence in Lebanon and Syria and, generally, across the northern African states, the disaster in Indochina and, now, Suez as he faced a return to an impending debacle in Algeria.

The Algerian war was one of the last and most important of the grand-style European colonial wars. It toppled six French prime ministers and the Fourth Republic and was close to bringing down General de Gaulle and his fifth republic and threatened metropolitan France with civil war.[15] Algeria was French *chez elle* for 132 years and my father's spiritual home. Most of the European settlers in Algeria, *pieds-noirs*, literally 'black feet', thought they were carrying the White Man's Burden. Many a French para gave his life believing he was defending a bastion of European civilisation; the bogey slogan of the 'soviet fleet at Mers-el-Kébir' retained its force right until the last days. Although most mainland Frenchmen lived unaffected by the war, it was undeniably and horribly savage, bringing death to an approximately one million Muslim Algerians and expulsion from their homes of about the same number of European settlers.

It was, perhaps, inevitable that my father fell more closely under the influence of Salan, who was now commander-in-chief of French forces in

Algeria from 1956 and the darling of the *pieds-noirs*. My father was the backbone of the premier regiment under his command, a survivor, a much-decorated NCO, a believer. His witness to the French decline across the globe, I am sure, pushed him over the edge into fanaticism. In 1958, Salan called for the return to power of de Gaulle hoping he would deliver on his repeated promises to protect French Algeria. That May, right-wing *pieds-noirs* after bloody fighting in the streets won control of Algiers and set up an emergency government called the Committee of Public Safety. These activists won Salan to their cause.

And then – the betrayal. One of de Gaulle's first acts as president was to retire Salan who continued to live in Algeria. De Gaulle made a devastating TV broadcast late in 1960 stating that 'my new path leads not to an Algeria governed by France, but to an Algerian Algeria'. Salan was exiled to Spain, then moved to France, and was banned from entering Algeria.

All the while, the men of 1er REP fought and died. For what? The battle honours flew thick and fast. First, the regiment sought to restore order in the capital and spent almost a year living in apartments and villas in the city conducting daily patrols to flush out the National Liberation Front, FLN, rebels. The high walls that surrounded the squalid exteriors of houses in Algiers' casbah concealed delightful courtyards in total privacy. They exemplified the FLN's instinct for secrecy, developed over five generations of French suzerainty. This was heightened to the point where few leaks crept out during eight years of clandestine warfare of the many internal splits that threatened to crack open the FLN leadership.

The occupation of the Arab city was interspersed with operations close to the Spanish Sahara, in Medea, in the Kabylie region, and, back in the capital, the capture of rebel leader Saadi Yacef, the killing of Ali Ammar, the second most important FLN leader, and, finally, the detention of Abderrahmane Benhamida, the chief of the FLN's political bureau in Algiers which ended the uprising. Until 1961, through the putsch that took de Gaulle to power, the referendum on Algerian independence, a refusal to obey orders by three of the regiment's officers in fear of more needless deaths of their men, 1er REP fought over twenty major battles and operations, killing, wounding and capturing 3,507 rebels.

How much was my father involved in the extraordinary events that followed? Quite a lot, I surmised, based on his pivotal position in the regiment and his history with Salan. Salan, at first, publicly opposed de Gaulle expecting him to undermine the Algerian rebels, but when this hope was lost, began to plot to keep Algerian French. In Spain, from where my father's last letter was written whilst on a 'walking holiday', Salan formed the Organisation Armée Secrète, the OAS, in response to the referendum on independence with the motto *'L'Algérie est française at le restera'*.[16] The OAS brought a second terrorist force onto the Algerian streets, planting plastic bombs in cafés, buses and crowded meeting places, which reached a crescendo in the following year.

In April 1961, four French Army generals, led by Salan on his secret return to Algeria, began a putsch against France, particularly de Gaulle, the very man they had helped put into power. The move had been presaged by General Navarre five years before. They saw de Gaulle as a betrayer of the French settlers in Algeria and of the fallen French soldiers in the Algerian War. The generals, with 1er REP at the core of their supporters, believed the Algerian rebels could be defeated. 1er REP moved to Algiers to take control of several strategic points. Following an emotional plea by de Gaulle to the soldiers of France, the generals capitulated within four days. Three of them, including Salan, moved with 1er REP to Zerelda, a suburb of Algiers. Within days, all the unit's captains were condemned by a special court to up to two years' imprisonment, later suspended; all lieutenants were detained, then released. France's most elite force was dissolved on Camerone Day never to be re-established. Tens of legionnaires deserted to fight for French Algeria as partisans. In his absence, Salan was condemned to death for treason, later commuted to life imprisonment. He was arrested in April 1962 in Algiers and pardoned in 1968 along with 3,459 others.

Algeria became independent in July 1962. FLN forces entered Oran where they were fired on. No one knows how many French settlers died in the angry response; the numbers vary widely. French troops were ordered not to intervene. At the same time, to the great shame of France, perhaps 100,000 *harkis*, *spahis*, cavalry, and *tirailleurs*, infantry, Algerian men who fought with the French from the Prussian wars of 1870 through to Dien Bien Phu, were killed by the FLN as they were refused permission to escape to France.

Camus, in the *First Man*, tells of the reaction of an old Algerian settler when the order came for the *pieds-noirs* to evacuate the country. The man said nothing.

His grape harvest was over, his wine was in the vats. He opened the vats and he went to a spring of brackish water that he had diverted long ago and he turned it back to run into his fields, and he equipped a tractor with a trench plough. For three days, at the wheel, bareheaded, saying not a word, he uprooted the vines all over his property. Think of it, that skinny old man bouncing around on his tractor, pushing the accelerator lever when the plough wasn't getting a vine that was bigger than the others, not stopping even to eat. All this from sunrise to sunset, without even looking at the mountains on the horizon, nor at the Arabs who had soon found out and were watching him from a distance, they weren't saying anything either. And when a young captain arrived and demanded an explanation, he said to him, 'Young man, since what we made here was a crime, it has to be wiped out. I'll stay until the bitter end and die here. We'll kill each other for a while longer, cut off each other's balls and torture each other a bit. And then we'll go back to living as men together.

I was not correct when I said that what I have just written came from my father's last letter. There was one more letter in the pile I received in Paris. At first, I took it as just an envelope, but, in the Algerian embassy, I realised it for what it was. It was written in Paris late in 1962 and was received at my grandmother's house after her death where it was unopened. All I knew from my conversations in Le Mouffetard was that she had been killed by chance by a bomb placed in a crowded Arab market in one of the poorer parts of the city. The most probable culprit was Salan's OAS which over the year amassed 2,000 souls to their credit and twice as many wounded. But only one of them was my grandmother.

Reading between the lines, my father was on the run. It seemed obvious that he had followed Salan into the OAS, or, at least, onto its fringes. There were no incriminating admissions, just hints and two names. One of these was Jacques Prévost, a sergeant paratrooper at Dien Bien Phu, mentioned warmly in earlier letters. I picked up a paperback listing the thirty-one attempts on de Gaulle's life, mostly by the OAS following the Algerian declaration.[17] The most famous assassination was a fictitious one, invented by my old acquaintance, Freddie Forsyth.[18] In his novel, Forsyth begins with a real execution in a French prison after another attempt, another failure. This attack at Petit-Clamart, a Paris suburb, on 22 August 1962, was organised by Jean Bastien-Thiry, a lieutenant colonel in the French Air Force. Several men ambushed a Citroën in which de Gaulle and his wife Yvonne were being driven into the city. Despite spraying the car with automatic weapons, to everyone's surprise, including that of de Gaulle, no one inside the vehicle was hurt and only the proprietor of a roadside café was slightly injured.

A message went out to the conspirators: '*Le canard est toujours vivant,*' 'the duck is still alive'.

After a lengthy and sometimes lucky police investigation, many of the perpetrators were captured and tried. Their leader, Bastien-Thiry, was sentenced to death and quickly shot at Fort d'Ivry on the Seine. He refused to be blindfolded and clutched his rosary at the end. Two of the would-be assassins, also condemned, had their sentences commuted to life imprisonment and were later pardoned. One of these was Jacques Prévost.

My father mentioned one other, Jean Canteloube, one of de Gaulle's former security officers who provided information to Bastien-Thiry's organisation. Canteloube organised an escape plan for Bastien-Thiry, but it was abandoned.

I do not know what role my father played in the assassination attempt, or the failed escape, but I am convinced he was closely involved, so involved that he had to disappear. His unopened letter gave another clue, perhaps to put his mother's mind at rest. He praised his political and military leader, General Salan, and talked of how happy he had been when he first met him.

I had nothing else to do. I was also on the run. I decided to follow him. It was a Sunday. I went, with a slight ironic smile, to Charles de Gaulle airport and caught the Vietnam Airways flight just before midnight to Hanoi Noi Bai. With a French passport, an open return ticket, I avoided suspicion or the need for a visa.

1 Townsend, *Légion of the Damned.*

2 Young, *Foreign Légion.*

3 Greene, *Quiet American.*

4 Townsend, *Légion of the Damned.*

5 Fall, *Street Without Joy.*

6 Fall, *Street without Joy,* 'It should be remembered that at the same time, exactly on 24 October 1950, the Chinese "People's Volunteers" made their appearance in North Korea and inflicted on the American forces near the Yalu losses in men and equipment which made the subsequent retreat from North Korea the most expensive defeat since Corregidor in the Philippines in 1942.'

7 Ainley, *In Order to Die.*

8 Stuart-Fox, *History of Laos:* On a large plain in northern Laos, there is an unrecorded megalithic iron-age culture characterised by standing slabs and giant stone jars (Colani, *Mégalithes du Haut-Laos*). Hilsman, *Move a Nation:* Two sites on the plain are littered with several hundred each. They stand about four feet and are carved from solid rock, many with well-fitted lids. The jars were already there when the first Lao people arrived.

9 Rogers, *Trauma.*

10 Macdonald, *Giap.* Colvin, *Volcano Under Snow.*

11 Fall, *Hell in a Very Small Place.* Boylan & Olivier, *Valley of the Shadow.* Windrow, *The Last Valley.*

12 Navarre, *Agonie de l'Indochine.*

13 Fall, *Street Without Joy.*

14 Heal, *Disappearing.* Warbey, *Ho Chi Minh.* Warbey was a English MP who strongly opposed Wilson and Stewart's position, resigning the Labour whip in protest in 1966. He took part in the early peace negotiations and later wrote *Vietnam: The truth* in 1965 and *Ho Chi Minh* in 1972, both scathing interpretations of Wilson's manoeuvrings. Some of his comments have relevance to the Brexit debate of today: 'When someone tries to tell the truth of what is happening, or what people are thinking [around the world], unless what he is saying happens to suit the momentary convenience of the Government, the BBC and the Press Lords, we will be denied a hearing in any public forum … and if he succeeds in making himself heard, he will be ignored, cold-shouldered … or, in the last resort, denounced as a traitor.'

15 Horne, *Savage War of Peace.*

16 'Algeria is French forever.'

17 Plume & Demaret, *Target: de Gaulle.*

18 Heal, *Disappearing.* Forsyth, *Day of the Jackal.*

14. DEATH AND HOPE IN INDOCHINA

Some say that phantoms haunt those shadowy streets,
And mingle freely there with sparse mankind;
And tell of ancient woes and black defeats,
And murmur mysteries in the grave enshrined;
But others think them visions of illusions,
Or even men gone far in self-delusion;
No man there being wholly sane in mind.

Thomson, *The City of Dreadful Night*, S VII

I booked an indulgent hotel in Ly Nam De Street which backed onto the ruins of the Citadelle in Hanoi's Old Quarter. For the first two days, I fought my single sheet and shouted at the housemaids as I tried to shake off the six-hour jet lag. I guess it's an age thing: no matter if I fly club class, drink only water, take the pills, I still end up a wet rag, desperate but unable to sleep.

I was following in the footsteps of Field Marshall Joffre, hero of the French empire on the Marne, without whom the First World War would have been lost in weeks. Joffre superintended the construction of the Kayes to Bafoulabé railway to enable the march on Timbuktu, a city which he then captured. He also built the fortifications on the northern point of Madagascar and was chief of the engineering department in Hanoi in the 1880s. Flushed with prestige after the Great War, Joffre embarked on a grand goodwill tour visiting the United Sates, Indochina, Siam (Myanmar), Japan and China. The celebrations brought a rash of 'Joffre' landmarks. In Saigon, it was the *Place de Maréchal Joffre*; in Hanoi in 1922 a main thoroughfare was named after him which was later subdivided as fresh heroes appeared. During this triumphal return, Joffre toured the town in an open motor surrounded by indigenous lancers on horseback. When the Vietnamese finally threw out their colonial masters, most things French received new names: rue Maréchal Joffre became Ly Nam De Street.

In my experience, most heroes, like Joffre, are ordinary people who come to a time when, with little thought, they take on a monster. Some writers seek to make them larger-than-life as they 'venture forth into a region of supernatural wonder, fabulous forces are there encountered and a decisive victory is won, the hero comes back from the mysterious adventure with the power to bestow boons on his fellow man ... Where is the guide which will give us the courage to face the monster and the means to then find our way to freedom when the monster has been met and slain?'[1]

My father had fought his many monsters year after year, but he was not running to, I thought, but running away. How was I different? I had increasing knowledge of him while he carried only a small and diminishing memory of me. For the first time in my life, I felt warmth to a father, no matter how crazy this father might have been, and I felt something new inside. I loved him, loved him unconditionally in the way I had always wanted to love somebody. I knew that this longing was deep within me. I also knew it made no sense.

I took an early walk through the Ban Mon Gate into the Citadelle ruins and realised that the area had been used by the French as its army headquarters. Any hole in the blank wall of my hotel room would lead straight into the Général Commandant's office where my father would have stood ramrod straight as he received orders. I felt somewhat at home. For the first time since I walked out of my life in England and settled in Marrakech, I enjoyed the frenetic atmosphere of a new place. It was freedom of sorts mixed with the excitement of new purpose.

At the Hanoi Military Museum in Dien Bien Phu Street, I gazed at an old map of the Ho Chi Minh Trail. It didn't look at all right. I read that by the end of sixteen years, there were seven entry routes from North Vietnam. The Viet-Minh then used neutral Laos to by-pass the demilitarised zone (DMZ) to get men and supplies through five main exit points into the heart of South Vietnam. Laos was planned as the Trail's fast lane. I realised what was wrong. The map showed no Trail in Laos, the politics of the 1970s reaching down even to today.

I took a taxi to the Ho Chi Minh Trail Museum, a dazzling white building set in fields 15 kilometres outside the city where I found more answers. The maps here showed that most of the Trail was in Laos: over 20,000

General Jean de Lattre de Tassigny, 1946. *Willem van de Poll*

General Raoul Salan with Lao Prince Sisavang Vatthana, Luang Prabang with Sergent-Chef Gaston Albert among the escort party, 1953. *Wikipedia*

Ho Chi Minh reads the Declaration of Independence in Hanoi, 1945. *Wikipedia*

1er BEP jumps into the valley of Dien Bien Phu, 1953. *ecpad*

Aerial view of Dien Bien Phu valley, 1953. *Wikipedia*

General Vo Nguyen Giap presents his plans for the Battle of Dien Bien Phu to Party and State leaders including Ho Chi Minh, second left, 1954. *Vietnam People's Army*

Albert Camus, 1950s. *Robert Edwards*

Viet Minh troops plant their flag over the captured French headquarters at Dien Bien Phu, 1954. *Roman Karmen, Vietnam People's Army*

Légionnaires of 1er Régiment Etranger de Parachutistes (1er REP) watch a large crowd of enthusiastic local people during the Algerian Putsch, 1961. *Foreign Legion*

General Vang Pao as a young man. *Muckrock*

De Gaulle's Citroen DS with marked holes from automatic weapons after the assassination attempt at Petit-Clamart, 1961. *Institut Charles de Gaulle*

Jean-Marie Bastien-Thiry after his arrest for the attempted assassination of de Gaulle, 1963

The USS *Gabrielle Giffords,* launching a strike missile, is one of two new Littoral Combat Ships (LCS) in the South China Sea to supplement the US Seventh Fleet, 2019. *US Navy, South China Morning Post*

The CIA's Long Tien airbase, 1973. *G R Jenkin*

Cessna Bird Dogs (rear) used smoke rockets to mark targets for Hmong pilots in two-seat North American T-28s. *Air & Space, 2003*

Hmong girls meet possible suitors while playing a ball-throwing game in Laos.
Oliver Spalt

Hmong village

Vang Vieng

Han Zheng, 2018. *Kremlin archives*

Xi Jinping and Winnie the Pooh, 2018. *SOAS Blog*

kilometres of tangled roads, mountain paths, shifting sub-soils, dense forest and waterways, some for soldiers and porters, for six-wheel Russian trucks, for cyclists and for the petrol pipeline which ran from near the Chinese border to just outside Saigon. The routes were not fixed, but grew and twisted to find shelter against American carpet bombing, sometimes aided by climbing vegetable plants formed into domes, and, all the time, to increase the volume of munitions and replacement troops devoured at the front line.[2] By the end of the war, over a million tonnes of supplies had been delivered and two million journeys competed by individuals. At its peak, there were 120,000 people working on the Trail of which 20,000 died, 30,000 were seriously injured, and 6,000 are unfound.

As I left, I read some useful words from an interview with General Giap, hero of Dien Bien Phu, the man whose vision and intellect had seen the Trail's construction through to the fall of Saigon.

We built the Trail because the Americans attacked us. President Ho Chi Minh believed that the war would last a long time. We were determined to be victorious ... from the Battle of Dien Bien Phu I knew that our logistics were a key factor, among many. I knew that if we were to win in South Vietnam, where there was already a guerrilla war, we would have to expand our front line and fight larger battles ... There were times when the roads [in Vietnam] became blocked and in May 1959, I ordered the west Truong Son in Laos to be opened [to a greater extent] ... At first, it was only passable on foot. Later, roads were opened. It was an area of hard limestone and vast mountains. The first time, my soldiers said it couldn't be done. The second time, they said there were too many rocks and stones. The third time, I ordered the stones to be cut. The road into Laos was called Ta Le [but was given the number Route 20 as this was the average age of the workers].[3]

I perched on a blue plastic stool at a pavement street food stall for a morning bowl of *pho*, the ubiquitous beef and noodle soup. A small group of children gathered respectfully to watch me eat. For 20,000 dong a bowl, one US dollar, I felt it reasonable to order for my newfound friends. As the children left with many bowings and thanks, an aging soldier with grey hair *en brosse* and a toothy grin, speaking perfect French, limped into their place. His used face stared at me. He was far away from a world of comfortable apartments, milk at lunch and chicken and relish sandwiches.

'I suppose you want a bowl, too?' I asked.

'Some *pho* would certainly help me through the day,' he replied. 'You were very generous to feed the vendor's children.'

'You're kidding me?'

'Not at all. On some days, she reckons they get six bowls each. Her foreign customers unwittingly pay her to feed her own brood. And she makes a small profit.'

'That's certainly a neat trick.' I looked at the lady of the sidewalk, but she remained po-faced, concentrating on her work. Or did I see a twinkle at the back of her eyes?

I changed the subject. 'That's an old legionnaire's uniform you have there, and the bullet hole in the back has only been roughly stitched.'

'I was at Dien Bien Phu,' he offered without a drop of embarrassment.

'So was my father,' I retorted with a straight face, 'and I am in my seventies.'

I made no dent in his demeanour. 'It's always a shock these days to meet someone with a knowledge of history, especially the French, but none of it changes the price of the *pho*,' he countered. He managed his noodles and chopsticks with the dextrous hand of a veteran. 'The French today have base instincts, they are easy to seduce, they have a past but no future. They are obsessed with their little privileges. I fought for them, but I want nothing more to do with them.' He held out his bowl for a refill.

'Footloose Americans like me are no better,' he continued. 'As an old soldier, I'm still disgusted at the US government for avoiding the blame for the My Lai massacre. There is no such thing as a war crime. War is the crime.'

'I'm not sure I can agree as far as Lieutenant Calley was concerned,' I retorted.

'Huh, that's all you know. I am outraged by a court sentence that condemned Calley for the murder of "human Orientals" – as if "Oriental" needed "human" to qualify it.'[4]

He mulled matters over and then got down to business. 'So, what brings you to Hanoi? My name is Pyle.' There was no trace of embarrassment at the barefaced appropriation from Graham Greene.

'Bit of military tourism,' I offered. 'As a man of advanced years, you'll remember the ambushes and massacres in the 1950s on the supply road from here to Hai Phong and then up the coast to Cao Bang.'

'Much of the drama has gone,' Pyle said wistfully. 'The roadside has been cleared for farmland and gasoline stations, but the jungle is still the same. We will need a car and a *bounyoul* to drive it. I will be happy to be your guide. How many days would you like to go for? I suggest three nights?'

I was impressed that he freely used *bounyoul*, the French Army slang for natives, and by his well-timed assumption of control. I was beginning to enjoy the man's company. He was anything but quiet, but, perhaps, he had some good stories to tell. I soon learned that whenever he began with, 'I knew a man who …' or 'a friend …' or 'an Englishman who was travelling with me …' you could be sure he was talking about himself.[5] It didn't mean, of course, that it was a true story, but it meant that it might be nearly true. They were always stories worth hearing.

'May I suggest that you take a stroll at the West Lake?' He pointed. 'It's fifteen minutes that way by *xe om*, the motorbike taxi. Make sure you agree the price first. Have a small late lunch of *bánh tôm Hồ Tây*, fried prawn cakes to you and me. You can see the Tran Quoc Pagoda, if you wish. It's on a small island and is the oldest of its kind in Hanoi. I'll pick you up at your hotel in your car at four. That'll give me time to make the arrangements. No money in advance.'

I nodded in agreement, wondered what I was letting myself in for. He moved off into the crowd. It was five minutes before I realised that I hadn't told him where I was staying. When I got back to the hotel to pack, I could tell my room had been searched. Everything was tidier.

On the morning of the third day, Pyle and I were sipping *ca phe den da*, black iced coffee, under the flame flower trees at a delightful café on the colonial Hai Phong waterfront. We watched the multi-coloured boats waiting for the coaches from Hanoi bringing the tourists to visit the Halong Bay islands. The junks and the fishing fleet nudged each other in the gentle current. It was already hot, the sky a burnt blue. Pyle knew a great deal about France's eastern colonial wars, although I did tease him about his timing of some of the battles and the names of the regiments involved. However, he knew his strategy. He handled the tour well, managed the driver and kept him cheerful through our sudden stops. Pyle pointed out the wrecks of the military hedgehogs, the road pinches and the ambush sites. Many times, he barked an order to park and we walked a few feet into needle grass or cloying jungle to find an important earthwork or some rusted scraps of war machines. Everywhere, we found shell cases and even a bayonet and scraps of uniform.

'Someone told me,' he began, 'that the event that brought the Vietnamese to open violence happened here in this town in 1946. There was a row about customs control and there were shots exchanged over a Chinese junk accused of smuggling. The French replied with aerial bombing and a naval bombardment by their cruiser *Suffren* of the native quarter of Hai Phong. Estimates of the dead ranged up to 6,000. Some claimed 20,000. The riots went on for days.'

He paused and then continued: 'You'd think the French would learn. The parallels with the *Duguay-Trouin* which bombarded the town of Kherrata the year before and inflamed every Muslim in Algeria are so obvious.'

I grunted agreement and wondered anew what Pyle knew about me. My father had deftly entered a casual conversation. Was it a coincidence? Had *La Moqueuse* been part of the attack at Hai Phong as it had been at Kherrata?

'Ho Chi Minh rose to the occasion,' continued Pyle. 'He headed to the highlands in the north and declared war. His speech was prophetic and is famous hereabouts and I have learned part of it.'

Fellow countrymen throughout the land!

Impelled by love and peace, we have made concessions. But the more concessions we make, the more the French colonialists take advantage of them to trample on our rights and reconquer our country.

Can we allow this?

No! It would be better to sacrifice everything that forfeits our country and sink back into slavery. Compatriots arise! Let him who has a rifle use his rifle, let him who has a sword use his sword! And let those who have no sword take up pickaxes and sticks!

Even if we should have to endure the harshest privations and the worst sufferings, let us be ready to sacrifice everything, including life itself. Forward to victory! Long live an independent, united Vietnam![6]

'Well done,' I offered. 'It's hard to know where your heart really lies.'

Pyle then pushed me for information on my father, but I held back on the details. He professed a mild frustration. 'An inquiry is bound to be superficial about a man who must be dead, but it is not known when. There is a risk of only limited information,' he lectured.

I criticised him once for an outright invention. 'You do need wonder,' he answered, 'to touch and inspire. There is deep creativity in the smallest nursery fairy tale – as the flavour of the ocean is contained in a droplet or the whole mystery of life within the egg of a flea.' It is difficult to argue with that kind of stuff. This was no briefly educated US marine.

Pyle chose our accommodation and eating places with taste and character, shunning the conspicuous and garish. He pre-booked where necessary although, I noticed, he seldom used a phone. I was pleasantly surprised by the overall price he suggested. I walked to the cash machine and returned to lay out the money with what we both agreed was a generous *pourboire*. As usual, we began a game of Quatre Vingt-et-un to decide who paid for the drinks. His luck with the dice was beginning to irritate me. From further along the promenade, there was a clash of symbols, an incessant drumming and a steady chant directed by hand-held loudspeakers. The crowd of angry men in dirty T-shirts numbered over a thousand.

'Should we be worried?' I asked as Pyle separated some notes to give to the driver and pocketed the rest.

'No and yes,' he offered. 'There won't be a war this time, but the Chinese are so arrogant and stuck up their own arses that it won't be long before they go too far. Vietnam and China have been close at the party level; the locals owe their big communist brother a lot for support through their independence struggle. In 1978, the Vietnamese invaded the Chinese-backed Pol Pot regime in Cambodia and, partly in retaliation, the Chinese invaded Vietnam. That prolonged and vicious border war, little reported in the West, lasted more than ten years. It also drove the Vietnamese closer to Russia.

'The Chinese never forgave the Vietnamese for winning or, for that matter, repressing their large Chinese community who took to their boats in great numbers. You remember the Chinese 'boat people'?

'Now, the Chinese claim ninety per cent of the South China Sea as its exclusive economic and military zone. Look at the map. They've pushed their supposed sea border right up against Japan, Vietnam, Taiwan and the others. It's preposterous. Of course, it's mostly about huge untapped oil and natural gas which are in international waters or waters owned by national states.'

'So, what's brought it to a head here?' I asked.

'The Chinese moved onto some of the Spratly Islands with military and exploration vessels. They've built airfields, radar domes, missile shelters, underground munition storage and naval harbours. They've done the same on Fiery Cross Reef off the Philippine coast. The South China Sea provides about one-tenth of the entire annual global fish catch. The Chinese have now rammed and sunk two Vietnamese fishing boats off the Spratlys for "invading their ancestral waters and not stopping when commanded". Beijing oversaw the replacement of traditional Chinese wooden fishing vessels with steel-hulled trawlers fitted with modern high-tech navigation systems. The local boats don't stand a chance.'

Pyle waved an arm towards the demonstrators. 'These guys are demanding that their government stands up to the Chinese bullies and lets them fish around the Spratlys in safety, as they used to. Neither side can afford to lose face.

'If real trouble starts, it's very likely the US could get drawn in. Their Seventh Fleet out of Japan has over fifty ships. Just last year, the US sent two brand new Independence-class littoral combat ships into the area to ensure "freedom of navigation". Those are powerful beasts.'

'You know an awful lot more than the average man about the situation, Pyle.'

'Yeah, I guess I do. I keep a close watch. I think, sooner or later, it's all going to blow. These Chinese reds are going to ruin my preferred existence. I don't want to go back to what I used to call home.'

I started to wonder what this well-informed old soldier was doing acting as a tourist guide to someone like me.

Back in Hanoi, I picked up my Laos visa and booked a flight to Dien Bien Phu. Pyle offered to come, but I decided to take a break from his ministration and to visit the battle site on my own. I wanted to use the closeness of the border crossing to go by road into Laos while letting him think that I would be flying back to Hanoi.

I moved to the Metropole Legend Hotel at Pyle's suggestion and was delighted. Bernard Fall described it as the 'last really fashionable place left in Hanoi'. Charlie Chaplin and Paulette Goddard honeymooned there in 1936. Graham Greene was a guest as was Jane Fonda when she infuriated the USA with her widely condemned broadcast to American troops. 'To be a revolutionary you have to be a human being. You have to care about people who have no power.'

Pyle and I spent a couple of days touring the capital. We always ate at street stalls, washed down wherever possible with *Bia hoi* mild draught beer poured straight from the barrel into greeny glasses. The mustard-coloured colonial architecture was always the star. I paid homage at the mausoleum of Uncle Ho and gazed at his body with the devoted local pilgrims while being rushed through by uncompromising guards.[7] Pyle remained outside, 'seen enough of the old bugger', on a bench in the big concrete parade ground.

'Did you know this is the same square where Ho give his 1945 victory speech?'

He proclaimed again,

[The French] have built more prisons than schools. They have mercilessly slain our patriots; they have drowned our uprisings in rivers of blood ... They have invented numerous unjustifiable taxes and reduced our people, especially our peasantry, to a state of extreme poverty ... In the autumn of 1944, when the Japanese fascists violated Indochina's territory to establish new bases in their fight against the Allies, the French imperialists went down on their bended knees and handed over our country to them. Thus, from that date, our people were subjected to the double yoke of the French and the Japanese.

We moved for some balance to Hoa Lo prison, 'Hanoi Hilton' to the captured and tortured American air crews. Pyle also organised a drive to the Museum of Ethnology, out past the West Lake, which had stunning displays of Vietnam's fifty-four ethnic groups. I couldn't help but spend most time among the Hmong-Yao-Meo displays. This Pyle observed while quietly muttering to himself about the accuracy of the Kinh exhibits, the majority

Vietnamese group, who, like the Hmong, had their roots in Southern China.

My aircraft slid softly down through the hills after a one-hour flight. I could make out the battlefield site in the near distance. There were a few history buffs among the passengers, but most were Vietnamese about their business. Several of them wore largely pointless cotton masks in fear of China's latest contribution to medical science, the Wuhan coronavirus, which had just reached Saigon and was spreading around the world. The virus was the main topic of conversation in the newspapers and on board.

What was it about the Chinese way of living that produced H2N2 Asian flu of 1956–8; H3N2 Hong Kong flu, 1968; H5N1 avian flu, 1997; Sars, 2002; H7N9 flu, 2012; and the recurring coronavirus of 2020?[8] Swine fever was devastating the country's pork industry with 100 million pigs slaughtered and driving up pig meat prices in Europe.[9] The consensus was that little care was given to the quality of life of their animal population. In China's hectic and heavily populated 'wet' food markets, live wild game, including illegally imported pangolins, although officially banned, mixed closely with the slaughtering and open-fire cooking of more common bred animals.[10]

Some careful thinking was required. In the summer months, it makes no sense to buy butchered meat to take back to a shack with no electricity or refrigeration. It is far better to buy live animals and to kill at home. Since 2002, virologists have warned that the viruses in horseshoe bats, and the Chinese custom of eating exotic animals or using them for traditional medicines, was a 'time bomb' for the world's health. China did nothing to limit the danger. How many people across the world have to die so that Chinese men can improve their sex life through ingesting ground pangolin scales?

There was considerable anger in the newspapers about a Chinese political culture built on lies and censorship. The first instinct of officialdom was always to control inconvenient news rather than to discuss and alert the wider community about possible pandemics. The death toll of Mao's great famine, twenty to thirty million, just two generations ago is still not admitted. When a regime views the lives of its own people as disposable, there seems little hope of quick improvement. In 2008, the government permitted a cover-up that led to 300,000 babies being poisoned by contaminated milk formula in order to avoid embarrassment ahead of their Olympics.

Pyle had insisted on making my hotel booking at the Muong Tanh where I slipped gratefully into the swimming pool to assuage the heat. I ate that night at his recommendation at an excellent vegetarian restaurant in a dusty lane just outside of the small town. Next day, I saw the town as one large historical site which offered little to the uninitiated. Of course, without the battle, there would be no reason to visit such a sleepy place. A small museum with a three-dimensional map showed the progress of the Viet-Minh to their great glory. The French fortified positions on the small hills at Beatrice, Isabelle and Eliane, and de Castries' bunker were preserved in a relatively good condition. The whole area was dotted with memorials and the rusty wrecks of French Chaffee tanks and anti-aircraft guns, but, as usual, the saddest place was the lines of grey-marble headstones of the Viet-Minh dead marked only with a red and gold star. Their names were probably unknown even to their commanders.

On my last day, I was driven 30 kilometres to the Viet-Minh complex at Muong Phang village. The shelters and trenches and an underground tunnel connecting the headquarters of Giap and General Hoàng Văn Thái, his chief of staff, are nearly as they were. To be honest, I was pleased when my individually guided tour came to an end. While I knew my father had lived in hell in this place, I did not feel the hoped-for strong connection.

After lunch, I was prompted to a drive to Pa Khoang for a reflective and solitary lake cruise. As we purred our way through flocks of pelicans and geese, I asked my official guide about any French who escaped the battle. He said nothing at first and all but ignored my question. Later, he slipped me a piece of paper as if committing a crime. 'If you should make it to Vientiane,' he explained, 'please visit the university. Here are two names who may well be able to give you some help.'

That night, I returned to my vegetarian restaurant to explore more of the menu. I was welcomed like an old friend. Halfway through the meal, an elderly Vietnamese gentleman, who had clearly been invited to attend for my benefit, introduced himself as Lia while leaning on his white stick. He wore crisp Western clothes topped with a Panama and was knowledge personified. I explained my father's role in the battle and he was able to elucidate many small details. We drank beer as I asked about the men who got away.

'You raise a difficult subject, my friend,' Lia explained. 'Official ears everywhere will likely perk up at your preposterous suggestion. According to the clear direction of the local all-knowing authorities, no one escaped. The French forces and their colonial lackies either died or were captured; such was the stranglehold of the glorious Viet-Minh army of independence.

'From the later French perspective, "running away" did not fit with the patriotic martyrdom necessary to ameliorate this great failure. You must remember that, by this time, the Viet-Minh had captured almost the whole of northern Laos including reaching close to Luang Prabang and the Plaine des Jarres.'

Lia smiled. 'However, you mentioned the Hmong. There were, perhaps, over 200 of them at the battle; many of them worked with French NCOs and the Thai Dam, 'black Thai' soldiers from the north, to protect the main airfield with 37mm mortars, machine guns and small arms.

'One force of Hmong that you will probably never hear about, led by Colonel Jean Sassi as head of the local *Maquis*, and Vang Pao, a young Hmong leader, fought their way in four weeks from the Plaine des Jarres to within sound of the battle in an attempt to relieve the entrapped men. A few miles to the south of Dien Bien Phu, they heard that the French base had fallen. Ignoring orders to return, Sassi, born in Tunis, you know, changed his mission to harass the Viet-Minh flank and to gather up survivors. I heard that they collected about 300 Frenchmen and, exhausted, fought their way slowly to safety. They had no food and had to eat bamboo shoots and leaves. The French could not handle the privation or the diet; their feet and legs were ulcerated and bleeding. Only thirty survived the jungle and the ambushes.

'It was the same Sassi who later transferred tons of equipment to the Hmong among others to be hidden on the Plaine des Jarres in case the French decided to pull out and to disarm their former allies.'[11]

With some bitterness, Lia explained that some 2,000 Hmong captured in the battle and in later skirmishes in the hills were not released by the Vietnamese until the beginning of their Chinese war in 1979. During their twenty-five years in captivity, most of the Hmong died and, during all that time, in contrast to the efforts of the French and, later, the Americans to reclaim their own nationals, no international agency tried to secure the Hmong's release.

I wondered whether Lia was Hmong but didn't ask him. I did find out later that 'Lia' was the Hmong descriptive middle name for 'red'. I explained that I planned to cross into Laos the next day at the land border crossing but had not made any plans.

'If you would like,' he offered, 'I can make some arrangements for you. I have family on both sides.'

I nodded as he smoothly suggested that a son would drive me the 35 kilometres to the Vietnamese post at Tay Trang. 'This would be an advantage for you,' he suggested, 'because he has a cousin among the guards and so, for a small offering, will be able to drive you the 3 kilometres to the Lao side and save you the walk and carrying your suitcase.'

Lia smiled again, a little more broadly, enjoying his influence. 'Now, at the Laos border, I have the son of a nephew who owns an air-conditioned limousine. I know he is free because yesterday was his birthday and there was a big celebration. He will be able to drive you south at your own pace to at least Luang Prabang and visit some parts of the Ho Chi Minh Trail and some of the lesser-known river crossings. He speaks excellent French.'

I started smiling.

'You may know that the Trail is a criss-cross of paths and roads?' he continued, pressing home his sale. 'Ask any Lao where the Trail runs and he will say "everywhere".'

My new friend flipped open his up-market mobile, made a couple of calls and all was fixed. I was reminded of the smooth arrangements made by Pyle just a few days before. Had I been passed effortlessly along a chain?

Before noon the following day, I was comfortably ensconced in a black modern Mercedes equipped with cold water and beer and some snacks with Binh and his driver as we bumped our way along the soon-to-be tarred road into the northern heart of Laos. The rice fields shone under the sun, the fisher's cranes hovered over the fields like mosquitoes, the mollusc hats of the girls with their bright dresses worked at repairing the road edges. We made slow progress; five hours, on the 100 kilometres of winding roads with glimpses of stunning mountain scenery to Muang Khua; stopping briefly at Khamu, Hmong and Lao villages on the way.

I took a two-day break at Muang La and the Khamu village of Pak La. Every half an hour, an articulated truck laden with hardwood trees thundered in the distance, not stopping or caring for pedestrians.

'They often kill people with their speed,' said Binh. 'Trees are one of Laos' greatest assets, but they stand in the way of Chinese damns, roads and mines. The Vietnamese have been logging here for decades and have barely made a dent. There is so much more for the Chinese to steal. They are wolves in sheep's clothing. America likes to make a fast buck, but they have made way for China to make two fast bucks.'

Binh suggested the best way forward was to travel to Nong Khiaw by small long-tail boat along the Nam Ou river while the car did the rugged bit. Small villages lined the banks. Gardens stretched down to the water's edge. Buffalo stood and stared. Children waved and jumped into the flood pools. Their mothers stood knee-deep, clothed in tightly embracing sarongs that shimmered in the afternoon sun while they beat their clothes on flat stones. Cramped for legroom and wishing for a cushion or two, I got the third degree from Binh as we chugged along with the current. He was well read on my military interests and explained his version of the Ho Chi Minh Trail which snaked and branched along our route. Binh assured me that his grandfather and his two brothers, rice-farming peasants, had been forced to hand carry mortar shells all the way from Hanoi.

'It took about three months. They carried three shells each and had to walk. They arrived and reported to their captain. He said, 'Thank you,' aimed the shells the same day at an American strongpoint and then sent the men back for three more. My grandfather couldn't believe it. He thought he would have a break as a reward and then join the fighting.'

Binh's grandfather said the second trip was by far the worst. The porters had to cross the Truong Son mountains, accessible by just a few passes, to reach the Trail in Laos.[12] It was during the monsoon and for four weeks their clothes were never dry. South-west from Ha Tinh to the Lao border was the Mu Gia Pass, the 'door of death'.

'Once the Pentagon saw the gaps for what they were, bottlenecks in the Viet Cong's lifeline, they started round-the-clock bombing,' explained Binh. Already exhausted from the climb, the heavily laden human pack animals broke into a run at Mu Gia. The American B-52s dropped three million tons of munitions on the Trail, a million more than were dropped on Germany in World War Two. Some days there were 300 flights. Opposing them were as many as 80,000 anti-aircraft gunners, infantrymen and engineers whom Hanoi stationed in Laos to keep the Trail open.

A Vietnamese soldier poet wrote at the time,

The crab lies still on the chopping block
Never knowing when the knife will fall.

Binh returned to the horrors of his own family's story. 'One brother died as he fell from a bridge of vines and bamboo into a ravine. Leeches dropped from branches and sucked their fill. There are both common and king cobras and green, Malayan and Russell's pit vipers.

'Have you heard of the two-step snake?' he asked. I shook my head. 'If it bites you, you take one step and then on the second you fall dead.'

The two remaining brothers both got malaria which killed as many as ten per cent of the people on the Trail.

'That was the least of their worries,' explained Binh, as he warmed to his story. 'What they really had to look out for was dengue fever which is ten times worse. We call it break-bone fever because you feel like every bone in your body is broken. It's the worst thing you can get and not die, not counting Japanese encephalitis, a mosquito-borne disease which swells its victim's cerebrum. If you survive, you get left with mush for brains.

'My uncle became a twice-decorated officer. At the end of the war, he expected a decent government job. Instead, he was ordered back to the rice paddies because the Party learned of his bad marks in seventh grade.'

After a few minutes of reflection, Binh slid into my father's story. 'What did he do when he was in the Army in Vietnam and Laos?'

'Binh, I have never talked to you about my father. How do you know he was ever in any army anywhere?'

'You must have mentioned it.'

'No, never.'

He thought for a bit then, relieved, said that his 'uncle' Lia must have mentioned something when he made the booking on the telephone.

'No, Binh, he never said that because I was there. Now, why don't you tell me what is going on or you'll get no tip?'

'I am a poor man,' he responded. 'I am just carrying out my uncle's wishes.'

'I suggest you drop the subject forever, Binh, and next time you are on your phone tell your uncle to drop it as well. I have lost my patience.' We sat in silence as the plethora of green, more varieties of greens than I had names for, passed by.

Back in the car, just north of Luang Prabang, Binh ordered a half-hour detour. We arrived at a barren stretch of hillside where bulldozers followed by heavy-duty track-laying vehicles and hundreds of Chinese labourers ploughed a wide straight trench heading north through the landscape. The gangs looked as if unchanged from the south of China in the 1880s when the English referred to these workers as 'coolies', from *kuli*, or 'bitter strength'. Here they were toiling on a section of Laos' first ever railway connecting Vientiane to Boten and the intended Yuxi-Mohan railway on the Chinese border. The ambition of the six-billion-dollar project, begun in 2016, is breathtaking. A link in the south will cross a new bridge connecting Thanaleng to Nong Khai and the high-speed rail network in Thailand. The route north to the Chinese system will have thirty-two stations spread over 250 miles with 167 bridges and viaducts and with almost a half its length inside seventy-five tunnels.

A bumptious official in yellow jacket and hard hat rushed over and ordered us away. 'Dangerous, forbidden,' he shouted. There were armed guards in the background.

'The Chinese will overrun this country,' said Binh. 'Every time they offer the Government an infrastructure, they add crippling loans which mean they will soon become the majority owners. Then, they bring their own workers. When it is all done, the workers stay. It is the new colonial capitalism.'

Mostly, I read, the workers didn't remain from choice. They were under orders. They were particularly bad colonists with an overwhelming pride in themselves and their cultural identity. They tended to have strong ideas about race, rarely respected religion and had trouble considering a non-Chinese point of view. They did not tend to go to foreign places, learn the local language or mix with the local people. In the 5,000 years of their history, it was striking how little interest the Chinese had in exploration. 'They seem completely content to be Chinese.'[13]

At Vientiane, I made for the rue Samsentai and the Constellation Hotel. The heat and dust of the day covered everything in a thin layer of grit and dried sweat.[14] In 1960, the city became a four-day civil war battleground. Armoured cars fired indiscriminately. 'Much of the small downtown area of wood shops burned to the ground, sometimes with the store owners and their children inside.' Half the city was destroyed and most of its population fled. As the war wound on, the Constellation Hotel become home to all members of the 'wandering press': an old, decrepit, hot, mosquito-infested place with one toilet per floor. It was also the contact hub for pilots of Air America, the CIA's airline, and the privately run Bird Air and Continental Air Services which successfully bid against them, and embassy personnel and spies from around the globe, including the Russians and the Chinese.[15] I had read of its owner Maurice Cavalerie who acted as counsellor, intelligence chief, money changer and friend to the assorted hacks. 'I never break the law because, in Laos, everything is legal.'

But, today, the Constellation had gone. Binh was confused, and I ordered him to the peaceful, side-street Ansara Hotel.

I decided on a short walk in the garden before dinner, relieved to be on my own for the first time in several weeks. As I rounded a corner where the path was framed by short banana plants, I came on a stone-viewing bench. Why was I not surprised to see Uncle Lia in residence, for all the world a regular casual visitor puffing on a small cigar? I stood in front of him, balanced, legs apart.

'I've had enough, Lia, what with the ludicrously named Pyle and Binh, your juvenile spy. You better come up with an explanation quickly.'

He played it entirely the wrong way. He was too confident. 'The cultural gaps between Europeans and the Lao are almost entirely unbridgeable,' he offered. 'Also, the huge income disparity precludes integration. I, we, feel that you are on some quest. We feel that you might need some help and that you might move too quickly.' His smile brought bile to my mouth. 'Do you know the acronym for the People's Democratic Republic of Laos, "Please Don't Rush"?'

I picked him up by his crisp lapels and dangled him among the bananas, a small hand of tiny fruit hanging over his nose making the situation almost comical. He was much shorter than me and, perhaps, half my weight. His stick fell to the ground which was reassuring considering what I knew of their potential subterfuges. Lia went yellow in the face.

'You have just one chance,' I told him. 'If I am not happy with your answer then I will hurt you badly.' I hoped he would answer quickly as my arms were tiring. I was no longer used to this sort of thing.

The light went quietly from his eyes. 'You have the same French name,' he said. 'It's very unusual. We were alerted in Hanoi by some friends in the police department. We thought you might be related and that you had come to look for him. You are French, you have the same name. The Hmong might help you. They won't help us.'

'Goddammit, Lia. Who are you talking about?' The name on my passport, the only name that Lia and Pyle knew me by, was that of my birth mother. It was a passport I had secured as a young man when I found out that I had been adopted.[16] I had to drop Lia back on the bench as my arms gave out.

'The Frenchman, the soldier, the one who lived in the mountains with the Hmong.'

'If you stop now, you won't walk away from here,' I told him. 'What's so important about this soldier?'

'We know little of him but, among the Hmong left in Lao, he is well known. He appeared with General Vang Pao about the time of the useless Geneva ceasefire and worked with him for many years. We think he might have left information that could make us money.'

Lia glanced up at me. 'We could share the money with you. Would you like that?'

'This is your very last chance. I'm waiting.'

He sighed and the life seemed to drain from him. 'We used to have a very good business helping the Americans finding the bodies of their pilots and special forces killed in Laos, their MIA, their 'missing in action'. We would find bodies in the jungle, in crash sites, and the Americans were so corrupt that they didn't really care if they were genuine or not. Then their thefts were exposed in Congress and the money dried up. The Americans put a new organisation in place and, while they still pay good money, their laboratories check the DNA. We have to find real body parts.'

'And what has this to do with this French soldier?'

'I told you,' he said, looking bewildered. 'He was the man who led the Hmong guerrillas into the jungle to rescue the downed pilots. The Americans dropped them in by helicopter and they searched for survivors.

They saved a lot of men. They lived in the jungle for months on end. He knew where many of the bodies were and still are, the ones they couldn't bring out. We hoped he might have kept a diary or papers or something. We wanted to find his village.'

I slapped him once across the face and slipped my hand inside his jacket for his wallet. 'Stay away from me. Give up and leave me alone. There is no connection between me and this mythical French soldier.'

As I walked back to the hotel, I knew that what I had said was wrong and, probably, stupid. I had spoken in anger and shock. There was obviously a connection. My father had returned to Laos and used the name of his lost love in Rouen. He lived again with the Hmong. Where? And for how long? I sat on the veranda, called for a *beerlao* and was handed a dinner menu. Just as the waiter came back with the drinks, notepad at the ready, an old man in a white suit staggered out from the garden onto the small lawn. He cried out, clutched his chest and fell prone. The waiter told me later that he was dead. They didn't know who he was. He was not a guest and had no identification.

'How sad,' I said and ordered dinner. I remembered some words from Ibn Khaldun, 'Be in this world as if you were a stranger and a passing traveller.'

1 Campbell, *Thousand Faces*.
2 Morris, *Road to Freedom*.
3 'Interview with General Giap', Morris, *Road to Freedom*.
4 Chatwin, *Songlines*.
5 Camus, *First Man*.
6 Warbey, *Ho Chi Minh*.
7 Steele, *Ho Chi Minh*. Warbey, *Ho Chi Minh*. Fenn, *Ho Chi Minh*.
8 Coleman, Emeritus Professor of Demography, *University of Oxford*.
9 *Daily Telegraph*, Wallace, 11/2/2020.
10 *Daily Telegraph*, Samuel, 25/1/2020.
11 Hamilton-Merritt, *Tragic Mountains*.
12 Hunt, *Sparring with Charlie*.
13 Hessler, *River Town*.
14 Kurlantzick, *Great Place*.
15 Hamilton-Merritt, *Tragic Mountains*.
16 Heal, *Disappearing*.

15. LET SLIP THE DOGS

Life is a bridge. Cross over it, but build no house on it.

Indian proverb

I felt at the mercy of forces that are more easily ignored than faced.[1] Forces out of childhood, forces from present causes and conditions, forces as enigmatic as life itself. They all told me that I must try to achieve something or to get somewhere. In this moment, my escape, my journey, seemed the product of whim or accident. The authorities did not connect me to the dead stranger in the garden. Why should anyone think that we had even met? Was there any point in trying to hide from any blame that Binh and his friends might attach to me? It was time to trust to instinct.

Next morning, I took a tuk-tuk to the university's Dongdok campus and asked for either of the two names I had been slipped by my guide at Dien Bien Phu. Doctor Vang Tshua of the agricultural faculty answered his mobile and said that he would be happy to see me, even at short notice, if I went to the balcony on the third floor.

Security was non-existent as I plodded my way up the stairs passed smartly dressed young people engrossed in lively conversations. A group of about a dozen was clustered around their tutor and making fine adjustments to an expensive telescope set on a tripod and pointed towards the heavens. I introduced myself. The doctor was in his late thirties, tall for a Hmong with a long almost European face sprouting wild, black hair.

He gave me a broad grin. 'I'm Tshua,' he announced in French. 'You are not expected. Have you come to see the rocket? You are most welcome.'

'You have the advantage of me. What rocket? I hope I am not intruding on a special event?'

Tshua deliberately lost a little of his smile. 'You disappoint me, sir. This is the biggest day of my academic life and you don't know what's going on.'

I spread my hands in apology. He led me to the edge of the balcony and pointed west.

'Out there,' he said, 'about 2,500 kilometres away is the Indian island of Sriharikota in the Bay of Bengal. What does that mean to you?'

'The Indian space centre,' I replied, pleased to redeem myself. 'I think it's named after one of their scientists, Sati Dhawan. It's their Cape Canaveral from where they launch their rockets.'

'Satish Dhawan,' he corrected gently. 'You are almost forgiven. At 11.05, in about ten minutes, the Indians will launch their second Mars orbiter mission. We are ninety minutes ahead of them. Aboard the MOM is a spacecraft called Vimāna, like the mythical flying chariot of their gods, which will separate and float down to the surface of Mars, Ganesh and Allah willing, in part deference to the souls of all of our Lao elephants, you understand. I hope I have not used the wrong deity, though. We don't want a bumpy landing.'

He waved a hand at the young people clustered round the telescope. 'Frankly, we have little chance of spotting the speck of light, but we live in hope.'

'And how is Vimāna important to you? Your work is with plants, isn't it?'

'Rice, sir. Fast-growing, disease-resistant rice that requires little water and a lot of sunlight. When Vimāna lands, our self-contained capsule will be ejected and we will watch on our cameras, or rather the Indians will watch and sends us transmissions, and we will see whether we can grow food on Mars. Not bad for a Hmong boy from the hills, eh?'

'It's a staggering achievement,' I offered. 'Your people must be very proud. And you must have impressed the Indians for them to include you.'

'We have had good results in Laos and the Indians are keen to counter the influence of the Chinese in our part of the world. The Chinese have a lot of investment at the university. They have the Confucius Institute. They have made it clear that our experiment should have been aboard a Chinese rocket. We may need their money, but we are not in their pockets and not all of us like their style. This, of course, you must not repeat.

'Excuse me ...' and Tshua rushed to a large-screened laptop as the student monitoring the launch issued a squeak.

I stood and watched the excited group, struck by my good fortune to attend such an event with so charming a host and his committed students. A chilled coconut water was thrust in my hand by a young man. Amid the chatter and exclamations, I did have a personal problem. Why had Tshua called for support from Allah and an Indian deity rather than a spirit from his own animist world? I knew that the Hmong spirits and supernatural forces were referred to as *dab* and were divided into several groups. The most important were the *dab nyeg* and the *dab qus*. The *dab nyeg* included the household spirits, *dab qhuas*, which inhabited and protected the household. The *dab qus* were the wild, forest spirits that roamed around the home areas to attack or capture Hmong souls.

There was a cheer and Tshua returned. 'Success,' he beamed. 'MOM got away all right and on time. We have pictures of the launch and we have a little shiny streak recorded from our telescope which we will share with the TV people.'

'Wonderful. You have my congratulations and admiration. Tell me, why were you not at the launch?'

'Money and privilege,' he replied. 'The university's leaders and a few politicians have gone, but there was no room for the people who did the work. Besides, I spent many weeks in India helping with the specifications for our little tray. We did not have the technology to build it ourselves. Our contribution was the seedlings.'

'And, why, forgive me, did you mention Allah?'

'الحمد لله، أنا مُسلِم,' he said, 'that is, "thank God I am a Muslim".'

'الله في عونِ,' I replied, 'that is, as you know, "May Allah be with you".'

He looked at me in surprise then broke into another of his infectious smiles. 'Perhaps, you would join me for lunch?'

We took a packaged rice and chicken dish from the cafeteria and found a quiet place outside at a trestle in the shade of a flowering hibiscus tree. The scent was enough to make one drowsy. From time to time, students and staff came up to shake Tshua's hand in recognition of the famous day. A Chinese contingent two tables distant pointedly looked away.

'In many ways, the Chinese we get here are children,' commented Tshua. 'Intelligent in their subjects, but petulant, spoiled, bullies and very self-centred. They are not trained to think for themselves about life, about politics. Our own glorious government wishes the Lao population were more like them. Conformity within the Party is everything. Good Chinese believe as a people that they have a unique destiny among nations which excuses any action. For instance, I have two brazen spies in my faculty, recording all that I do.

'Face is everything. Other people are just means to an end, have no essential value, but this is also true between themselves. They are there to be sacrificed if the need arises. Every semester, we lose a couple of them, reported to their masters for becoming too closely assimilated, for making friends with Lao students, and they return home in shame.'

'How did you find Allah with so many *dab nyeg* in your home to protect you? He is not a natural bedfellow for the Hmong.'

'An accident of birth.' He waved the subject away making clear the direct question was not welcome and gave the standard Lao answer to difficult questions, *Bo pen yang*, 'never mind'.

'In truth, I am a bad Muslim by the tenets of the Middle East. I do not look down on non-Muslims. If I did, I would have few friends in Vientiane. I respect and enjoy women and work hard at their education which is still shocking to some in Laos. There was an interesting disclosure about this in *Time* magazine last week. Opportunities for women in education is one of the few benefits of our socialist system.

'We really have only one congregational mosque in the city, the Jama' Masjid, in a narrow lane just behind the Nam Phu Fountain. We even have our own miniature minaret. You must visit with me if you can. There is one other small Azhar Mosque in the suburbs which the Cambodian Cham people built for themselves after they escaped Pol Pot and the Khmer Rouge.'

'Any Muslim would have great reasons for antipathy towards the Chinese right now,' I suggested.

Tshua heaved a sigh and his eyes misted. A dam burst within him.

'There is clear evidence,' he said, just under control, 'that the Chinese are conducting systematic brainwashing of hundreds of thousands of Muslims in a network of high-security camps built over the last four years. These camps are in the Xinjiang region. About a million people, mostly from the Uyghur community, have been detained without trial and forced to renounce their religion. Leaked papers, including a memo sent in 2017 from Zhu Hailun, then deputy-secretary of the Communist Party, confirms this and orders indoctrination, strict punishments and no escapes. Families are separated. Every aspect of their lives is monitored and controlled: when they get up, roll call, washing, toilet times, housekeeping, language, eating, studying, sleeping and so on. It is this century's most serious human rights crisis.

'The Chinese, of course, deny everything. They say that are conducting passive programmes to explain the dangers of Muslim extremism. Yet a comment piece in China's state media publicly stated that the aim is to 'break the Uyghur's lineage, break their roots and break their connections.

'As the *Washington Post* said in an editorial, "It's hard to read that as anything other than a declaration of genocidal intent".'

I joined in the denunciation. 'I hear that the repression of Islam has spread to ethnic Kazakhs and other Muslim minorities. These are people who have moved freely across the Chinese-Kazakh border for centuries. They are also being locked up.'

The Uyghurs called their land Turkistan or Uyghurstan. The Chinese called this province Xinjiang Uyghur Autonomous region. Xinjiang means 'New Frontier' and for more than 2,000 years it slipped in and out of China until the Communists took firm control in 1949. Difficult to govern, it bordered Tibet, India, Pakistan, Tajikistan, Kyrgyzstan, Kazakhstan, Mongolia, and constituted one-sixth of China's land area. It had a wealth of oil and minerals. It was also decidedly Muslim.[2]

'What frightens me,' Tshua continued, 'what shows the power of the Chinese, is that it has taken the Americans to blacklist some thirty Chinese surveillance and security organisations involved in these abuses. American companies are banned from buying and selling their products without approval from Washington. What do we hear from the oil-rich Muslim leaders in the Gulf in defence of the *Ummah*, the Muslin brethren – nothing?'

He paused, then abruptly changed track.

'But this is far, far too much of my story and my concerns. I have been remiss. You sought me out so there must be something you want of me?'

I decided to trust him and told him of my quest for an old French soldier whom I believed lived in the high mountains with the Hmong for some years in the 1960s and, perhaps, 1970s. I had heard that he was a leader in search missions looking for downed Lao and American pilots during the secret war and, perhaps, the MIA long afterwards. I had been given Tshua's name with one other by a sympathetic Hmong guide at Dien Bien Phu where the soldier had fought.

Tshua's mood changed instantly. I couldn't identify what piece of my story had grasped his attention. He looked me hard in the eyes and then studied the dirt ground for what must have been five minutes. He seemed to come to a decision.

'The war was only secret to the American government and the American people even though they paid for it,' he began. 'It was no secret to the CIA or anyone in Laos or North Vietnam or China. Anyway, I have some questions of you. First, what is your name?'

I told him the name on my passport and his eyes flickered. 'I have other names, too, Tshua. I have a complicated past. I am not a criminal, but I have done many things that have upset people. They would be happy if they could find me. You could say that I am trying to hide.'

'What was the soldier to you if he ever existed?'

I said I believed that the soldier was my father. I had found some letters from him in Paris in the last few months. I could show them to him, but they were written in Arabic. One of the letters suggested that he was on the run and had come to Laos to escape. He had lived with the Hmong before and after the battle at Dien Bien Phu.

'What was the other name you were given?'

'Vang PajYeeb, who I was told is also at this university. I found you first by chance. Isn't "yeeb" opium?'

'PajYeeb means opium blossom, an important crop for the Hmong. She is a sort of cousin of mine. She is a medical doctor and works in our environmental faculty and is also connected loosely with the Indian space programme. Our clan name is Vang. Do you know of any other people with that name?'

'Only Vang Pao, the great Hmong general who fought the communists for the whole war. I think he went to America after the Pathet Lao's victory. I suspect he knew my father.'

'What do you know of the MIA?'

'Very little. I want to find some books on the conflict and also get on the internet. I believe I need to find out a lot more.'

'And, lastly, Mr Man-on-the-Run, what do you know of the old Vietnamese gentleman who died of a heart attack yesterday evening at the Ansara Hotel?'

This was unexpected. My whole visit to Laos might be in jeopardy if I shared what had happened with Tshua. I took the plunge. 'I met him shortly before he died but haven't told the police. His name was Lia and he also wanted to find this French soldier to make money out of his knowledge of crash sites. This is why I need to understand the MIA programme,' I finished, a little lamely.

'OK,' he concluded. 'You are in deep water here. You ask about things that are private to the Hmong. You may be trying to hide from your past, but you are in danger here and now.

'I have to go back to my students. I will talk to some people. It may take a few days and, while you wait, you will become a tourist. You will not contact anyone else about this until I come back to you. You will not try to contact me or PajYeeb. I suggest that you spend some of your time on the hotel computer learning about the MIA.

'Agreed?'

'Agreed. Thank you for trusting me.'

'Trust is not decided yet. That is what the next few days are about.'

We nodded our mutual understanding and he was gone.

When I reached the campus gate, Binh was waiting in his air-conditioned limousine. It was too tempting to pass and I climbed in.

'Was Lia really your relative, Binh,' I asked? 'You don't look too upset at his death?'

'I didn't know it was him until you told me,' he replied as he threaded his way through a waiting convoy of university buses. 'All I knew was that he was going to try to see you. Did you see him? Did you kill him?'

'Come now, Binh. You must know that the man in the hotel garden died of a heart attack. What could that have to do with me? If you want any more information you must answer some of my questions first. Was Lia really your relative? I don't see any tears.'

'He was a sort of distant uncle,' he admitted. 'I didn't see him often at all, but he was kind to me. He often gave me jobs to do like the one for you. Just driving and delivering, you know. I wasn't involved in his business. I don't even know what it was really except that it involved finding bodies of Americans dead from the war.'

I decided to trust him, at least on a long string. 'Would you like to work for me for the next few days, driving on call, errands, information?' Binh nodded and we agreed a daily price plus expenses.

'OK. We'll see how well it goes. First thing, I want you to tell me all you hear about Lia. Second, I want you to check quietly among your friends about the American MIA programme and to let me know. Third, find me the best Hawala banker in Vientiane. And last, what's the story about Hmong villages in the high mountains that have not made contact since the end of the war?

'Don't get yourself noticed. Do it all softly, softly.'

Binh nodded. 'Perhaps I should have asked for some more money,' he ventured. I added another ten dollars to the agreed price.

'And here's an extra,' I said and passed him Lia's wallet minus a page of notes and numbers that looked like MIA intelligence that I decided to keep to myself for now. 'Your Lia's closest next of kin that I know about so I guess you should have it.' His eyes opened wide at the wad of money it contained, US dollars, Lao kip and Vietnamese dong. Then the eyes narrowed as he grasped the implication of my having the wallet.

'Truth and trust is one,' I said, 'even though wise men speak of it by many names.'[3]

He nodded again and passed into my service, I hoped. I arranged for him to pick me up the next morning.

The hotel agreed to leave open an internet line for the afternoon for the in-room laptop along with a *beerlao* and a snack and I settled in for a session discovering what I could about the MIA. First, I checked on my covert money arrangements. All was well, except that I needed to top up some accounts. There were no alerts or danger signals.

The Americans probably head the nations' league table for concern, identification and return of their war dead. The issue is a highly emotional one for the families and is usually handled with kid gloves by the US government. There are vociferous and persistent MIA activists watching every development. Broadly, the missing are split into possible prisoners of war and those whose bodies have not been found, but are believed dead. Numbers are complicated because some servicemen just walked away from their battle area and, if still alive, could be living quietly in, say, Thailand. The searches of the Indochinese wars cover Vietnam, Laos, Cambodia and China with offices in Hanoi, Vientiane, and Bangkok. There are equivalent operations for other semi-recent conflicts, for instance in the Middle East, Korea, and France and Germany.

Some activists maintain that there has been a concerted conspiracy by the Vietnamese and US governments to hide the existence of continuing prisoners of war. Both sides have always denied this. Popular culture has continued the speculation, through songs, TV series like *Magnum PI* and the *X-Files*, a Newsweek cover using a hoax photograph, and films like *Good Guys Wear Black* (Norris 1978), *Uncommon Valour* (Hackman 1983), *Missing in Action* (Norris 1984) and *Rambo: First Blood Part II* (Stallone 1985). Several wives of missing servicemen organised tragi-comic attempts to identify POW camps, often led by dubious, semi-military figures and conmen. Congressional investigations culminated with the large and thorough *US Senate Select Committee on POW/MIA Affairs of 1991–1993*, led by Senators John Kerry, John McCain and Bob Smith, which found 'no compelling evidence that proves any American remains alive in captivity in Southeast Asia'. Trust in the US government on the issue was low with seventy per cent of Americans in 1975 believing that their leaders were lying.

The *Joint POW/MIA Accounting Command* (JPAC) for all Americans from past wars and conflicts had the motto, 'Until they are home'. The command was deactivated early in 2015 following a series of embarrassing scandals and damning revelations in reports and testimony to Congress concerning failures in the effort to identify missing war dead. JPAC management was declared woefully inept, even corrupt, mismanaged and wasteful and about to worsen from dysfunctional to total failure. Exposures included inadequate databases of missing personnel, use of unreliable maps, unnecessary and useless travel and failure to meet targets. Thousands of dollars were paid out to 'recover remains of fallen servicemen whose bodies had been planted on former battlefields'. This sounded like it could in part be Pyle and Lia's handiwork. Identification times of body parts and site artefacts by experts in state-of-the-art laboratories in Hawaii and Nebraska increased from four to eleven years, long after the bounty had flown. There were also phoney arrival ceremonies involving non-flying transport aircraft towed to position and, later, disgorging empty flag-covered coffins before grieving families.

The search and recover organisation was reconstituted as the *Defense POW/MIA Accounting Agency* (DPAA). Conveniently, it posts on the internet the names of all the lost individuals. In Laos, 573 Americans were originally missing of which 287 have been identified and part repatriated. Of these, eleven are known to have perished, but the remains could not be recovered.

That left 286 bodies lying somewhere in the jungle, swamps, lakes and hilltops, most of them pilots. Everybody knows they are dead, but they stay on the list until remains are found. Less than eighty of them have an unknown fate. A US investigator is stationed full-time in Vientiane to pursue leads and to direct several large search missions each year. These missions often last over a month and can involve up to sixty-five US personnel plus their Lao counterparts.

The MIA teams never expect to find entire skeletons neatly sitting in cockpits. The impact of a plane hitting the ground can sheer teeth off at the jaw. All that can be expected at a crash site are bits of uniforms or fragments of hair or bone. Observers, especially if they have never served, feel that treating a dental filling to full military honours sounds a bit silly.

The rub was that paying for bones meant separating fact from fiction. I noticed that, in 1995, scratching sixty names off the list cost $160 million. Reading between the lines, a professional body finder in Laos with the right connections might expect $50,000 for a successful identification. With the endemic corruption and huge budget available just five years ago, anyone involved in the racket on the ground might quickly become very wealthy. For men like Pyle and Lia, the closing of the corrupt side of their business would have been devastating.

At today's reduced rates, with 286 men still missing, there was still a pot of almost $15 million waiting for a knowledgeable and committed local discovery team. I could see how a diary or papers from a leading crash team from the war might be valuable and worth risk and death in its recovery today. If this all added up to dangerous men wishing to find my father's village, if it ever existed, then I was an important pawn in the game. Once found, I would be immediately, indeed necessarily, expendable.

I made a phone call to the US Embassy using the name on my American passport and made an appointment for the next morning with a member of the DPAA team. Binh came to pick me up and shared the early results of his investigations. His main worry was that he was in dangerous territory. It was clear to him that some of his more questionable contacts were very aware of underhand MIA activity and they weren't talking. It was easier for Binh to discuss the death of his uncle and reactions suggested people didn't believe his professed ignorance of Lia's ways of making money. He had had no chance to find out about any secret Hmong villages, but he had found me an Hawala banker.

'You need to be careful with Hawala in Laos,' he said. 'I have never used it. It is run by the Muslims and I don't know whether they can be trusted. The police keep a very close eye on them because people say they are used to move opium money. But, then, if there is opium money, the police will be involved anyway. It is a question of balance and respect. There are police cameras trained on the front and back doors to check who is going in and out, but you can go in three doors down and pass through an internal passage. I got these for you.'

I put on the robe and beard, feeling a little obvious, and shuffled down the street losing three inches and made it to the anonymous green door. Inside, curtains were moved aside without question. I found everyone most helpful.

Over a relaxed lunch, I quizzed Binh about his own family. He had a girlfriend in the city who had just told him she was pregnant. Her family were in the dark so far. He needed to get some quick money to pay a bride price before matters became obvious. The need for cash explained his happiness to work for Lia without asking questions and, also, he admitted his immediate agreement to my terms. Handing over Lia's wallet had been a master stroke. The girlfriend was applying real pressure on her man to cater to all my needs no matter how personal or extreme in order to raise his income.

'So, you let me know if there is any comfort you need,' he said as he dropped me outside the new US Embassy. The building was in Thadeua Road, 9 kilometres from the city centre in the Mekong River loop that forms the border between the city and Thailand. Dozens of new palms were working hard to manage the heat among some desultory shrubs that looked as if they may have met their match. The futuristic cantilever-wing shade, which looked fit to deflect hostile satellite signals and imagery, was studded with cameras and aerials.

'I may be gone some time, perhaps a few hours,' I said to Binh. 'Watch the walk to the car park. If I am driven out, follow at a distance. Don't show yourself.'

'Yes, sir.'

I declared myself to a marine at the booth by the front door amid a stand of Harley Davidsons. My name, the only one, was checked against the day's list. I felt my first cramp of panic. This visit was a large and, perhaps, unnecessary risk. I had to admit that finding more about my father, about flying to Hanoi in the first place, was making me do things that were incompatible with my safety. I was on the run for heaven's sake and in a country where life was cheap. Laos had close ties with France and, therefore, with the EU which was still hungry for someone to charge with the assassinations of Juncker and Selmayr.

The name I was using here was not the one registered at my hotel or that I had given to Tshua or Binh. The US passport I handed to the receptionist, and which was placed immediately in an internet scanner, was the dirty blue descendant of the green one I had taken from the body of a mercenary in Morocco over fifty years before.[4] It was a biometric issue and while its content would tally with my body, the information could be sent in a blink to be checked against US archives and many of the world's police forces. My saving grace, I hoped, was that no one else had these details. Also, the passport had by law to be accepted in the embassy as proof that I was who I said I was and that, as an American citizen, I would be afforded the protection of a zealous state. I made a point of collecting the passport before I was escorted to a small, but well-appointed, air-conditioned office on the same floor.

I was in difficulty from the start and already beginning to rue my impetuousness.

'Welcome,' said the sharp-suited, clean-shaven, middle-aged man with cropped military hair. He smelled slightly of lavender deodorant which I thought an odd choice. He was already running to fat and needed to do more exercise. 'My name is Brody,' he continued after I took my seat. I suspected my chair's front legs were slightly shorter than the back pair to keep visitors unsettled.

'We don't get many casual drop-ins asking about MIA. Especially by older gentlemen, excuse me, like yourself about whom we have very little on record. I must ask you first to tell me about your background.'

He didn't offer me his hand, but then who does these days with Chinese-born viruses everyone's regular companion. He gave me the hard eye.

'You are entitled to your privacy, but you are, at the moment, on US soil. For our co-operation, you would be advised to remember that. As you would expect, we have close ties with the Lao authorities. We are here, in part, as their guests.'

'Of course,' I smiled, with my nerves just in check, 'just like in the 1960s.' I realised I had forgotten how old my passport said I was supposed to be.

'I was born in the US, as you see, entered the armed forces, as you can check. What may not be apparent was that for a while I was stationed here as a young man, in Laos, and my work was classified. I don't know if you can see that. After discharge, I worked as a mercenary in Biafra around 1969: a matter of conscience supported by many in your government of the time. Since then, I have lived wholly outside the US. I have another passport which I use for travels from my country of residence, which is France. I have independent means.

'An interesting life,' he smiled back. 'I see you have a property on St Kitts in the Caribbean.'

That was an unwelcome surprise. 'Yes, I do. I bought it about four years ago as an investment. It has appreciated very well. I have been to the island only once. I can't imagine I will ever live there. When the time comes, I will sell it. I have no family to leave it to.

'As you have stated, I am a walk-in, here of my own free will. I have information which may be of use to my homeland. I would like my presence to be kept confidential and my motives to be respected. I am not seeking any personal gain only information. You can do what you will with what I tell you.'

I suppose our little contest was a draw, which was the best I could hope for. He wanted to know more about me. I was a blank for fifty years on his files. But he also wanted to know what information I had. It wasn't in his interests to bully me so much that I walked away. Dealing with the CIA was always a matter of standing your ground and, he would be guessing, that I was probably an old employee of the Company lost in a chaotic filing system with who knows what troublesome information and contacts.

'I think we understand each other,' he offered. 'However, I have to tell you that the MIA team are all away on a search mission. I am standing in for them, so to speak. I am, though, familiar with their work. What do you have for them?'

I parried. 'Do you think I could have a coffee?' It always makes sense to establish a little authority. His eyes flashed, but he picked up the phone to place the order.

'Good idea. I'll join you. Cream?'

'OK,' I said. 'Please excuse me if this story isn't presented with military precision. It's been a long time. It is high on uncorroborated fact with a good smattering of speculation.'

He waved his hands in understanding.

I explained that I had been adopted, that my birth father was French, that he had been in the Foreign Legion and had served in Laos. I never knew him and, for want of something to do, was trying to track down his history. He had fought at Dien Bien Phu and had escaped. So far, it seemed that around the mid-fifties he went missing, rogue even. I suspected he worked with the Hmong and General Vang Pao, going native. I also believe that he led one of the Hmong units that were dropped by helicopter near crash sites to recover Hmong and US pilots, who would have been equally valuable to him. Where he found planes with dead crews, it was suggested that he made notes of the locations. I have no proof of this.'

Now, for the first time, I had his full attention. His eyes narrowed and he used a newly sharpened pencil to make notes on a yellow jotter. Just like I was sure his name wasn't Brody, which was probably his idea of a TV joke, I was confident that our conversation was being recorded on camera. I was also sure that he had just pressed a button concealed under the desktop.

'Please go on.'

'OK. I arrived in Hanoi about three weeks ago and entered Laos a few days ago after visiting Dien Bien Phu. Here, I won't go into details, but it has become evident that I am being followed. I have spotted the same men in different unlikely places. My room has been searched, twice. I know two names, Lia at Dien Bien Phu and Pyle in Hanoi. Some kind of literary joke, perhaps?'

If Brody got the joke, he didn't comment.

'We have had dealings with both these men. Are you in touch with either of them now?'

'No, neither. But I did find myself in the position of being able to ask some questions. It seems there is a gang, run by Vietnamese possibly with

Chinese backing, that wishes to discover if my father did indeed keep papers, as long suspected, and if they still exist. To do that, this gang needs me to identify the Hmong village where he lived. They are hopeful that I may gain trust where they could not. I suspect that this village is one of those that are still sought by the Lao military, people who survived attacks of yellow rain and never surrendered to the communists. I do not know the gang's motives, other than the obvious one that an income source dried up with the exposure of the JPAC scandal and they wish to replace it. However, you may have information that suggests another answer, especially with the Chinese connection.

'What I am here for is to pass on most of what I know, to ask for any information, rumour, you may have, and, if it comes to it, you will know the situation and be able to provide some unspecified assistance if I ever need it.'

'Quite a story,' muttered Brody as he templed his fingers. He phoned for sandwiches and more coffee which were brought in by an identikit agent who gave his name as Mathison. Was there no end to this? For the next hour, they questioned me closely, testing and retesting my facts and ideas. At one stage, I requested a bathroom break and I was escorted by a marine across the hall. 'Procedure,' said Brody.

When I came back, I picked up the chair and turned it around resting my arms on the back. 'Getting tired,' I offered. I gave them nothing more about my sources and did not mention Binh or my visit to the university.

'Give us five minutes, would you? More coffee?'

I declined and sat calm and still while my prospective handlers deliberated outside. They returned smiling but serious.

'We are impressed by your story,' said Brody. 'There is more than a ring of truth in it and it chimes with other intel that we have. You will understand that we need to do some checking before we can contemplate going any further.'

I nodded understandingly.

As a small offering, Mathison told me a story that I already knew. In 2006, fourteen years before, a group of 438 half-starved Hmong came out of hiding in the mountains after being chased and hunted by the Laotian and Vietnamese military for over thirty years.[5] This group had been visited after a trek of several days by an American journalist, Roger Arnold, who said that he found a 'forgotten, terrified people, living in squalid conditions, foraging for wild plants and animals, suffering malnutrition, many shell-shocked and injured from bombs, bullets and chemicals'. Their leader Blia Shoua Her said that more than ten families were still in the jungle and were waiting to see how his group was handled by the authorities. A helicopter was used to ferry the people, fifty at a time, from the village of Na Khae near the mountain of Phou Yeui to the Muang Mek landing strip.

'You may also not know,' Arnold wrote, 'that in the last decade the Lao military have used Vietnam People's Army troops to hunt down Christians and animists, even independent Buddhists, who seek to worship outside of strict state monitoring and control.[6] This is particularly targeted against minority groups like the Hmong, who have been hunted, brutally tortured and killed.'

'We have proof positive that four Lao Hmong Christian women were summarily executed in 2011 in Xieng Khouang Province,' interjected Brody.

'Look,' added Mathison, 'we are telling you these public domain stories because when we come back to speak to you in a few days, we would like to talk to a warm body. You are on the edge of very dangerous territory. Relationships between the US and the Laotian government have only recently been normalised. We must tread very carefully. A dead American would not help.'

It was my fourth warning in as many days, Lia, Binh, Tshua, and now the CIA. I was close to something. Far from clap me in irons, or get me thrown out of the country, agents Brody and Mathison were contemplating making use of me and that promised both new information and a degree of protection.

I hesitated for effect. As hoped, Brody decided that I needed to be scared a little more.

'The PDJ is a minefield of unexploded munitions. We dropped more stuff there than on Germany and afterwards over a third of them were still in the ground undetonated. Every rain, something new and horrible works to the surface and another Lao child loses its legs. In the three decades after the civil war ended, 20,000 locals were killed or maimed. There is a big trade in scrap metal. Off the tourist routes, you see piles of rusting bombs at every track corner. Last year, a woman took some grenades to market on the roof of a bus. Someone threw a case on top of her sack and, boom, forty dead villagers.

'Don't forget, too,' he concluded on a roll, 'that in 1975 the Vietnamese-Pathet Lao forces announced plans to wipe out the Hmong in revenge for them siding with us. The next year, they started dropping coarse mists of oily yellow rain on Hmong villages to force the clans from the mountains. These are *trichothecene mycotoxins*, bleeding agents, defoliants and skin burners.[7] They can last a long time.

'Don't go wandering off on some fool errand,' he concluded.

At least, I now knew my destination: the mountains to the south of the Plaine des Jarres.

'OK, guys. You win in spades. I'll be sensible.'

'Good man. We will provide you with a car back to your hotel. Call this number each day in the late afternoon until you get a firm response from us. It may take a few days.'

So, the CIA would know where I was staying, but also find out the French name under which I was registered. It was a fair swap, I thought, for information and some personal safekeeping. And, in amongst the havoc, I had let slip three dogs who could lead me to my destination – each unknown to the other. I collected my jacket from the back of my chair trying to decide what to do with the tracker I could just feel under my lapel.

As we swept out of the compound, I noticed Binh pull discreetly in behind.

1 Salak, *Cruellest Journey*.
2 Hessler, *River Town*.
3 Campbell, *Thousand Faces*.
4 Heal, *Disappearing*.
5 Kitchen, *Hmong Today*, 17/11/2006.
6 *Centre for Public Policy Analysis*, Washington, DC, 15/4/2011.
7 *Nonproliferation Review*, Tucker, 'Yellow Rain Controversy', 2001.
8 Shakespeare, *Julius Caesar*.

16. CHINESE FREEDOM

To every nation a term; when their term comes they shall not put it back by a single hour nor put it forward

Du Fu, *Spring View*

The nation is shattered; mountains and rivers remain.

Qur'an, 7:34

Binh was upset when he accosted me under a jacaranda tree in the hotel garden. He waited for the embassy car to disappear before pouncing. I wasn't sure what had disturbed him most: my length of time inside the compound, that I might be working for the Americans or that his friends with unpleasant motives might have seen me dropped off and come to a dangerous conclusion.

'Whatever,' he told me, 'you were not wise to accept the lift.'

I decided that his fear was a combination of any possibilities that might be detrimental to his income.

'You will have to take very good care of me, Binh. Anyway, I've decided to take a couple of days off as a tourist. First job, put this tracker on a bus to Luang Prabang. Can you arrange a lengthy massage for me tonight and pick me up at 0930 tomorrow morning for a day's sightseeing with a street lunch? Your decision.' And off he went, shaking his head.

We had a religious morning at the Wat Sisaket, the oldest in the city where the Siamese, in 1828, and the French, in 1893, brought the cowed Lao nobility to swear fealty, and at That Luang, the stunning stupa, glowing golden in the full sun. On our drives around the right-angled streets, it seemed there was building work on every corner, some Thai, some Vietnamese, but over half were Chinese projects with loud noticeboards and native construction crews. Binh took me to the morning market for lunch, a crispy baguette lathered with pâté accompanied by the obligatory *beerlao*. We sat facing each other under a shared umbrella on the rough pavement amongst the bedlam. For a small man, he had a large appetite. He told me he had no extra news as yet, but he had some leads. 'Perhaps tomorrow.'

'Well, are we being followed?' I challenged.

'Yes,' he replied triumphantly, 'but very badly. 'Twice, I had to slow down to allow them to catch up.'

I didn't rise to the bait so, after a minute, he could hold no longer. 'It is the Americans in a black 4x4 with darkened side windows. They both have crew cuts. They are so obvious. They are having a drink over there by the fruit stand.'

'They are not following exactly, I think,' I said, 'but giving us a little protection in case of trouble. You should be honoured by such an escort.'

'They are dangerous to be near. Where you want to go this afternoon?'

'This beer's going down so well. I thought the Mines Advisory Group followed by the Beerlao brewery where we could get a tour if you phone ahead.'

'OK. Can do.' Binh made a call.

'Would you like another massage tonight? It went OK, I think?'

'How do you know how it went?'

'Bong,' he said without any hint of a smile, 'is a sort of a cousin of mine. She is very high class. She tells me what goes on so I know everything about you so I can look after you. Bong thinks that she should bring her half-sister this time. She thinks you would enjoy extra company. Special price for good customer.'

'Tell Bong that I am in her hands. I look forward to seeing her and her sister this evening.'

Binh made another call.

The Mines Information Centre was a sobering commentary on the continuing effects of unexploded munitions. The designers' trademark was graphic imagery. At least, among the horror and blasted Lao and Hmong, I got some sense of the various types and sizes of the many nasties the Americans had left behind. It was a first visit for Binh. The photographs shook him despite his personal experience. The free samples at the brewery were a welcome antidote for both of us. At the end of it, a brewery is a brewery. We went next door to Buddha Park which, after a brief look round, I decided to escape. One can have too many buddhas.

A message from Tshua back at the hotel asked if I was free for lunch the following day. The receptionist was eager to confirm the meeting for me. Sengdao Kitchen is on Heng Boun Road with the more upmarket Lao Kitchen next door. I rang Binh and gave him the day off, saying I wanted to do some work and have a rest. It was a small restaurant and the crowded tables were taken by relaxed, chattering locals, professionals and academics it seemed. I must have looked confused. A woman waved at me from the back and I edged over.

'Sabai dee,' she said with a broad smile while rising in courtesy and bringing her palms together in a nop, templed to her chin. 'You must be the man I am to meet. I was told to look out for Denzel Washington. I am PajYeeb, Tshua's big sister. From your look, you were not expecting to see me.'

I may have been in my seventies, but my legs went to jelly. She was not as short as most of the Hmong women I had seen and read about. This was no squat mountain walker with bulging calves and thickened hips. She was ready for the Parisien catwalk, in her late thirties, I guessed. Her coal black hair was cropped like Mia Farrow; her tan skin was flawless porcelain with almost no make-up. She was cool, confident and unflustered in a white dress that showed off the exquisite colour of her face, arms and legs. This woman might never age. Several of the diners, male and female, looked up at her and then me in what I hoped was jealousy.

I struggled for words and went too far too fast like an awkward teenager.

'Hello, PajYeeb,' I managed. 'I was expecting Tshua, but then the message may have been wrong. But I have to say that I am very glad it is you. I am going to have to sit down. I feel that I am in the midst of opium fumes. You are the most beautiful woman I have ever seen.'

I sat down abruptly with, perhaps, my jaw hanging a little as I studied her with rude admiration.

'I am sorry,' I stammered. 'This must be very embarrassing for you? Not what you were expecting from a polite, elder European gentleman?' I loved the way she sat down.

'Well, I admit to being taken aback. I have never had a greeting like this, especially at a business meeting. I must own up. I find it exciting. I am delighted. You are not so bad looking yourself, for an old bloke, I mean.'

Her tongue relished the word 'bloke'. Her smile was something I could dive into. She placed a hand on mine and I thought I might die from the electricity.

'Shall we order? It is a broad menu, almost the same as next door, but the prices are about half.' I couldn't waste time looking at any menu.

'Do you like Lao food? Would you like me to choose for you?'

Without waiting for a reply, she took charge and gave a rush of instructions to the waiter. Within seconds, a *beerlao* arrived and a glass of perspiring white wine.

We talked like old friends for over thirty minutes as a stream of small white sharing dishes arrived which allowed us, perhaps, two tastes from each. Crab, snake, bugs, snails, river fish, a wonderland of experiment and delight. As a doctor, she had helped construct the tropical part of a medicine kit for future manned spaceflights. The subject did not interest her greatly. It was a career decision to participate. Her real interest lay in the Hmong people and their specific problems in the mountains, especially with those tribes still in hiding and without access to care.

'They have to rely on the old ways, on shaman and on their spirits,' she said, 'but some are gradually learning to rely on me. Of course, if I cure a wart, the word spreads.'

PajYeeb was forty-one, unattached, a widow; her husband, also a doctor, had died in a landmine explosion while visiting an injured child on the Plaine des Jarres fifteen years before. Since then, she had lived alone and thrown herself into her work. Her grandfather, she was told, was an American in Laos during the civil war. She didn't know his name. She was only distantly related to Tshua, but they were treated everywhere as brother and sister.

'My current worry is what happened to the Hmong who had recently been captured or given themselves up. The rumour is that they were stripped of their organs before they were killed. The organs were then shipped to China.'

I demurred, shocked at the accusation.

'You may have heard of Sir Geoffrey Nice, the British QC who prosecuted Slobodan Milošević, the former President of Serbia. He chaired an independent tribunal that found unanimously that it was "sure beyond reasonable doubt that in China forced organ harvesting from prisoners of conscience has been practised for a substantial period of time involving a very substantial number of victims". These organs were for use and sale in their burgeoning transplant industry.[1] In doing so, they breached six articles of the Universal Declaration of Human Rights.

'The tribunal concluded that these actions amounted to a crime against humanity and that anyone engaging with the Chinese should do so in the knowledge that they are "interacting with a criminal state".'[2]

'Good God,' I managed.

'Why be shocked?' she asked. 'Think about everything else they do, just because they can. Chinese self-belief is nothing but the original stack of myths and primitive rationalisation. Cleared of the mechanism of experience and contemplative vision, they can be manipulated without emotion.

'That's enough of me, mystery man,' PajYeeb changed gear. 'You wanted this meeting to find your father, I understand. Even if we could help, why should we trust you? You learn about this father's history, you make an inadvertent slip, Hmong people get captured, some die, the rest the Pathet Lao or the Vietnamese give to the Chinese and the Americans buy their body parts for their elderly relatives and their sick children. You could even be working for the Americans. No one speaks for the Hmong. You ask a lot so that you can complete your family tree.'

I just stared at her, appalled by the consequences she had outlined.

'You are right, PajYeeb. My motives are entirely selfish. What do my emotions count against a tribe that has been forsaken by the world, especially by the Americans?'

'I want to rub in the point of "forsaken",' she said. 'The final battle was at Vang Pao's mountain headquarters and airbase at Long Tien.[3] There were almost 50,000 guerrillas and refugees living in and around the airstrip. Aircraft brought in new troops, took out casualties, and kept delivering supplies of rice, tools, seeds and building materials. The final defensive outpost fell leading to the site's evacuation. Vang Pao, my grandfather, finally agreed to quit. About 2,000 CIA and their employees and Hmong, mostly leaders, were evacuated by heavy transports to US bases in Thailand. Vang escaped by CIA helicopter leaving thousands waiting in vain on the runway. Old People. Children. Women, including my own mother, one of his many daughters. He went to America.

'Forsaken! Gone were the American advisors and their vast stocks of supplies. Gone were the power and the glory of US hi-technology and their "can do" attitude.[4] Where were the Americans who worked and played in Laos in "the American time"? Where were the USAID workers and their families who once inhabited the modern American compound at "Kilometer 6"? Where were the "civilian" pilots with their heavy gold link bracelets, their big salaries and their daring? Where were the Raven spotter pilots who flew clandestinely in Laos to direct airstrikes in support of Hmong soldiers on the ground? Where were the CIA paramilitaries, with their gusto for counter-insurgency, women, drink and freedom, who had worked intimately with the Hmong since 1961? Had they just walked away and abandoned their friends of fifteen years?

'Then the Vietnamese shelling began. When the communists closed in, my mother and the others fled into the jungle. Some of them wanted to keep fighting. Some thought the Americans would come back and save them. They had given the Americans everything. Many CIA-trained Hmong fighters and their families had been at war for twenty years. Some made their way overland to Thailand during the next several years. There they lived in appalling, squalid camps, which still exist, queuing to get to France and to the USA.

'The Thais tried to force the Hmong back into Laos and the arms of the communists; over 15,000 Hmong escaped the camps in dread of being returned to a genocidal Pathet Lao. In America, Hmong people made a living in their communities by keeping alive a dream of returning to Laos.[5] Still others lingered in the jungles, their villages often unknown to the Lao government, their futures blighted by their erstwhile alliance with the Americans.'[6]

We were both crying.

'Do you know,' she said, 'that under the Carter presidency, the Department of State's annual *Country Reports on Human Rights Practices*, 426 pages long, did not even list the country of Laos.'[7]

Her face had crumbled with the violence of her feelings and her magnificent speech. I held her hands and said that I was sorry, for what, for me, for my request, for my father, for America, for the world's cruelty? What distant ancestors had given me this conscience? Surely they were free of it when they raped and killed in the palaeolithic world.[8]

PajYeeb began to quote a Hmong survivor who had resettled in the United States,

The communists know that we were the American's hands, arms, feet and mouths. That's why they believe they must kill all Hmong, soldiers, farmers, children. We suffer and die just like the Jews in World War II, but the world ignores us.[9]

After a while, as much to myself as to PajYeeb, I said that my father, a European with his reputation and record, could have got on one of the planes.

'If I am right,' I reasoned, 'my father decided he owed most to the Hmong. He stayed.'

She searched my eyes. 'That is why,' she said, 'Tshua and I have decided to help you.'

This was not a spur of the moment decision. Conditions had been decided before our lunch. Yet, I felt that PajYeeb had the final say and that, during our meal, I had passed a test. Something had been decided within me as well. I now had a more important objective than finding my father's story. How could I, thirty years PajYeeb's senior, spend as much as possible of the rest of my life with this rare woman?

PajYeeb's list comprised $1,000 to buy medicines for her Hmong or rather to pay the backhanders to get the medicines she needed. I was to go with her alone into the mountains, to hidden places. I was never to disclose where we went, not now or in the future whatever the circumstances. She wanted another $500 for food and a final $1,000 for hiring a robust 4x4 and paying bribes. We would be away for at least ten days and I should be ready to leave at midday in three days' time. I pulled out my wallet and gave her $500 on account with the rest promised for tomorrow.

'Can I see you before then?' I asked. 'I want to very much. You are, all at once, so important to me. More important than our adventure. I hope that does not offend you.'

She lowered her head and then looked up slowly. 'I feel the same way too. Impossible and ridiculous, isn't it. We should not be seen together before we go. You will need an alibi for your disappearance.'

She thought for a moment. 'You will receive a sealed envelope at your hotel. If it has been opened ignore the contents. It will be a safe address unconnected with me. Come there when it is dark tomorrow evening. You can stay the night. I would like you to stay the night.'

I kissed her hands. 'I should check outside. We should not be seen to leave together.' My caution was well placed. Across the road, sat Binh in his limousine accompanied, several metres down the road, by a 4x4 containing the American cousins.

'Is there a back way,' I asked, 'for you to leave now? I have unplanned escorts.'

She kissed me lightly on the lips and left. I felt like I had been split in two. I sat with my head against the cold wall. I cried quietly without tears. In my seventies, every year is a stay of execution. I knew I was coming to the end, not tomorrow, but the end was in sight just as I had found that I wanted very much to live. I would like to die in peace and dying frightens me. I have felt I had accomplished nothing, but maybe I could do something useful in whatever time I had left.[10] I was told there was nothing to pay.

After five minutes, I dodged across the busy street and tapped on Binh's window. He was deep in conversation on the phone and jumped.

'Fine watchdog you are,' I said. 'How did you find me?'

'I had a cousin follow you in a tuk-tuk. I need to protect my income.'

I borrowed his phone and checked in at the US embassy. There was a message. Could they collect me at 1000 in the morning for a meeting in the compound? I agreed but said I would make my own way.

'US Embassy tomorrow morning,' I told Binh. 'I need you to take me.' He looked hard at me. 'And bring me back, of course.'

I thought for a few minutes and then said, 'And would you tell Bong that I will not need her or her sister for the next few days. I'm feeling a bit tired. And tomorrow, I need to talk seriously to you about a mission. There will be a good bonus.'

'So, it was a woman you had lunch with,' he charged. ' She must have been special.'

'Careful, Binh. You could get to know too much. I may have to kill you.'

I spent the afternoon in the pool, had a quiet solitary dinner on the terrace, and went to bed early. In the middle of the night, I began to plan the rest of my life I had still somehow to live. I sorted out memories. I was practised. I had lived major changes before. I knew what was needed and I felt I could do what was necessary, except that I was much older and lacked the energy that brings confidence.[11] However, I saw the beginning of a way.

Next morning at the embassy was an altogether cosier affair. A flunky was at the door to save any delay at reception and I was taken straight in to see Brody and Mathison. Coffee was on the go, some French biscuits were on display, and there were arm bumps all round. Brody was pleased to tell me that he had approval to make a deal. It would entail sharing information of mutual benefit.

But first, I had to listen to a briefing, some of which was surprisingly frank.

The Chinese had long eclipsed the Russians in America's defence planning. The red flag's military and economic march across the globe was a significant concern especially with their single-minded moves in the South China Sea, ridiculous though they were in law.

'I have seen plenty of examples of Chinese expansion here in Vientiane,' I offered to show willing and interested. 'Particularly with the railway from the north that I checked out on my way here. Once it gets to the first Thai-Lao Friendship Bridge and joins China directly to Thailand it makes for a disturbing strategic link. Although, I'm not sure why Laos is so important?'

'It's not the half of it,' continued Mathison. 'Vietnam protects against a Chinese incursion into the west of the South China Sea along with half-hearted support from Cambodia; in the east it's the Philippines; Malaysia, Singapore, Brunei and Indonesia in the south; and Japan and Taiwan in the north. If the Chinese decide on even a localised hot war in the region, it's likely everyone, and that includes the US, will be drawn in. We've got a carrier group around the USS *Ronald Reagan* on constant flag-waving patrol.

'The Chinese are very serious about this. You may have heard of a politician, Sam Dastyari, who represented New South Wales in the Australian Senate. Dastyari was caught in a donations scandal, leading to his resignation in 2018. He asked people with links to the Chinese Communist Party and to a Chinese education company to cover travel expenses and his exposure in a legal case. Prime Minister Malcom Turnbull accused Dastyari of accepting money in exchange for supporting China in its South China Sea territorial disputes.

'Your point about the railway is well made. Landlocked Laos is Vietnam's back door. The railway from the north is high speed. Chinese troops will have access to the whole of Laos within hours if they wish. It's made worse by a little known 10,500 feet runway they have built in the Cambodian jungle at Dara Sakor International Airport. It has a tight turning bay in a style often used by jet fighters. The airport is very near Cambodian ports and access to the Mekong. The river would provide the southern part of a pincer movement into the heart of Laos. Vietnam is vulnerable from front and rear.

'Between 2013 and 2017, China invested over $6 billion in Cambodia.'

Brody explained that a similar second pincer could be seen as a threat to the whole Indian sub-continent. The first arm was the new silk highway joining China to Tibet. The second was activity in Sri Lanka where the former president Mahinda Rajapaksa was desperate for votes in his home province of Hambantota. He struck a deal with the Chinese for a new international airport at Mattala. The lack of demand got so bad that planes were forced to the airport and made to idle for thirty minutes before being allowed back in the sky. By 2018, all the airlines had left and there was no income to pay off the Chinese loans. Nearby, on the coast, Sri Lanka's second largest port is being built, named after the president, of which eighty-five per cent was funded by the EXIM Bank of the People's Republic of China. In 2017, because of heavy losses, seventy per cent of the port was leased to the China Merchant Ports holding company.

'Chinese ownership springs from Chinese loans. The whole of Sri Lanka is in debt up to its neck.'

'This is all fascinating, guys. My compliments, but I can't see what any of this has got to do with my father and the Hmong.'

'Hold on,' said Brody. 'We've not finished yet. There's one more item on the agenda before we discuss any deal.'

I nodded and helped myself to more coffee with a glass of cold water.

'The Chinese have been hacking into the world's computers for years to steal intellectual property and trade secrets. The US Government is getting mighty pissed off.'

Brody reeled off a list of statistics. The People's Liberation Army Unit 61398 had five officers indicted on charges of theft of information and intellectual property in attacks on over a thousand organisations. Donald Trump called it the 'largest transfer of wealth in human history.' Brody added the graphene industry in the UK; solar panels in Freiburg, Germany (after which theft China doubled its global capacity in the industry); documented targeting in the US of fifty retired nuclear and military officials; attacks on managed service providers like IBM and HP and at least forty-five defence and technology companies; the records of 45 million US employees hacked for spy recruitment; the latest fuss over Huawei and 5G telecommunications. Brody paused for breath.

'OK,' he said, 'I get a little emotional about the bare-faced nature of it all. Back to Laos. The Chinese have thousands of students placed worldwide in strategic industries and in university research projects. Even in Laos at Vientiane University, they have a group that is here to spy on crop developments, particularly rice yields. There is a Hmong professor there called Vang Tshua who has made some remarkable developments in low-water products that are high-disease resistant.'

I went quite cold at this revelation.

'You know, it's not as if the Chinese wouldn't have got the information anyway. It's just that everyone else involved is putting money in. The Chinese want it for free.'

Brody told me the story of two Chinese individuals, Wieqiang Zhang and Wengui Yan, who were convicted of agro-espionage in 2016. The theft of trade secrets was estimated at $75 million. It was discovered when the luggage of a Chinese delegation was searched and rice seeds found.

'Even Wikipedia has a list detailing thirty-nine individuals accused by our government of spying for China.'

'OK,' cut in Mathison. 'Enough already. Here's the deal. You want information on your father in Laos in the 1960s. We have it and we will share it with you. We will help you all we can in getting to the Hmong villages that your father was close to, but we don't know where they are. We will provide you with medium-distance personal protection. We will also provide you with money and transport if you need it.'

'And ...' I said. 'In return ...?'

'You do what you can to get into the mountain Hmong villages. We want to know what they feel today about the communists, Lao, Vietnamese and Chinese. We know some of them are still fighting the old war.

'Also, we are sure that your father kept a record of the crash sites. Vang Pao knew of it and talked about it to our contacts when he got to Montana. If you find any records of our MIA, you hand them over to us at a fair price. Only you never mention your contacts with us, like today.

'We also want you to contact Vang Tshua and alert him to the Chinese espionage on his work. For various reasons, it is inappropriate for us to do that directly. Then you ask for his help in finding your father. He should be willing to help. We think he's, like, your nephew or a cousin or something. When you tell him your story he will know that, too.'

1 'The Independent Tribunal into Forced Organ Harvesting from Prisoners of Conscience in China', lecture, Gresham College, 6/2019.
2 *The Spectator*, Rogers, 20/12/2019.
3 Vater, *Golden Mind*.
4 Hamilton-Merritt, *Tragic Mountains*.
5 Cha, *Dia's Story Cloth*; Fadiman, *Spirit Catches You*; Moore, *Free People*; Pegi, *Tangled Threads*; Yang, *Latehomecomer, Song Poet*.
6 Vater, *Golden Mind*.
7 *Report submitted to the Committee on International Relations, US House of Representatives and Committee on Foreign Relations, US Senate, by the Department of State*, 1977, babel.hathitrust.org.
8 Greene, *Quiet American*.
9 Ly Chai, 1980, Hamilton-Merritt, *Tragic Mountains*.
10 Camus, *First Man*.
11 Greene, *Quiet American*.

17. FREEDOM OF THE MOUNTAINS

Time will restore us on its course. Centuries come and make their way, but mistakes will be repeated. 'Vicious cycles' as Joyce calls them in Finnegans Wake.

Burke, *Vico*

I said nothing when Binh pulled alongside unplanned and unbidden. He was sensitive enough to keep quiet on the trip back to the hotel. The American 4x4 followed dutifully but stopped some way from the entrance.

I now knew, courtesy of Brody, that my father had returned to Laos in the early sixties and had re-joined his friends. The Hmong were known to the French as *montagnards*, to the Americans as the 'little guys', a respectful not pejorative term; the opposition were the 'bad little guys'. The Hmong fought, foremost, not for the French or the Americans, but for themselves and their own land, freedom and families. Members of my father's Hmong village all followed Vang Pao as did thousands of others, many desperate for anything to eat as the war tore up the land. The CIA offered rice and salt to Vang's supporters. Vang married many women from different Hmong groups to unite several clans behind him. A Hmong man may have as many wives as he can afford, as a bride price is substantial; a Hmong woman can have only one husband. I wondered how involved my father had become to produce a Hmong child.

'The CIA's initial plan in 1961 was called Operation Momentum,' explained Brody. 'We wanted to train a thousand Hmong men. There was a budget of nearly $5 million. Hmong attacks would bloody the Vietnamese and Lao communists and then the guerrillas would vanish into the jungle in what was almost the reverse of the French war in Vietnam.' Within a year, Momentum's budget had grown to over $11 million, by the end of the decade it was $500 million, over $3 billion in 2016 dollars.

By 1962, it was obvious that the Vietnamese had no intention of leaving Laos. My father first made his mark soon after arrival by leading a parachute drop from a Dakota near the village of Khang Kho with 500 World War Two weapons taken out of storage in Okinawa. The CIA recognised my father's decades of practical experience which were an improvement on the limited skills of their own field operatives. They must have known something of his history because Brody's files gave his CIA codename as 'Legion'. Hmong recruits often brought spears and bows or flintlock muskets when they enlisted. My father's job was to move them from stone age to space age; to show them how to hold a gun and to kill Pathet Lao and Vietnamese. There was nothing that the volunteers could be taught about ground craft, stamina or courage. Within weeks, the Hmong were firing sub machine guns. Each dry season, the foot soldiers took ground until the Pathet Lao brought up heavy artillery. 'The war washed backwards and forwards like a polluted tide.'[1] The very best recruits were sent to Thailand for flying training on single, piston-engine aircraft. This brought much misplaced military opposition because few believed that primitive tribesmen with just a few years' schooling could ever handle a plane.

It was the Hmong and Lao pilots who made my father such a respected soldier. They flew or acted as interpreters in slow-moving Swiss Pilatus Porters and small American Cessnas that could take off and land in rough-hacked clearings. Their main job was to act as forward air controllers for the CIA, spotting enemy targets for airstrikes. For this, they often had to fly among the treetops. A very few graduated to fly T-28 fighter bombers alongside the Lao air force.

A Hmong T-28 pilot, keeping tabs on the Ho Chi Minh trail, ditched near a jungle village. One good chute was seen and a beeper signal received. Hmong T-28s were not fitted with ejection seats until late in 1968. My father's team leapt aboard a Jolly Green Giant rescue helicopter as it left Long Tien. There was no sign of life at the crash site. Numerous enemy forces were seen closing in. The team landed, found their man, and walked him back to his base. It was all over in the same day.

Shortly afterwards, a Cessna light observation plane crashed into a mountain side while on a routine training mission near the Plaine des Jarres. The team went in quickly and found a burned-out wreck which they were able to identify as flown by a Hmong. Modifications in basic cockpit geometry are required to accommodate many east Asian pilots like Hmong, Japanese and Vietnamese. With shorter arm and leg lengths than Americans, the control stick was moved about eight centimetres closer to the pilot and rudder pedals closer by ten centimetres. The pilot had been captured by Vietnamese. The party was tracked, ambushed and the man taken home.

Trail watch teams, Hmong men and boys, regularly ran into trouble as they operated from behind enemy lines and had to be rescued.

With the advent of American bombing of North Vietnam from Thailand in 1965, Hmong scouts with their radios watched from mountain tops for bail outs from crippled aircraft downed by communist guns. Over the next two years, the US installed top-secret equipment at Lima Site 85 on the remote heights of Phou Pha Thi in northern Laos to provide 24-hour, all-weather, precision bombing. The site was overwhelmed by communist forces in 1968 when fifty-five defenders were killed; the great shock to the Americans was their own twelve casualties.[2] The search for the remains of missing US radar technicians was a major focus that was never solved even though Hmong search teams quickly arrived.

There were no friendly forces in North Vietnam. Downed flyers were doomed to capture, cruelty, a POW cell or death. In Laos, or just over the border, a crew might be rescued in sneak helicopter landings. Often it meant a long walk to a rough landing site. Knowing the rescuers were coming, the Vietnamese often laid ambushes at crash sites. Many Hmong died while trying to save Americans.

My father and his men became feted heroes at Long Tien and at Na Khang, Lima Site 36, 150 miles west of Hanoi, which became an essential forward base for these operations. Each morning, big US rescue choppers flew from Thai bases to Na Khang to stand-by.[3] These Jolly Green Giants orbited at 10,000 feet near the border for a couple of hours then dropped into Na Khang to refuel.

Long Tien became the second busiest airfield on the globe, unknown to the American taxpayer. American 'ravens', forward air controllers, typically flying Cessnas from Thailand, called in jet strikes, F-100s, F-94s, F-84 fighter bombers, from six major Thai bases. There were up to fifty missions a day, some in major battles like at Nam Bac, the CIA's catastrophic repetition of Dien Bien Phu. Vulnerable Porters and short take-off, cantilever, high-wing Helio Couriers dropped Vang Pao's men onto dirt plots that passed as airstrips for guerrilla raids. A gouge on a hillside often denoted a village's willingness to join the fight. C-47s, my old Dakotas from Biafra, still proving their worth, and larger freighters used Long Tien as did H-34, HH-3E and HH-53 helicopters.[4] You must add to this, high-level bombers, planes launched from aircraft carriers, refuelling tankers, and converted 'Spookies', Dakota gunships that operated at night. The aircraft were 'sheep-dipped' to remove all identification marks, the crews flew in civilian clothes, all designed to preserve the fiction of American non-involvement dubbed 'plausible deniability'. Aircraft casualties were frequent.

My father's team became the undoubted experts at search and recovery. Their knowledge of crash sites around the Plaine des Jarres, and wider afield, where American, Hmong and Lao aircrews died or were saved, was extensive.

Brody hoped that it was also documented.

In the hotel driveway, I explained to Binh that I would not be needing him for at least a week. He would stay on the payroll and I had a special task for him. He would drive around the tourist sites for a few days, perhaps an out-of-town trip, pretending that I was his passenger while I got away. I left it to his imagination how he went about it, but I gave him some of my clothes to aid the deception.

'Are we working for the Americans, now?' he asked.

'The Americans will be worried. They might give you a little trouble when they find out I've gone. They won't know where I am and neither will you.'

I had to push my way through reception and got the evil eye. A small group of aggressive young male Chinese were checking in. They hadn't the dishevelled look of holidaymakers.

PajYeeb had chosen our tryst with care. I was able to slip away from the hotel just after finishing dinner. Two Chinese gentlemen sat at the next table looking a little uncomfortable. A few streets away, I picked up a tuk-tuk to the Settha Palace Hotel where I walked around the pool and then found another taxi. I walked the last three blocks.

She had dressed with great care in black with a camelia in her hair. Drinks were ready by the pool, but we ignored them and made our commitment to each other. She was more tender and more understanding than ever I could have imagined.

I had schemed, lied, deceived, evaded, killed even, to be alone and to be free. It had been my single focus: to be a modern-day nomad without attachments. There is a certain moment when all resolve goes, when even the most determined person faces the knowledge that they have done the most they want to do on their own. In that moment, the only choice, perhaps the last choice, is to give in. Even as I walked up to the bungalow and its heavy, sweet scent of ylang ylang, I wasn't ready to admit that I was at that point. When I saw PajYeeb, all hesitation slipped away. I knew this was what I wanted, for better or for worse.[5]

Near midnight, we slipped into the cool of the pool and kissed slowly. I had a lot to say as it was now my obligation to tell her everything. Trust had to be complete. We moved to the small patio and she brought out some delicacies to match the wine. She told me my money had arrived and her preparations were well advanced. She hoped to have good news for me.

Then I began my story with the last few days: the money and corruption involved in America's MIA; my involvement with the CIA; the threat to Tshua from the Chinese and, in a wider context, to Laos and regional peace; my father's military and Muslim history; his time with the Hmong in the mountains; my instruction to find any records he may have left; my purported blood relationship with Tshua, and how I wanted to spend the rest of my life with her.

PajYeeb stayed with me till late morning and then left to complete her arrangements. We didn't talk deeply after my long-life story. She asked a few questions, nodding all the while, trying to place me in her experiences. I knew that she would tell me what she thought when she had taken time to digest my weight of information. It seemed to make no difference to the way she looked at me and touched me. I stayed at the bungalow out of sight although I did take a long swim. I spent the night alone.

Just before midday, a Chinese 4x4 pulled into the driveway, the back filled with boxes and a couple of spare fuel cans. PajYeeb had brought two male Hmong companions, one the driver. We were not introduced. To me, they were polite and reserved, but they treated PajYeeb as delicate royalty. She spoke briefly to them and they broke into wide smiles.

'I told them you were my man,' she said.

Their main purpose became clear when we pulled up next to a remote shack set back from the road at the 20-kilometre mark and they returned from a quick visit with two well-oiled, aging M2 carbines and a box of M26 fragmentation grenades.

The bodyguards sat in front while PajYeeb and I sat in the back holding hands. It was 350 kilometres to Phonsavan, our overnight stop on the edge of the Plaine des Jarres. The driver estimated the trip would take seven hours with brief breaks.

'You said that you were Vang Pao's granddaughter?' I asked. 'What was he like? Did you ever meet him?'

'He left my mother pregnant with me on the runway at Long Tien when he escaped in his CIA helicopter,' she explained. 'My mother said she stood with a little group of some of his other wives and watched him go. They say he had at least twenty-five children so I must have many cousins around the world.

'No, I never met him because he went off to America. I did go there once on a training course, but I decided not to get involved. Everything I know is from family members. They told me he was squat with an oval face, high cheekbones, a wisp of a moustache that the girls say tickled when he kissed them.'

She understood that Vang spent his whole adult life fighting: the Japanese, with the French against the Viet-Minh and with the Lao government and the CIA against the Pathet Lao and its backers in Hanoi. At first, the Hmong had more of an inclination to rally to the Pathet Lao under the Hmong leader Lo Faydang. Lo, with perhaps a third of the Hmong, received substantial Viet-Minh assistance in the form of cadres, equipment, and training. However, many Hmong of the Vang clan found communism inequitable with their strong belief in personal freedom and joined Vang Pao.

I was immediately struck by the similarity with my father who also fought all his life: the Germans, Vichy France, Algerians, the Viet-Minh, the French government and the Pathet Lao. The two men may have got on well.

Vang was a strong man, unafraid in combat, a brilliant tactician, who led from the front. None of the Viet Minh ambushed by him and his men was allowed to survive. He executed many traitors personally with his handgun. He built himself a two-storey home among the wood and aluminium shacks of Long Tien.[6] The main room doubled as tribal and military headquarters and held a vast wooden table so that a hundred men could sit or squat around and eat and talk.[7] He had a softer side as a musician and played the thin Hmong bamboo mouth pipe while stomping a foot on the mud floor.

Vang was revered among the Hmong community in the United States. Several of his business interests were later investigated and some were forced to close and he lost influence. In 2007, he was arrested for allegedly plotting to overthrow the Pathet Lao government. With some 'co-conspirators' he was charged with inspecting heavy-duty weapons with a view to smuggling them to resistance movements inside Laos. In 2009, after widespread protests, all charges were dropped. He was also accused of war crimes and drug trafficking. He died of diabetes and heart disease in California in 2011, refused a burial with military honours in Arlington National Cemetery.

PajYeeb sat silent for half an hour, playing with her thoughts. As we left Muang Khoun, the old Xieng Khouang, much destroyed, she roused and waved her left arm towards the mountains.

'Long Tien is up there,' she said. 'Few people go there now. It is remote and the military try to keep people away. We are not going near there.'

'Did your mother tell you what it was like?'

PajYeeb laughed. 'She certainly did. It was dangerous. The Vietnamese were getting closer and closer and eventually encircled the site. She always felt they would be overrun. Many thousands of young Hmong moved there in 1962 with their families. The place was full of soldiers, CIA, Hmong, Lao, Thais. The footless and legless hobbled about on crutches improvised from tree branches.[8] It was a CIA military base, one of the largest US installations on foreign soil and one of the busiest airports in the world. To keep its location secret, it was called Lima Site 98, 30, or 20A. Sometimes it was called 'Happy Valley', '20 Alternate' or just 'Alternate'. One day, a US Air Force Phantom mistakenly hit the site with cluster bombs causing a fire that destroyed the CIA operations shack.

'My mother always remembered the mountains all around. They had chilly nights and cold fogs. It was a desultory, muddy, sewerless town of 40,000 people, the second largest in Laos, suspected, but initially unknown to the Pathet Lao. Long Tien never appeared on maps and had no road connections. It had a single paved road running through shacks often built from flattened red and blue aviation petrol drums and cast-off USAID rice sacks. Eating shops, food stalls and living quarters fronted the road. There was even a whitewashed Buddhist temple, built by the animist Hmong.'

She sighed. 'Yet, you know, it was my mother's home. It was the largest Hmong settlement in the world where my people ran noodle stands, cobbled shoes, tailored clothes, repaired radios, ran military-jeep taxi services, and interpreted for American pilots and relief workers.'[9]

We drove into Phonsavan, obliterated in the American's Vietnam war and hastily rebuilt.

'It still looks like it was thrown together,' said PajYeeb. 'No character.' I agreed.

We were passing another Mines Advisory Group information centre, this one brand new and housing a museum for the Paine des Jarres. I shuddered at my memory from Vientiane. We were booked at the Auberge Phouphadeng just outside of town. The landscaped grounds were shaded by pine trees and bougainvillea. The wooden cabins looked faintly Alpine. 'I'm told it's a bit rough inside, but it's the most romantic place around,' she said. 'The other places remind you of Lenin.'

We decided on a walk to dinner after the long day in the 4x4. Our vehicle with both bodyguards crawled behind at a discreet distance. We had a beer at the Bamboozle! bar on the way, surprisingly full of tourists, NGO officials and Chinese mining engineers, and then wandered a few more yards to Nisha, a bare-bones Indian restaurant that didn't waste money on padded chairs or carpets. The vegetable jalfrezi was top-notch. One peculiarity, at least I thought so, was the small display in both places of 'cleaned' unexploded ordnance. PajYeeb picked up a tennis-ball size bomb and handed it to me.

'Large cluster bombs were dropped from planes,' she said. 'The case was designed to open in mid-air releasing thousands of these, packed with nuts, nails and bolts, and detonated with a spring. The bombs needed to turn several times before exploding. Some malfunctioned and hit the ground in one piece. Children mistook them for toys, played with them and made the final turn.'

'I didn't realise you were an expert in these awful things,' I said.

'You forget I am a doctor,' she replied. 'Every doctor in Laos is an expert in UXOs. American planes pummelled Laos for almost a decade. Day in, day out, B52s filled the skies and carpet-bombed village after village into oblivion to cut the Ho Chi Minh trail. Pilots who failed to use their payloads were ordered to return to their Thai bases empty and dropped their remaining munitions anywhere over Laos. By the time Long Tien was captured, Laos and Cambodia were the most heavily bombed countries on earth.'

We were a few steps away from our earlier beer stop, my arm around her waist, when I pulled PajYeeb roughly to the ground.

'Steady, tiger.' She managed a surprised smile. 'Remember your age.'

'No joke,' I hissed. 'I've spotted someone who shouldn't be here.'

Our escort revved a little and began a rescue charge but saw my waving hand and moved on to park further up the street. I raised my head carefully and double-checked. There was no doubt. Pyle's soldierly frame lounged in the bar doorway, seemingly at peace with the world, but his eyes carefully checking the occupants of the uneven evening traffic. PajYeeb's head rose to join mine.

'There in the entrance,' I explained. 'He says his name is Pyle. He makes his money out of MIA. He picked me up in Hanoi and passed me on to Lia, the old man who died of a heart attack in the garden of my hotel in Vientiane. He passed himself off as the uncle of my driver, a chap named Binh.'

A sickness filled my stomach. I had trusted Binh, had told him most things. Had I been duped, taken for a literal ride? As if on cue, Binh's limousine pulled up. Pyle shook his head slowly, and Binh slipped back into the passing traffic.

Why here? Why now?

After a moment's thought, it all made possible sense. Binh knew that I was leaving Vientiane quickly and quietly without telling the Americans. He had taken me to the university himself and knew I had made at least one contact there. Surely, that was with the Hmong. Chinese interest suggested something was afoot. Binh knew I had a girlfriend. Could he have reasoned it was PajYeeb? I thought not. We had been discreet. Where would I be going? Probably to the mountains near the Plaine des Jarres to find my father's village. This was where his diary, if it existed, might be found. Phonsavan was the obvious place on any route to wait and watch for me if they got here first. Perhaps Pyle had been in Vientiane already, brought there by Lia's death, just waiting in the shadows?

I took PajYeeb's hand and led her back to the restaurant and down its dustbin-filled side alley, pleased I hadn't seen the rats before dinner. The back was open to noisy housing filled with small children. We ran through the garden debris. Across the back street, I could see a drunken sign proclaiming the Phoukham Bus Station.

'Call your men and tell them to meet us here as soon as they can,' I asked. She pulled out her phone and issued instructions.

It was too late. As we crossed a loop in the road, Binh pulled up behind us and he was half out, one foot on the dirt, with a blue steel Smith & Wesson Model 10 revolver with its trademark half-moon gun sight pointed directly at PajYeeb. Known to people who handle guns the world over, variants of this .38 Special had been in production since 1889. It had been a US favourite in all its South East Asian wars. I had carried one while flying in Biafra. At this range, I knew it would make a large hole.

'Well, this is a lucky meeting,' drawled Binh, enjoying his moment. 'Move, diary hunter, and she dies first, whoever she is.' At least that was two questions answered. PajYeeb's identity was unknown or even suspected. And Binh and Pyle had come to Phonsavan in hope as I had reasoned.

'You sound like something out of a bad Western, Binh,' I countered. 'I thought you were my friendly driver working on a special mission for me in Vientiane?'

'Money talks, white man. We want the diary.'

'"We?" Who's "we"?'

'Don't be smart, old man. Not if you want to keep your friend.'

'Well, if I don't keep her, you'll never find the village or the diary, if it ever existed.' In the background, I saw a friendly 4x4 turn the corner and begin creeping towards us.

'Oh, it exists.' He waved the gun towards the car. 'Get in the back.'

I dropped my voice to PajYeeb. 'We will have just one chance. Go first and when you step into the car, slip and fall. Lie flat on the ground and start moaning.'

As she dropped, I fell on Binh's gun arm and put everything I had into a throat chop. The gun went off, punching a hole in the car roof. Binh dropped like a stone. Our 4x4 was alongside blocking the view from the bus station which was all but empty. I helped PajYeeb up while one of the guards leapt on Binh and then got up slowly, congratulating me. He said a few words and PajYeeb translated.

'He thinks that you are a top man. This driver is dead. His larynx is crushed. He apologises for letting us get into danger. He is embarrassed and they both have lost face.' She paused and continued, 'I listened to all the stories you told me, but I am still surprised by how expertly you did what you did. I am going to have to reappraise you.'

Nobody came running to see the source of the shot. No child stopped playing. No dingy curtains twitched. People were too experienced to get involved. The war was not so long ago. Blindness was a virtue. We bundled Binh into the back of his car and drove in convoy to the hotel, taking the back roads so that we evaded Pyle. I was given a carbine while one of the guards pocketed the revolver. The men then drove off in both vehicles to make sure that Binh and his car would not be discovered for several days.

The whole episode had taken just ten minutes from leaving the restaurant. I was a bit out of breath, shaky even, and needed the toilet. When I came out, PajYeeb said it was her turn. As I sat on the bed, carbine to hand on the floor, there was a knock at the door, a hotel waiter, carrying a bottle of good quality Lao-Lao rice whisky, ice and four glasses. I handed PajYeeb a full glass when she came out.

'I probably said things badly,' she offered. 'Tonight has been a shock. I am not used to violence first hand. I usually deal only with its consequences. I admire what you did, your speed of thought, your skill even. As soon as my men get back for their whisky and to watch in case Pyle turns up, please make love to me.'

'I hope they hurry up. I don't think we have to worry now although we should be on our guard. Pyle doesn't know we're here. He'll just be confused about where Binh has got to. There is no reason that he should connect the two.'

The four of us left at six in the morning. Nothing was said. I even got a slight bow as I stepped into the 4x4. PajYeeb and I slid down below window level as we left the old derelict town of Xiang Khouang. We turned towards the mountains and worked our way up a pot-holed road, which became a muddied, narrow, crumbling track. We passed deserted villages with overgrown fields surrendering to the jungle. Some were burned ruins.

'Tell me about the people who lived here?' I asked. 'These are the sorts of places that used to be your home?'

PajYeeb reflected then opened up. 'Yes, places like these were my home until I was about fourteen and went to school. Hmong rely on swidden – slashing and burning. Villages move mostly because to remain too long on the same cultivated ground would mean a slide into poverty.[10] Of course, here, the main reason to move was the frequent attacks, even today, by the government. The Vietnamese also attacked the villages and conducted illegal logging driving many from their homelands. All our men had automatic weapons saved from the war.

'In the dry season we grew rice and then, when the rains came, we planted maize giving us double the crops for the same number of people. We also grew opium, which was the ideal mountain cash crop, grown at a different time from both maize and rice and easily portable. Opium is often six times more productive than rice. We were always busy in the fields.'

PajYeeb paused and let her mind flood back.

'Ideally land should be primary forest, the higher the trees the better the land. While the family is at work, a wild cock chicken is pegged out in the fields to attract its fellows who are shot. Gathering is important. In the rainy season, the forest yields abundant supplies of bamboo shoot and mushrooms. Without straying from the path, it is quite possible for a family to gather sufficient vegetables during a walk home for the evening soup.

'They were happy times. I was bright and got a scholarship. That was very unusual from a Hmong girl. Being Vang Pao's granddaughter certainly helped. My father was the long-term headman, *nai baan*, elected from the village.'

'Tell me about your family?'

'My mother just worked the fields, did the cooking and raised the family. She was like everyone else, but very jolly. She died early from some disease. It was one of the reasons I was sent away to school.

'The *tsev*, the house, was very important to us. We call members of a single household *ib yim tuan neeg*, "one family people". We always ate together in front of the ancestral altar except when male guests were present. Dogs and chickens wandered into the house, cleaning the floor as they went. We had a stable for our horse. Cattle, pigs, goats and dogs roamed the village and its surroundings. We were animists and believed in the natural spirits that lived in our homes and in the trees. They demanded respect and careful management. The eldest male, an uncle, was the household head, not my father. When he decided to move to new fields, he took with him his ancestral altar and symbolic ash from the abandoned hearth.'

Four hours up into the hills, seemingly no different from anywhere else, we pulled into the shade of the green canopy. After a few minutes listening to the chatter of birds well above and watching heavy drops drip from the leaves washed by early morning rain, two Hmong men carrying machine pistols appeared at our driver's window.

PajYeeb smiled at me. 'Now for your surprise,' she said. 'Here is your taxi. I had to look after my old man.'

Two dun two-seater microlights that had seen better days were hauled onto the path and some of the medical supplies were loaded.

'When we arrive, some of the village men will walk down here and collect everything else.'

There was no ceremony and no time to protest as I was strapped into one of the machines. The sewing machine engine spat into life and my pilot took off downhill into the wind. We quickly soared in the high-altitude currents. I twisted and saw PajYeeb not far behind and we waved. Seeing the terrain, I was glad I did not have to walk. The air was cold and I began to shiver. We flew between the rugged and forested mountains, the purple karsts with their stalagmite rock formations which appeared and disappeared in the twisting mists. Spirits were everywhere, guiding us. After fifteen minutes, we bumped gently onto a rough field that leapt up at us. The village was almost empty, just a few elderly people stood by. When they saw PajYeeb, however, their faces lit and they shouted a welcome and shuffled forward to hug her. The few boxes were unloaded and the microlights were gone, their engine sounds soon lost.

'I'll bet you couldn't walk home,' said PajYeeb.

I was taken to a nearby smoothed log and handed rice wine and a plate of grubs. PajYeeb immediately got to work with a clinic. Elders waited patiently in line as she dispensed medicines, treated wounds and sores and asked for news of relatives and friends.

'You'll notice some of these Hmong have American features,' she offered. 'Some of these people are second or third generation descendants of former CIA agents. They stay hidden for fear of Lao government reprisals. However, these people and a couple of nearby villages are relatively lucky so far. They have not been discovered and they can live in the old ways and grow and catch enough food.'

A couple of hours later, the younger villagers started trooping back from their fields laden with woven baskets. PajYeeb began her second clinic and supplies from our 4x4 started to arrive on the backs of men who seemed to regard their climb as a stroll. We were invited to a hut for dinner, rice and palm rat stew from memory, and sleeping accommodation which was very cheek by jowl. For the first ten minutes, the young women took turns to shout out to PajYeeb, asking, I was told, if she was all right and did she need any help with her grandfather? Each enquiry was followed by loud giggling. The headman called for quiet and we snuggled up. I was told to expect an early start although the march, even for me, would be less than an hour. It was surprisingly snug. I felt very content. No, I felt very happy.

Next morning, I was pleased that there was limited climbing. Four armed guards led the way. The walk mostly followed the contours of the hill on discernible, but narrow paths. Even so, I found the lower oxygen level caught my breath.

'Today, could change your life,' PajYeeb said coyly.

'You mean if we find my father's village?' I suggested.

'No, that's not what I meant. Haven't you realised that that is where we are going? The people there knew your father well. He is a famous man among the Hmong in this area.'

I took a few minutes. 'There's always hope, but I expected it to be more difficult than this. Do you mean we might find his diary?'

'No, that's not what I meant either. Although I do hope for your sake that we do find something. My village spies tell me it is possible.'

'OK. What do you mean?'

'Well, the first thing is, I think it is better to warn you now. You may find many of the villagers where we will be staying for a few days look a bit familiar.'

The obvious crashed into my head: Tshua, my nephew; a village where my father lived for many years.

'How many of my family do you think I will find?'

'I would think almost everyone in the village will be a blood relative, one way or another. Your father was quite prolific. I think he took his lead from Vang Pao who had several wives, one of them a Lao called Mae La, the 'youngest mother', to prove that he loved Lao people as well as Hmong. You father's wives are all dead now as, of course, is he. Having been with you, I can see his attraction to the local women. We call this the 'French village'. There are about seventy people.'

For the past fifty years or so, I had believed I had no family.

'You're right, PajYeeb. That would change anybody's life: to find seventy brothers and sisters and nephews and nieces in the same day and all that could follow. They know of my coming?'

'Of course. They are very excited and have planned a great feast. Goats have been killed. Rice has been brewed. You will soon realise how important your father was, and is, to his village. The headman, your baby brother, has even moved into a new hut.'

'Why, on earth ...?'

'Secret!'

I plodded on for a while, deep in thought, then I remembered. 'You said "the first thing". What's the second?'

'Well, we have been getting on well,' she said, almost hiding her face in embarrassment. 'And we are going to a big party in your father's village.'

'Well ...?'

'Well, I thought we could get married, Hmong-style. That is, if you want to. It probably wouldn't count in Europe, but it would count here and that would be enough for me. And, of course, there would be no bride price although I expect my pound of flesh.'

The guards hid behind a large tree trunk as we embraced. As they crept back out five minutes later, PajYeeb told them the news. There was a quick conversation and two of the men rushed off down the path yelling.

The village was a whirl. Not only the son of their father present, but I was to marry Vang Pao's granddaughter. PajYeeb set up clinic, but it sounded more like intense discussion with the elder woman as to the correct form the wedding should take to meet with tradition and to gain support from the spirits. Both of our parents were dead and neither of us had an acknowledged home in the village. In the end, a deputation of the elders met and a format was agreed. I had to be careful not to drink too much and to disgrace myself. I kept seeing mirrors of my own face in the myriad of children, young women and the over-sixties. Babies were prized possessions and were carried everywhere in their colourful slings, adorned with lavish embroidered hats and colonial silver coins to ward off evil. Each one had to be unwound and placed in my lap. The excitement was intoxicating.

It was decided to start with a *baci*, the Thai and Laotian ceremony in which people are symbolically bound through the tying of strings around each other's wrists and forearms. The ceremony lasted into late afternoon. In the first hour, I had twenty white strings tied around my arms. By nightfall, I was covered in strings, as people, relatives and friends, arrived from nearby settlements. There seemed to be no end of well-wishers crowding through the door who wanted to share their relationship and to see and touch the Frenchman who was the son of their clan leader.

Before the first feast of goat and chicken, I was declared *ib cuab kwv tij*, one of the household brothers, prostrating myself before my new headman and my home. PajYeeb declared what had happened to Binh and how I had saved her life. I was a true son of my father. The whirl became a blur until I woke mid-morning.

PajYeeb was brought before me and a rooster was swung three times around her head to prevent her old ancestors causing trouble.[11] I was handed a knife and told to slit the throat of a chicken to placate my own ancestors. I was then instructed to kowtow to all my household ancestors, living members of the household and relatives, which meant almost everyone, starting with the eldest and working through to the babes in shawls. At PajYeeb's adopted house, I was provided with a live pig to give as my ceremonial bride price. PajYeeb kowtowed to all my male relatives. We sipped at two cups of alcohol accompanied all the time by chants.

We were married.

A group of elders, PajYeeb in the background, led me to a deserted hut in the village centre. It seemed men had worked through the night to strip the roof and walls so that only the central pole remained. This hut was the fourth descendant of my father's own first hut and his altar and ashes from the fire had been moved with each new building as the village shifted around the mountain to virgin fields. With great ceremony and respect, men worked at the pole until it crashed into the ground and was rolled away.

I was led to the hole, made to kneel and some of my father's hearth ashes from its base were lifted and patted over my head. Then, a large flat stone was lifted and I was encouraged to reach inside. I brought out a small, crude black metal box. The lid was loose. Inside were two documents.

The first was the identity card of a French soldier, my father. I read his name and saw his face. On the inside, was a terse list of camps and campaigns: Marseilles, Oran, Algeria, Tunisia, Morocco, Suez, Vientiane, Hanoi. They recalled the heat of the North African desert, and the humiliations of Suez and Indochina.

The second was a meticulous diary with tiny writing. It gave dates, details and co-ordinates of every one of my father's fifty rescue mission from the 1960s until the collapse of Operation Momentum and Vang Pao's departure in 1975 when the Americans also quit Saigon.

1 Vater, *Golden Mind.*
2 Castle, *One Day Too Long.*
3 Hamilton-Merritt, *Tragic Mountains.*
4 Pratt, *Laotian Fragments.*
5 Salak, *Cruellest Journey.*
6 Long Tien, also Long Chieng, Long Cheng and Long Chen.
7 Kurlantzick, *Great Place.*
8 Hamilton-Merritt, *Tragic Mountains.*
9 Fadiman, *The Spirit Catches You.*
10 Cooper, *The Hmong.*
11 Cooper, *The Hmong.*

18. FREEDOM OF SPACE

Warfare is linked with a particular concept of religion: each people has its own patriotic deity, a sacralised version of themselves whose command entitles them to destroy or subdue their neighbours; each deity cares for only his own people whom he furnishes with a divine right to conquer without concern for the fate of their victims. Each ethnic group sees its deity as bigger and better than other people's gods and final proof of this is in victory. Much later, when the number of true gods has reduced to one, the feeling of the believers was that the one and only deity had chosen them above all others: victory furnished the proof yet again.

Crone, *God's Rule*

Vang Vieng might be the world's most beautiful village, much quieted by government edict since its hippy party days. Towering karst mountains rise around seas of rippling paddies where conical hats bob above the crops. Stilted huts sprout along the banks of the determined Nam Song. Women fish for *khai phun*, 'moss', from the stream and throw it on hot stones to dry or set traps for freshwater prawns. The older children walk slowly to school, one arm weighted with books, the other pulling the family buffalo to graze while they study. Younger siblings catch lizards and rice rats to carry to the leisurely market.

Vang Vieng had been our home for the past four years, the place where PajYeeb chose to set up her free clinic for the damaged young of the land. Waiting for Tshua, we sat in that calm half-hour before twilight with our pre-dinner drinks. The veranda breeze was just brisk enough to keep the mosquitoes at bay as we soaked in the view of fishing canoes and children splashing at the water's edge. All was wrapped in sadness for we knew that we were on the cusp of losing our freedom, even our lives, as the world boiled to its greatest catastrophe. The Chinese were rattling their carefree sabres, confident in their destiny and oblivious to failure.

My father's diary, authentic without question, had the CIA and their political bosses smacking their lips. In quick time, the tiny, pitiful remains of over twenty pilots had been found, identified and returned for a burial in front of their loved ones, sometimes just the literal sheared tooth in a coffin. There were more bodies to come as the ground teams worked through the list. The hard cash savings to the US government in winding down their Asian MIA activities and the warm glow of patriotic TV coverage were considerable. It was a political triumph.

I was well in the background, guarding my picture as behoves a wanted man in hiding. Admirers misunderstood when I declined all direct reward. My terms were almost all altruistic. After a not-too-hard day's bargaining in Vientiane with Brody and Mathison, now morphed into a team of fifteen anxious to share the glory, and just me, my requirements were all agreed and, to everyone's credit, rapidly implemented.

The US committed to fund a permanent and substantial team to the Laos government for at least five years to hasten the removal of unexploded munitions; 'to take them home', as some wag put it, mimicking the MIA slogan. Part of this programme included the building of PajYeeb's clinic near the Plaine des Jarres, the world's most bombed place, and the provision of medicines, equipment and prosthetics, mostly little legs, for twenty years. The Lao government's preferred site for the clinic was Luang Prabang, which had escaped the war unscathed, its spectacular sixteenth-century temples and twentieth-century colonial architecture too valuable for either side to destroy. It was the Lao government's most lucrative cash cow, a UNESCO world heritage site with a rapidly expanding infrastructure of hotels, restaurants and cyber cafés. It was not a centre that cried out for a clinic for casualties from lost bombs. PajYeeb also decided against staying in Vientiane with its mixed memories. Vang Vieng was accepted by all as a good compromise, only about three hours' drive away from both or thirty minutes by the new Chinese express train.

The US also agreed to speed an offer to all the remaining Hmong hiding in the mountains, descendants of the civil war who were still under threat from the Communist regime. In return for a free passage to California, where they could join those who had gone before, the Hmong had to renounce claims and plans to retake their homeland by intrigue or force.

The processes for this minor emigration were already in place. When the communists came to power in 1975, they launched a campaign to eliminate those who had not sided with them, especially the Hmong who had allied with the US. Some Hmong opted to hide in Laos, others headed for the Mekong and the Thai border where impromptu, crowded and insanitary camps waited. Many were forced back by the Thais to Pathet Lao persecution. In the US, Vang Pao and his followers and associates worked to reduce the deadly repatriations. By 1992, over 125,000 of Vang's veterans and their families who had proved their service to the CIA were made political refugees by the United Nations. These few were allowed to resettle in the United States, France, Australia and elsewhere. Their resettlement was dramatic, troublesome and for some unsuccessful. Unlike the Vietnamese after 1975, many of whom came from educated families, the Hmong were 'probably the least prepared of any refugee group for integration into modern America life, even less than the Somalis and Afghans of today. Many were illiterate, knew no English, had no capital and had never been employed other than in subsistence farming and fighting.'[1]

My requested solution was not perfect, but it did offer an end to misery to many of those left behind. Over 1,000 Hmong came down from the mountains to take up the new and well-publicised offer. Few from my father's village accepted and no one knows how many others remained. The Lao Government, prompted by a generous one-time aid package, also resolved to accept this as settlement of the dilemma without violence as long as resistance stopped. A small UN team monitored progress.

Finally, I hoped, I had contributed. Through all the upheaval, my real identity remained undiscovered. PajYeeb received a US passport to go with my own, and I received a Lao passport to go with hers. My only other condition was that I kept my father's documents. The CIA was allowed to copy, digitise, circulate, but the identity card and the diary were mine.

After a busy year, we settled permanently in Vang Vieng even more determined to enjoy our lives together. We built a raised house like the Lowland Lao, which looked over fertile lands studded with wet rice.[2] As PajYeeb treated the local children, we noticed that public assumptions by the Lowland Lao of ethnic and cultural superiority over the Hmong declined gradually. The term *maeo*, savage, used as a weapon against the mountain people became more of a gentle memory, flaring decreasingly. A nation was building out of the debris.

I liked the smell of opium. PajYeeb filled my first pipe and lit the small ball. She had persuaded me that mild use helped deal with the pains that came with later years and would relax me. She also enjoyed the ceremony of preparation, even its servitude. I appreciated the sense of quiet a smoke brought at the end of the day. I had reached the time when sex isn't the worry so much as the effects of old age. I woke up with decline on my mind and then I saw PajYeeb beside me and I became young again. I loved her scent and the rise and fall of her skin and the gentle hollows of her body. I didn't want to be alone in my last decade. I wanted to be with her.

'We had a child with a damaged ear at the clinic today. It made someone remember Tony Poe,' she said. 'I don't know if you ever heard of him? He was the wildest and craziest of the secret war warriors who lived in Long Tien. Remember Brando in *Apocalypse Now*? Poe's character was added to Conrad's creation. The necklaces of ears and teeth as trophies for the CIA, the skulls around his throne, were no invention. Poe offered money for communist ears.

'What I was told today was that a CIA pilot had flown to a remote site and noticed that all the tribal children who lived near the runway had their ears cut off by their parents.'

'The world's a crazy place,' I said. 'Everything goes around like Eisenhower's famous domino theory. China was funding communist insurgencies in Burma, Thailand, Malaysia ... When Laos fell, then Thailand, Cambodia, Korea, the Philippines and Formosa would go. Eisenhower thought that once the first country went, the last would go very quickly. It wasn't all true back then, but it's truer today. And, now, it's happening all over again.

'I bet my future harp that in five hundred years there may be no Paris or New York, but they'll still be growing rice in those fields down there.[3] They'll be carrying produce to market on long poles and wearing their pointy hats. The small boys will be sitting on buffaloes, but they'll be forced to believe what they are told. They won't be allowed to think for themselves. Thought's a luxury. Do you think the peasant sits and thinks about god and democracy when he gets inside his mud hut at night?'

Tshua was morose when he arrived with his new wife, Hnub, 'Sun', a Hmong with a high bride price whose doctorate in medicine had been accepted by the university for a junior teaching post. Tshua signalled that he wanted a quiet chat. We left the ladies discussing the clinic and walked around the small swimming pool with our *beerlao*.

'Well, Uncle Ho,' the title was Tshua's little joke, 'the first human landing MOM, the MLM, is ready to go.'

His rice seedlings carried on the earliest mission had been a great success, racing to growth. My half-nephew's stock had risen and he was known even to Lao politicians. He was invited to speak around the world, except China. India's space programme was fiercely independent, but had recognised its technology shortcomings and its cash limitation. The result was a politically astute 'equal nation' partnership with the US that had brought credit to all the contributors. An embryo, manned Mars base was to be established. China's nose was firmly out of joint. MLM1 next week was essentially a supply mission. MLM2 in a year would see the creation of extensive plant production areas and here was Tshua's problem. He was not yet confirmed to go and it was something he and Hnub desperately wanted. Their training time was running short. It would probably be a 'full-life' voyage. If they went, their children would be Martians.

'The problem is the cash contribution,' explained Tshua. 'While I am accepted as the "father of space rice", there will also be other edible plants on the trip and they each have their own fathers. All the scientists want to go and their countries have made small donations. It's a matter of half a million US dollars for the poor nations. It's meant to be a gesture of commitment. The Lao government hasn't got two pennies except from aid budgets. They are not allowed to redirect aid money.'

'What's the position with Hnub?' I asked.

'This mission wants two medics from the start so that's in her favour. We're married so that's a good thing, too, because, after rice, NASA wants to grow babies. As you know, Hnub's very keen to go. It's also a good time to get off the globe what with China threatening expansion and everything. It's also helpful that we are Hmong, minorities and all that stuff. Even the Lao government is coming round, partly because there are no Lao alternative candidates and partly because of the need for genocidal contrition in the eyes of the world. It's certainly not any feeling of guilt.

'The unimpeded transfer of your Hmong refugees to the US was a first step. I hear on the grapevine that there's some trouble in California. The transition isn't going so well with some.'

'So, Nephew Ho, where to go?'

'Money, money, Uncle. Always money.'

'Who is the minister in the government who holds the key?'

Tshua gave me the name of a senior general, notoriously corrupt with a list of war crimes behind him and a firm hand on Laos' position as the world's third highest exporter of heroin and opium. He was one of life's movers and shakers, well used to carrots and sticks, thongs and handcuffs.

'And, speaking of the general, you should watch your opium use, Uncle. Nobody beats the "Chinese molasses". Morphine and codeine are not a good mix.'

'OK, OK. Thanks for the concern. Let's join the ladies.'

'I had one other matter that I thought might interest you,' added Tshua as we strolled back. 'The university is holding a seminar shortly, examining the influence of the Huawei telecommunications company on 5G networks around the world. There are some international speakers. Our Chinese brothers at the Confucius Institute are very upset as this outbreak of free speech especially as their bully boys successfully closed a similar seminar at Cambridge University recently. I know you are interested in the subject and thought you and PajYeeb would like to come. You could stay overnight with us.'

Cambridge's timidity had created a major storm in London. Huawei's 'elite capture' had deep tentacles in British society. I thought this was no benign strategy and had sounded off to Tshua at length. The Chinese plan was to undermine rivals, kill questions about its actions and to use the openness of a liberal democracy against itself.[4] In Britain, Chinese students provided over one fifth of tertiary tuition fee income and took one in nine places at Russell Group universities. The effects of the coronavirus brought about a minor funding crisis as new students were told to stay away at the peak of the pandemic.

A busy tabloid press found that Huawei had secretly funded a Cambridge University study into global governance of communications and technology, in which, predictably, the authors praised their paymasters. Direct research funding of this kind is commonplace. Imperial College in

London receives millions of pounds from China and publishes more than 600 research papers with Chinese institutions every year. The London School of Economics has accepted funding from Huawei to study the company's role in the development of 5G technology; money has also gone to Manchester's National Graphene Institute.

Who now, in Western business, academia and the media can feel easy about selling parts of the British heartland to China? And, yet, Huawei's UK board is like a *Who's Who* of the British establishment.[5] 'Incredibly, in 2020, figures including Lord Browne of Madingley (ex-BP boss) and Sir Andrew Cahn (ex-UK Trade and Investment chief executive) welcomed Sir Mike Rake (ex-BT boss) as he joined them – all three fervent Remainers.'[6]

Chinese law states that all the country's companies must help its security services on demand, whatever claims Huawei's management made of its independence.

'I'll be there,' I told Tshua.

Over the years, I got used to Hmong faces of all ages appearing below the veranda waiting for permission to come up. It was one of my great pleasures for they were nearly all family and I was delighted to make them all warmly welcome. I would see flashes of my own face and that of my father. As government oppression fell away, villagers brought excess crops, often opium, to market and then caught a bus to Vang Vieng. Some children lodged locally as they made their first steps in the schools. Older people with great faith in PajYeeb's healing powers brought their ailments for her inspection. Other times, people would just come to visit.

A couple of days before the Huawei seminar, in the mid-morning, a Hmong man in worn peasant clothes, tired as if from a long journey and wearied by his uncomfortable years, stood looking hard up at my veranda. I gave him a wave.

'*Koj puas nyob zoo? Kuv tuaj yeem pab koj tau licas?*'

'I am well. Perhaps, I can help you,' he replied. 'You speak the language of the Hmong people?'

'I am learning. My wife is Hmong. Would you like to come up and take some food and drink?'

'I would gladly take a rest. I have walked from Nam Yao, one of the camps in Thailand. I have been there for many years. I couldn't get to America even though I fought for them with Vang Pao. I could find no one to speak for me. They were all dead or gone home to California.'

He settled gratefully in a chair with a *beerlao* and a baguette. He said nothing until he had finished both. I got up and replaced them. A few tears trickled from his eyes.

'It is a while since I have experienced kindness. So many wasted years. The Thais are closing the camp and I finally decided that I had to begin my life again. I will seek survivors from my clan village. Rather than be transferred to the communists, I made my own way here. I was in that prison of a camp for over twenty years, at the end not daring to dream any more. Hope deferred makes the heart sick.'[7]

'How can I give you some hope? If you will not be offended, I will certainly give you some money to help your journey. You can stay here for a few days to get your legs working again.'

'You are more than kind. The reason that I have broken my journey at your house is that I heard of you in Nam Yao. I have come to see you. My name is Vang Kai.'

'Me,' I stuttered. 'Kai, why on earth …?'

His face split in a drained smile.

'You are the son of "Legion", are you not? That is what I heard in the camp. You will know how well the Hmong network passes news.'

My heart started a dangerous dance. No one had been able to tell me how my father died, just that one day he had disappeared. Memories were fickle or perhaps details were deliberately kept from me. Could this man bring a conclusion to my mission of the last few years and deliver it to me freely without effort on my part? Had the spirits heard me and decided to be kind?

'Perhaps, if I just tell you the story,' he continued. Kia talked for over two hours until I felt guilty and took him to a shower and a camp bed and persuaded a passing boy to go into the village to buy him some clean clothes. He agreed to answer more questions when PajYeeb returned.

This was the essence of Kai's story, some of the background only too familiar,

The American war in Vietnam ended in 1973. In June the following year,
the last Air America plane and the last US military personnel left Laos

to the Pathet Lao and over 40,000 North Vietnamese troops. In 1977, the Americans quit Vietnam altogether with their tails between their legs. The communists set about exterminating the Hmong. They massacred thousands in the Phou Bia area and began hunting down those left in the mountains using conventional and chemical-biological weapons. Survivors fleeing the terror sought a bitter sanctuary in Thailand. Over the next few years, all high-ranking Lao military, police, and government officials who had stood against the reds were arrested or fled. The extermination of the royal family remains a hidden, shameful story. Then it was the turn of the teachers, the nurses, the mechanics and the merchants. Many would never be heard of again.

Some of the Hmong soldiers, and what remained of their families, decided to stay in the mountains and to fight. They realised that they could never beat the Pathet Lao, but they might be able to hold on for the day when the Americans would come back and they could live their lives freely in the old way. One of these groups was based loosely on the search and rescue teams, a tight and hardened unit numbering about 200. My father, in his fifties, was the military leader; a young Vang Kai was one of his junior lieutenants. He was angry that Vang Pao had left his people on the runway and had not persuaded the Americans, who they had died for, to save them, particularly the children.

After months of hit, run, hide and hardship, the group while on a foraging mission was caught in the open by a slow-flying plane which fired three rockets.[8] They exploded in the tree canopy, releasing clouds of red, yellow and black smoke. Many of the men were immediately dizzy and fell to the ground, bleeding from mouth, nose and ears, some in agony with chest pains. Ten died within the hour. My father and Kai were on the periphery and thought themselves unharmed. Within days, all the survivors had fever, diarrhoea and could not eat. By month end, a further twenty-three were dead.

The group was pursued endlessly. Its members split into smaller units to evade detection and to make it easier to find food. A price was placed on my father's head. 'He kept cool and saved many of our lives.' Kai felt, and still feels, that many times he owed his life to my father.

Each sub-group was hit time and again with yellow rain. Sometimes *it would take fifteen days to die. They took opium when they could find it and this kept the lucky ones alive; it also slowed down the red diarrhoea and allowed them to move, albeit slowly. There was also a wild, white squash that helped.*

For months they fought on, always on the run, leading the communists away from their families in their caves. The men were virtually defenceless, reduced to using crossbows and clubs, eating leaves, bugs, lizards, mice, buds, and bark and desperately digging holes, hoping groundwater would collect. The new babies all died as their mothers had no milk. The Hmong were like animals, trapped, almost naked, emaciated and, increasingly, without hope.

Word reached America from a Pathet Lao defector that 50,000 Hmong had been poisoned and another 45,000 shot, died of starvation or tortured to death.

The day came when my father's small group could fight and run no more. They lay exhausted in a glade where the Vietnamese found them. Only Kai, as the youngest, had the strength to slip into the undergrowth. He followed the captives to the nearest town where my father, easily recognised for who he was, was taken for interrogation while his last men were driven away in a lorry to disappear.

Kia hid nearby for ten days with a Hmong family who shared their rice with him. He told me what he saw the Vietnamese do to my father, how he suffered and how he died. Then Kai left for Thailand, hoping he would find peace.

I do not want to share the details with you. I do not want to remember them. They are not the memories anyone should keep. When PajYeeb came home, I cried in her arms into the early hours without explanation. A few days later, Kai insisted on leaving and I bade him farewell and made sure he was well provided.

'Do you want to know where your father died?' he asked at our last meeting. I heaved a sigh and nodded.

'It was here, in Vang Vieng,' he said. 'Walk with me and I will show you.'

He stopped at one of the local primary schools, a little run down, but bustling with small children playing in the street while keeping watchful eyes on their precious buffalos and waiting to be called for lessons.

Perhaps I had become complaisant in the ordering of my world. I suspect that it stemmed from my life with PajYeeb. I was an old man for whom a need for comfort and stability was to the fore. I was settled, not seeking and not running. Some years had gone since I was hunted across Europe and North Africa. After my brush with the CIA, I lived in the open, but admittedly, my 'open' was a small Laotian bubble. I was no threat to anyone if I was left alone. I had found my version of freedom by luck and was satisfied.

I had come to terms with my father's life and his legacy, but not, in truth, with the way of his death. I was proud of his strength, tenacity and loyalty. If I had an obligation, it was to continue his work and to protect his family. Even though, at that time, I did not know his whole story, that had been my obvious aim in helping those Hmong who wished to come down from the mountains and in establishing PajYeeb's clinic.

It was a monsoon day when I travelled by bus for a meeting in Vientiane with the general who held a passing interest in the manning of MLM2. The sun at last burned through as I made my way to the ministry housed in a dowdy French colonial relic. There were double guards with Russian machine pistols at every bend of a dripping garden path and at each door. The crook was short with grey tight-cropped hair; his uniform shirt buttons strained under pressure. His hand was damp and the demeanour of his aide suggested I would be lucky to get five minutes. The general's eyes bore into mine as he assessed my likely worth.

'We have heard good things about you and your wife and her clinic in Vang Vieng,' he opened, as he sat down. The office was large with bulky French oak furniture to match. It suited a man of power. The walls were well covered by important European artworks from the local galleries. There was nothing light or Lao about this room.

'General, you are most kind and I know you must be a busy man. I am grateful for your granting me an audience. I wonder, if it is not an impertinence, if we could speak alone and in confidence. I have a financial matter to put to you.'

The general flicked a little finger and the aide glowered out of the door.

Thirty minutes later I left, deal agreed. The general would nominate Tshua and Hnub for their place to Mars as worthy representatives of their country. I would arrange payment of $500,000 to the joint Indo-American holding company to guarantee the places for two well-qualified Lao citizens who had already contributed so much to its success. The general would reap the benefit for finding the funding from a private and anonymous donor and thereby bringing about a great reconciliation between the Lao and Hmong peoples. When he made the public announcement, I would pay $50,000 into his numbered overseas account. The day the rocket launched with my little family aboard, I would make another identical payment. We would never meet again, except if either of us broke our word. Then it would be a question of who managed to kill the other first.

I left the general to break the news. I think my father would have been pleased.

I stayed that night with Tshua and Hnub in order to attend the Huawei seminar the next afternoon. PajYeeb would not join us as she had been called to an emergency in a distant paddy field. Each monsoon, the heavy rains worked more, ever more, bomb casements a metre nearer to the surface and the pressure of unsuspecting feet. At this time each year, she sat on our veranda in the evenings, tense and waiting for her mobile to ring or for some bloodied urchin to run wildly towards her rocking chair.

The hall was already crowded. The Chinese had crassly and rudely sought to close down the meeting issuing threats about funding. The irony of proving the organisers' argument was lost on them. It was enough to stir some excited patriotism among the students and staff which heightened when, in a show of arrogance, pictures were taken from behind an hibiscus in full flower of many of the attendees. It was a further irony that through economic migration and flight, many of the Laos present were of long-term Chinese and Vietnamese descent.

The speakers were from Thailand, the United States, France and Australia. Britain was considered too tainted with its associations with Huawei. I have collated some of the arguments reported in the *Daily Telegraph*.[9] While in their way they contain nothing original, the collective statement was new because it constituted open disdain and criticism in what the Chinese increasingly saw as their own back yard. They believed, openly stated, that the whole of South East Asia was a natural and historic part of their hegemony.

We had no reason to worry when China was permitted into the international trading system, we were told, because Beijing would observe international norms and laws. As China traded more with the west, it would import the greatest of Western products: the desire for personal and political freedom. And as China's economy became more market based, so its state would accede to the demands of it people for freedom. Our leaders seemed convinced of these things, yet, in truth, they were horrifically naive. China has abused the international trading system by over-producing goods and dumping them on other markets. It has engaged in mass industrial espionage. It has set debt traps for other countries to win leverage over them. Its state has not become more liberal and democratic, but even more oppressive.

Thirty years after China's communist elite signalled its determination to cling to power by crushing anti-government protests in Tiananmen Square, the regime's relentless pursuit of economic dominance has even prompted senior officials in the Trump administration to regard Beijing as posing an existential threat to world peace ... A powerful constituency among senior Tories that was led by the UK's fallen chancellor, Philip Hammond, argued that the best way of persuading China to be more co-operative in its international undertakings was by developing close trade ties ... The problem with this approach is that China cannot be trusted to observe the norms of international conduct. The more logical conclusion is that Beijing's increasingly insidious behaviour is ignored at our peril.

Surely the solution must be strategically right before it can be technically justified. Five Eyes is the name given to the UK's closest intelligence and security relationship with the US, Australia, New Zealand, and Canada. The UK is getting perilously close to a situation in which it is forced to choose between Five Eyes and 5G.

There is no line between state and individual in China. In scientific research, its leaders talk of a 'military-civil' fusion that would be unthinkable in the West ... A recent paper published by the Australian Strategic Policy Institute details the startling degree to which China's military scientists are benefiting from open collaboration with Western academic institutions.[10] Their top two destinations are the US and Britain. The relationships involve scientists from a variety of Chinese military technological institutes coming to the West to study subjects *related to advanced weaponry, ballistics, and military supercomputing and then going straight home. These students are managed intensively to ensure that they do not go native and start getting funny political ideas.*

In the 'supermicro scandal', some of the largest US companies were infiltrated via a tiny chip inserted on Chinese motherboards. Western companies have become doubly wary of Chinese supply chains.

At Vientiane, that day, the Chinese state felt itself humiliated. The seminar became an exemplar of an ungrateful disrespect for China's rightful destiny. The event was placed by the Party hierarchy on a level with what happened in 2019 with the extensive street riots in Hong Kong. The former British colony, occupied in the shaming First Opium War in the middle of the nineteenth century, was returned to Chinese rule in 1997 in a semi-autonomous contract under the principle of 'one country, two systems'. The deal allowed Hong Kong its own laws with its residents enjoying civil liberties unavailable on the deeply flawed mainland. The city's puppet leader, Carrie Lam, was forced to withdraw an extradition bill which would allow suspected criminals, including, perhaps, religious and political opponents, to be extradited to China. I say 'puppet' because the first Hong Kong riots, the 'Umbrella Movement', was triggered by Hong Kong being allowed to directly elect its chief executive, but only from an approved shortlist. Local people believed that with this new law, China tried to renege on the agreement and, in doing so, put at risk judicial independence and the city's status as a world financial centre, the source of its wealth. In short, it was a matter of life and death, freedom and trust, rich and poor, good and evil.

The damming stories came in a regular and worrying flow. A leading UK-based firm, Imagination Technologies, based in the US, was summoned by British MPs worried that its ultimate Chinese owner, China Reform, had renewed efforts to transfer ownership of sensitive security software to companies controlled by China. Their expertise could be used to fine tune the 'back doors' into strategically important digital infrastructure. Several senior executives resigned in protest. 'There's no point in taking back control from Brussels, only to hand it over to Beijing,' said one MP.

The point is that if China cannot be trusted over Hong Kong, then why should it be trusted over its Belt and Road Initiative. Over protestations that Huawei is independent? Over South China Sea claims? Over protestations about what is being done to the Uyghurs? Over infrastructure loans to many poor countries? Over denials about coronavirus?

I remembered the day when George Osborne, then chancellor of the UK exchequer, decided to make Britain China's best friend in the West. Even its advocates called the policy 'Operation Kowtow'. Osborne's 'judgement, powered by a curious mix of arrogance, naivety and cynicism, has been proved foolish'.[11] It has brought British silence as China abrogates its treaty responsibilities over Hong Kong. Yet, under Chinese pressure, British ministers will not meet the Dalai Lama and, like other Western countries, refuse to recognise the independence of Taiwan.

The following week, one of three Vietnamese fishing boats suffered engine problems and the little fleet drifted close to the Spratly Islands. All three were sunk by Chinese patrol boats and their crews taken away. China's twenty-five-year deal of 2019 with Iran for the direct supply of oil, gas and petrochemicals was renegotiated into a rolling five-year contract with payment in yuan bypassing the established petrodollar system. Iran increased its discount from twelve to fifteen per cent in return for a confirmation of a Chinese injection of $280 billion, a further $120 billion to shore up Iran's transport system in the face of American-led sanctions and the deployment of 5,000 security personal to protect its assets, including oil tankers bound for China. A further $500 billion was allocated for investment in increasingly scarce rare earth metals such as antimony, magnesium, tantalum, and tungsten in Africa and South East Asian, including Laos, all vital materials for wind turbines, capacitors, computers and healthcare equipment. Deals concerning copper, nickel, lithium, and cobalt, particularly important for the development of domestic and car battery manufacture, were included.

There are shoots of a fightback from the West against China's dominance.

Bruno Le Maire, the French Minister of the Economy and Finance, noted in 2020 that over eighty per cent of pharmaceutical ingredients taken in France were made in China. 'Do you actually think we can maintain a long term dependency of medication being made in China?' he asked. He called for deglobalisation of the economy so that supply chains were closer to the centres of consumption.

Julian Reichelt, editor of *Bild*, called in his tabloid for China to pay reparations of £130 billion for the damage done by the outbreak of the coronavirus. The Chinese embassy in Berlin called his style 'infamous'.

Reichelt responded, 'You shut down every newspaper and website that is critical of your rule, but not the stalls where bat soup is sold. You are not only monitoring your people, you are endangering them – and with them, the rest of the world ... China enriches itself with the inventions of others, instead of inventing its own. The reason why China does not innovate and invent is that you don't let the young people in your country think freely. China's greatest export hit (that nobody wanted to have, but which has nevertheless gone around the world) is Corona. Would you like to explain this to grieving widows, daughters, sons, husbands of Corona victims?'

Taiwan's Tsai Ing-wen won a third term as lady president, securing over two-thirds of the ballot. She opposed closer ties with China and repeatedly told her neighbour to abandon its threat to take back the island, by force if necessary, after it was lost at the end of the Chinese civil war in 1949. As democracy riots flared again in Hong Kong, Mrs Tsai continued to offer sanctuary for protestors, infuriating Beijing. Refusing to bow to Chinese demands to cease dealing with Taiwan and to recognise China's sovereignty over the island, three European countries, led by Czechoslovakia, cancelled trade deals over a 'bullying' contract clause. Official contacts and cultural ties were suspended. China moved part of its South China Sea fleet close to Taiwan's waters to evidence its displeasure. The Americans reciprocated.

China's readiness to act the bully stretched far and wide and included, for instance, the refusal to give Anastasia Lin a visa to attend the Miss World 2015 pageant, held in China. Lin was Chinese born, but a Canadian citizen, a graduate of the University of Toronto, an award-winning actress and holder of the Miss World Canada title. Her title bid wished to extend 'light and courage to those who still find themselves in the dark'. Her stance on human rights fell foul of China's thinking and her banning caused widespread criticism of China's willingness to extend its influence far beyond its own borders.

Under Xi Jinping, China became more controlling, more confident and more assertive. Driven by its own sense of pride in millennia of history, it was determined to 'take back' its place in Asia and in the world and consign to history forever what it calls its 'century of humiliation' imposed by the British after the opium wars.[12] Ownership of Taiwan was a popular policy on mainland China. After the Long March, all that remained were 80,000 men when they reached the northern Shaanxi province. They 'established a base and grew steadily in power, conquering the nation village by village, province by province, and in every town where they spread their doctrine, which was a sort of bastardised Marxism based loosely on the Soviet model. Fourteen years later, Mao Zedong established the People's Republic of China. The Communists opposed opium, foot binding, prostitution, and gambling and they had a great deal of support from the Chinese peasants who had no affection for the grasping landlords and the corruption of the Kuomintang who had retreated to Taiwan.'[13]

As we now all know to our great cost, in China 'face' and the dominance of the Party is everything even when, in the eyes of the free world, both are demonstrably in the wrong.

1 Kurlantzick, *Great Place*.
2 Hamilton-Merritt, *Tragic Mountains*.
3 Greene, *Quiet American*.
4 Timothy, *Daily Telegraph*, 17/2/2020.
5 Farage, *Opinion*, 'Freeing Britain from Brussels only to bow before Beijing', 22/2/2020.
6 Charles Moore, *Daily Telegraph*, 18/4/2020.
7 Park, *Travels in the Interior*.
8 Hamilton-Merritt, *Tragic Mountains*.
9 Nick Timothy, Con Coughlin, Charles Moore, Juliet Samuel, Jeremy Warner.
10 ASPI: China Everywhere, 12/1/2018; Exploring the military and security links of China's universities, 25/11/2019; Mapping China's Tech Giants, ongoing.
11 Nick Timothy, *Daily Telegraph*, 20/4/2020.
12 Magnus, *Red Flags*.
13 Hessler, *River Town*.

19. THE LIFE OF WINNIE THE POOH

Liberal historian H A L Fisher confessed in his History of Europe that wiser and more learned men had discerned a 'plot, a rhythm, a predetermined pattern' in history. 'These harmonies are concealed from me,' he admitted. 'I can see only one emergency following upon another as wave follows upon wave, only one great fact with respect to which, since it is unique, there can be no generalisations, only one safe rule for the historian; that he should recognise in the development of human destinies the play of the contingent and the unforeseen ... The ground gained by one generation may be lost by the next.'

Irwin, *Ibn Khaldun*

On the morning of Friday 28 June 2024, PajYeeb and I were standing with Tshua and Hnub near the entrance to the night market in Luang Prabang. We had come to town for a celebratory lunch. In one week, the space travellers would leave for Thailand and then the Indian Space Centre to enter lock down until the launch of MLM2. It would be the last time we would all meet. We would never see each other again other than by satellite relay.

There was forced joviality, raw excitement, tears and a few shared fears. As cover, a lively debate surrounded the choice of restaurant. Tshua favoured the *Manda de Laos* with a veranda table skirting the UNESCO classified lotus ponds. He craved a last charcoal-grilled buffalo steak. PajYeeb, unusually, wanted style for so important a farewell and plumped for *La Belle Époque* at the Luang Say Residence.

Hnub and I mostly listened knowing PajYeeb would eventually give in to her favourite young man. They bickered happily as we moved to the middle of a crowd lining the corner of rue Chao Fa Ngum. It was the street that led to the Maison Souvannaphoum, one-time royal residence now an up-market hotel, at least in the main building. Everyone was waiting to see a tyrant drive past.

Today's tyrant was Han Zheng, one of the leading members of the Chinese Politburo Standing Committee, who was in town to attend the formal opening of the new railway link north to the Chinese border. After lunch with the Lao government, he was to cut the ribbon, then ride in state to Vientiane and then on into Thailand for further talks on South East Asian funding. Senior as he was, Han was only just emerging from the Shanghai pension scandals and the dismissal of its leader, Chen Liangyu. Han led the probe into his former boss and the city's corruption and was feared as a result. The bodies of the guilty, half-guilty, and an unusually high number of irritating political opponents were strewn around. In a wider investigation called for by Xi Jinping across the country, almost two million officials were indicted. They faced isolation, sleep deprivation, torture, imprisonment of parents, and death.

For his successful suppression, Han was given the street title of 'Wang Han', after his clan's supposed dynastic antecedents in the second century, often shortened to 'Archduke Han', which displeased the central committee. Han's handling of his tour of Laos and Thailand was a final test of his return to the inner sanctum of the Party, but not too close, all understood, to threaten President-for-Life Xi Jinping.

A respectful cheer greeted a six-vehicle motorcade. A large contingent of watching Chinese workers ordered to attend developed signs of ecstasy for the official surveillance cameras. A small group of Buddhist monks held out ritual begging bowls before being ushered away. Small Chinese and Laotian flags were handed liberally to the tourists then snatched back and rushed ahead of the slow-moving convoy to be re-issued. Coloured lanterns and snarling masks hung limply from lampposts in the heat. The air was full of the people's beloved interest in any celebration. There was little innate enthusiasm from the many European onlookers.

In the first limousine, the mayor of Luang Prabang, Soukan Bounnhong, hair slicked for the occasion, waved gaily to the tourists and got a bemused response. Alongside, the bemedalled Major General Vilay Lakhamfong, joint minister for public security, scowled as befitted his office. As the second open car inched along, Han, Vice Premier of China and leader of the Communist Party in Shanghai, and his female escort, waved professionally. Opposite them, to my surprise, sat my current business partner, the general who had facilitated Tshua's trip into space, sitting starchily to attention, collar well-buttoned, and accompanied by his Chinese counterpart. The next two cars contained stern-faced Chinese special forces charged with Han's protection.

What the general did not know, nor did the Lao security forces even suspect, was that seven terrorists organised in two cells had gathered in the city during the preceding days.

They positioned themselves at intervals along the route. Strapped around their waists were bombs no bigger than cakes of soap with detonator caps and twelve-second chemical fuses. In their pockets were loaded revolvers … If one man was searched or arrested or simply failed to act, another stood by to take his place. Each carried a packet of cyanide powder so that he could take his own life when the deed was done.[1]

Street security was farcical. There were no troops lining the kerb and others, destined to be in the convoy, had been left behind in the crush at the Chinese Embassy. At the last minute, the first bomber, faced with the enormity of his task, froze. The second freed his bomb and broke the detonator against a lamppost. Han's driver saw the bomb flying towards his car and sped forward out of the way. The explosion wrecked the third car and wounded many of the Chinese soldiers inside. The assassin ingested his powder and threw himself from a bridge. The cyanide only burned his throat and he fell onto a sandbank where he was quickly captured by a shopkeeper, a barber armed with a handgun and two police officers. The other young and inexperienced would-be murderers all missed their chance.

My little group was not hurt and I ushered them quickly away and down an alleyway towards the Mekong, lunch momentarily forgotten.

'We can't afford to get involved,' I argued. 'We all have too much to lose. There will be a witch hunt among anyone who was just standing nearby.'

I guess that what happened next will be debated for years to come, that is if there are years to come. As we reached the Khem Khong road where the ferries meet the riverbank, I was surprised to see Han's car travelling alone heading back towards the Royal Palace well away from its planned route.

People were milling about the crossing terminal going about their normal business, unaware of the drama. The car was reduced to a crawl.

One of the assassins had made the same journey. I saw him leaning against a wall corner lighting a cigarette. His jaw dropped as he saw his target. The man didn't hesitate and drew his revolver. I pushed my family into a nearby café and watched as he walked to the car and shot Han and his female companion. A mob wrestled him to the floor and his gun skittered away as he tried to take his own life.

The next part is obscure. More shots were fired from close range hitting the foreheads of my general-in-crime and the Chinese aide-de-camp as they groped for their own pistols. Both men died instantly. Some said that the assassin fired all four shots, others that a man among passers-by picked up the assassin's gun to complete the work. There were reports of a gun fired from the ferry terminal. If there was a second man, he disappeared and was never found. I didn't stay to see as I dived for the café as the driver, unscathed, forced his car through the crowd to the palace. I heard later that when a doctor finally arrived all four of the car's passengers were pronounced dead.

I gathered up PajYeeb and the others and we caught a ferry just leaving, found a small restaurant for our subdued celebration, and eventually made our way back by taxi to Vang Vieng. As I climbed the steps to the veranda, I realised I had saved $50,000 and Laos was well rid of a war criminal.

Tshua and Hnub left early for India to make sure they were not caught up in any investigative delays.

It was as if a tinderbox had been lit. All the assassins were taken and some gory interrogations began. Two were dead within the day. None admitted to firing the second two shots. The young men were all Vietnamese, living in Cambodia or Laos; three of them had strong connections to Shanghai, Han's political base. The Chinese demanded that the survivors be forwarded to China and this soon happened.

The first theory was that the men were victims of Han's Shanghai purges and sought only revenge for their lost illicit businesses. Lao police, anxious to move the blame elsewhere, built up the Cambodian and Vietnamese links. The Chinese seized on the latter and moved more of their warships close to Haiphong, Da Nang and Saigon. Then the Chinese 'discovered' a link to Taiwan where all of the men were supposedly members of the Taiwanese 'Black Hand', dedicated to undermining China, and had been trained in assassination techniques by dissident officers. It was not long before the Chinese found a connection between 'Black Hand' and the USA and all was laid bare. The capitalist master criminals, the dogs of war, and their island running-mates, disrespectful curs, had jointly mastered the murderous plot.

China's aircraft carrier, *Shandong*, was sent to the inner edge of Taiwan's territorial waters.

The Chinese propaganda machine was in full flood. We learned sitting on our veranda, listening to the radio and reading the newspapers, that the killing of Han was part of a chain, long-planned by the Americans and the Taiwanese, a chain with links that reached Hanoi and Bangkok.

The fourth wave of China's Chernobyl, an even more deadly mutation of Coronavirus, had reared in central China throwing populations and what was left of the money markets into panic. Prices surged and it became impossible to get some basic goods. Few news organisations bothered to report Chinese food riots. This was something the Party was meant to control. The authorities had learned nothing from their previous experience and tried again to suppress early warning systems and their 'false comments and rumours'.

In some respects, a genie had been loosed. Chinese people remembered their hero, Li Wenliang, the original whistle-blower who had been questioned and warned before dying while treating his patients. The conversation about freedom of speech that followed was quickly reopened. Dissention was a direct threat to the legitimacy of the Party. More local officials were replaced for 'dereliction of duty', but these were the people that the Party encouraged after the first fiasco.

The Central Committee squirmed as they became an international laughing stock.

Official stories began that it was not China, but the US military, which had released the virus when they visited Wuhan late in 2019. Derision at this claim could be heard around the world.

China bought up most of the world's stock of epidemic equipment and then launched a global charm offensive by using its vast aid budget to curry favour with those countries worst affected by the virus by giving back the respirators. When the European Union ignored Italy's desperate pleas for aid, Beijing filled the gap by airlifting thirty-one tonnes of medical supplies. Many other countries in Europe, as well as parts of Africa, were grateful recipients of Beijing's largesse.

China sought to take advantage of the 'Wuhan flu' to replace the US in its global leadership. 'The rank hypocrisy of China's attempts to profit from its own pandemic will not be lost on countries like the US, which are under no illusions about the CCP's ruthlessness when its own survival is at stake.'[2]

The outbreak was the biggest challenge to China's autocratic rulers since the Tiananmen Square protests over thirty years before. Just as in 1989, 'all the indications are that the authorities are determined to use brute force to quell any attempt to defy the government's will'.[3] Some thought that the earlier crack down had 'cemented the dominance of the Party and kicked off three decades of a rising China'.[4] Chinese autocracy worked before; it would work again.

More billions of dollars were needed to re-stimulate an economy badly damaged by medical and leadership incompetence. The value of the Chinese renminbi was deliberately depressed to gain a 'quick fix' export advantage in a move that damaged the struggling western economies. Set on a path of confrontation to cover its own failures, China manipulated markets and embraced a currency and tariff war with a combative Donald Trump coming to the end of his second presidential term.

China's current account surplus essentially vanished. Capital reserves more than halved. The money for world-dominatory projects through road, rail and sea links, a modern silk road with China at its centre, dried up. Xi Jinping's personal stock took another personal hit when it was finally announced that the Belt and Road initiative, Xi's signature foreign policy which entailed large-scale financing of infrastructure projects in over 100 countries, was on semi-permanent hold. The policy was dogged by complaints ranging from 'ineptitude, inefficiency, poor governance, and debt diplomacy'.[5]

At the modern-day centre of China's corporate implosion was the self-made man, Xi Jinping. His credentials were impeccable as a survivor of the cultural revolution, displaying the right mix of persecution and perseverance. His father was a prominent propagandist and politician in the Party until he was purged when Xi was ten and sent to work in a factory. Like so many other talented Chinese, Xi's father was banished as an intellectual, or chou laojiu, 'the Old Stinking Ninth', the lowest of the low, the ones who could only be saved by the basest and most tedious labour.[6] The family home was ransacked and a sister killed. Xi's mother was forced to publicly denounce his father and Xi was sent into the countryside to work where he carried backbreaking loads. After a few months, Xi ran back to Beijing. Arrested, he was sent to a work camp to dig ditches.

Conformance was expected and failure criticised and promptly corrected. You were right or you were *budai*, 'not correct'; there was no middle ground. China had bypassed modern democracy because of the iron hand of the Communist Party to which all the country's inhabitants were subject and indebted whether they chose or not.

Xi was a member of the Communist Youth League in 1971 and applied ten times before joining the Communist Party. He studied chemical engineering at Beijing's Tsinghua University as a 'worker-peasant-solider student'. In the early 1980s, Xi married Ke Lingling, the daughter of China's ambassador to the United Kingdom. They divorced within a few years, 'fighting every day'. Ke moved to England. In 1987, Xi's second wife was a prominent Chinese folk singer Peng Liyuan, then more famous than he was. Their daughter graduated from Harvard University in 2015 where she studied under a pseudonym.

Xi was a man, so the story went, who understood the time in which he was born. He sensed the secret forces. He felt in himself something cognate that drove him forward on a path neither hedged nor defined by concepts, with no trust in public opinion, empty phrases and the gods of the day. As a real leader, he was distinguished from the mere politician, those who play for the pleasure of the game, who sought wealth, rank, and acclaim, and could not grasp the real mood, those who would not demand sacrifices, and would not be capable of the deeds which were necessary.[7]

The CCP could not resist pumping out false propaganda which highlighted the superiority of the communist system. It even published a book in several languages praising the role that President Xi Jinping personally played in curbing the coronavirus outbreak. Meanwhile, detractors were imprisoned or disappeared.

If anything, my life had been a distrust of the order imposed directly on me by those who knew best or, if they had the time for honesty, what suited them most in their quest for power and money. So, I cursed the politicians, the industrialists, the bankers, the generals, the high priests. Intellectual pessimism was a characteristic of my age.

In both Ibn Khaldun and the Chinese versions of the cyclical theory of history, the fall of settled dynasties was inevitable brought about by the nomads, the tribal conquerors. Some saw the passing from dynasty to dynasty, or nation to nation, happening every 240 years.[8] Others posited the inevitability of decline.[9] It was pointless to seek to reform political institutions or society since their failings merely reflected the dreadful failings of human nature.[10] Man is the source of all evils which befall him.

Xi had made misjudgement after misjudgement when it came to relations with the West. In particular, he had not understood that American patience had snapped. China's economic model involved bribery, corruption, sucking up western industrial secrets and buying up foreign business while refusing access to its own markets. China's admittance to the World Trade Organisation on lax and uncensored terms had been a disaster.[11]

Xi was seen to have over-reached which worried many in his politburo. The Silk Road looked more and more like a vanity project where his ego had outgrown his position. Trying to become emperor for life was not turning out to be a wise move. Other innovations, like the app containing the thoughts of Chairman Xi, were worryingly reminiscent of an uglier era.[12] Meanwhile, the British circled like lapdogs letting a professed enemy into their most delicate infrastructures.

The first instinct of bullies is to bully. As Xi's prestige crumbled, dissent on the internet was quashed. Within the space of a few days, criticism on China's social media was subjected to heavy censorship. Dangerous banned phrases included, 'I don't agree'; 'migration' (Uyghurs); 'overreach' (Belt and Road); 'debt traps' (every nation on the Belt and Road); 'Taiwan' (doesn't exist); 'emigration' (better life away from the Party); 'whistle blower' (Li Wenliang); 're-election', 'election term', 'constitution amendment or term', 'proclaiming oneself an emperor' (all considering the implications of 'president for life' in 2018 with its lack of provision for an orderly succession).[13]

People everywhere talked about *Gaige Kaifang*, 'Reform and Opening', which included both increased contact with the outside world and the capitalist-style economic reforms that one of Xi's predecessors, Deng Xiaoping, had initiated in 1978. To a certain degree, 'Reform and Opening' was similar to the Russian concept of *Perestroika* and *Glasnost*, with one critical difference, the Chinese term lacked an explicit political component, as the country's leaders had no intention of opening the political system in the manner of Gorbachev.[14] Everywhere there were slogans blazoned on giant posters. 'Historical Materialism', the 'People's Democratic Dictatorship', 'Socialism with Chinese Characteristics' and which were never explainable in simple language, if they were understood at all. It was, as Orwell said, a case in which words and meaning had parted company. All that mattered was that the correct terminology was used in the correct political framework. Understanding was not a requirement.

With tensions over military intervention at a high level, BBC TV ran a three-part ruler over 'A New World Order'. It conjectured about Xi's family's personal wealth in companies and accounts controlled by his sister-in-law and other family members. Assets were later sold down to avoid scrutiny in any clampdown on corruption. Bloomberg disclosed a fortune of $380 million and its website was closed in China within minutes. Relatives of highly placed Chinese officials, including seven current and former senior leaders of the Party's Politburo were named in the Panama Papers links to graft, including Deng Jiagui, Xi's brother-in-law. Deng had two shell companies in the British Virgin Islands which quickly became dormant.[15]

The disclosure brought the children's bear hero, Winnie the Pooh, to the heart of Chinese politics. Winnie the Pooh was the recognised internet nickname for Xi Jinping initially allowing criticism of him to escape the censor's net. The subterfuge was recognised and that meant that Winnie's days were numbered; the bear had to go.

The cult of personality built around Xi since he entered office included books, cartoons, pop songs and dance routines. He was often called *Xi Dada*, 'Uncle or Papa Xi'. His village was now a shrine. Could Xi separate himself from the official worship and not be enmeshed in its enthusiasm?

I shared with PajYeeb some words about the inevitability of it all as I stood over my grandfather's grave at Soissons a few years before, but a lifetime ago: 'The soil was strewn with children who had been fathers of greying men who thought they were living in the present time. In the dizziness of that moment, the statue of every man eventually erects and that hardens in the fire of years, into which he then creeps and there awaits its final crumbling, that statue was rapidly cracking, it was already collapsing.'

In my case, all that was left was an anguished heart, eager to live, rebelling against the deadly order of the world that had been with me for over seventy years, and 'still struggling against the wall that separated me from the secret of all life, wanting to go further, to go beyond, and to discover, discover before dying, discover at last in order to be, just once to be, not for a single second, but for ever'.[16]

Xi went where all tyrants go when their power base is failing. He refused to accept that death must conquer in the end. He invented an external enemy in a final bid to unite 'his people' behind him. He took the great gamble for his own futile purposes. He risked the future of the entire population of the world. Bertrand Russell recognised his trait during the first great world war, 'We blow out a soap bubble as long and as large as possible, although we know perfectly well that it will burst'.[17]

The Chinese sent their fighter bombers to Cambodia's Dara Sakor International Airport. From there, airborne troops moved south to the ports. Incoming freighters, already at sea for a week, unloaded dozens of high-powered patrol boats which took control of the Mekong to the Laos border for 'joint training exercises'.

Xi waited a week to note the international reaction. Vietnam mobilised, moved forces to its western and eastern borders and called on the Russians for assistance. Putin threatened intervention but did nothing more except than to move deeper into Crimea. North Korea said its rockets were trained on Seoul and Tokyo. South Korea went to a war footing. Japan, Taiwan, and the Philippines followed suit except that they called for support from America where Trump was bellicose but placed no more warships in the South China Sea. The EU and the Pope and Keir Starmer begged for calm. World markets collapsed, currencies halved in value, and those countries committed to globalisation saw their vital manufacturing imports fall to nothing.

Standing shaky amidst the wreckage was China's 'Made in China' plan, announced in 2015 and due for part-completion next year. While the world might have come to China for cheap, low quality goods, increasingly the offer included higher value products and services built on stolen information. Chinese self-sufficiency came from a significant upgrading of its industrial and technological capacity by nearly seventy per cent, seen by Beijing as a means of boosting self-reliance and averting the middle-income trap.[18]

The Indians decided to press on with their Mars flight. PajYeeb and I stood on our veranda and raised a glass of rice wine to the invisible speck of the rocket launch far away to the west. We felt the push of the massive engines, felt every shudder as the atmosphere sought to stop the escape, held our breath and then they were free. We hoped that it was a 'cruise into infinite space and liberty, as a brief escape from the thousand fetters mankind has placed upon man under the pretence of progress'.[19] It was a rival existence, we prayed, ignorant of good and evil, living with limited effort and without petty regulation, an upright and a good life. It was, in short, a flight from all the falseness and corruption that civilisation has put into the heart of man, the realisation of the dream, which, though played with many philosophies, had been accomplished by none.

The next day, the Chinese invaded Taiwan, landing thousands of troops at five points. The Americans gave an ultimatum, 'Withdraw within twelve hours or face the full consequences.'

Xi called on 'his people' to stand tall in the attacks from all quarters on China and the Party. Five special trains left Boten, laden with soldiers, heading for Luang Prabang and Vientiane at the 'invitation' of the Lao government in order to protect the country from Vietnamese attack. Thailand and Myanmar sought to remain neutral. The Russians moved huge forces to its eastern borders.

My arrogant search for freedom had come to rely on a rocket heading for a hostile planet. PajYeeb and I sat on the veranda, hand in hand, long into the night waiting for the Chinese to arrive in our town. I read to her extracts from some recent articles about what we might expect from the Chinese surveillance society. High-definition cameras were mounted on buildings, in cars, in buses, on police officers' jackets, helicopters, drones alerted by algorithms, all interlinked in a surveillance net which took us far beyond anything that Orwell ever imagined. This was not restricted to video or facial recordings, day or night, all recognised now as functions of childlike simplicity. This was thermal imaging and motion tracking and directional microphones which captured every single movement of every person in sight of any camera. Data was instantly analysed to predict subsequent movements and then linked to any technology that the individual had ever used, from X-ray scanners to credit cards to mobile phone GPS to body temperature in hospitals. On the one hand, it could predict a heart attack, or a fight in a school playground or, on the other, anything that the state wished to stop their citizens doing.[20]

Every Chinese had been allocated a place in the 'individual social credit information system' which records all convicted criminals and all misdemeanours like smoking in public areas, travelling without a ticket, crossing the road at the wrong place, insulting a neighbour or behaving in a disorderly way. Every government department provides input to the system. Only good, state-defined behaviour is tolerated, any malpractice, anywhere, against deemed correct actions results in demerits and punishments. At the lowest level this includes broadcasting faces, names and addresses on public billboards; more seriously, it includes travel restrictions, lost availability to buy favourite goods, curtailed driving licences, and loss of employment.

I puffed slowly on my pipe and PajYeeb thought it might be the right time to join me. It would be our last moment of freedom? We wondered what the Americans would do? How long would the Taiwanese and the Vietnamese hold out? Would some lunatic in North Korea press the wrong button?

'Perhaps some later writer, aided by the divine gifts of a sound mind and solid scholarship, will penetrate these problems in greater detail than I have here. God knows and you do not know.'[21]

1 Clark, *Sleepwalkers*.
2 Coughlin, *Daily Telegraph*, 25/3/2020.
3 Coughlin, *Daily Telegraph*, 12/2/2020.
4 Magnus, *Red Flags*.
5 Magnus, *Red Flags*.
6 Hessler, *River Town*.
7 Spengler, *Der Untergang des Abendlandes*.
8 Khaldun, *Muqaddima*, Vol. 2. Lewis, *Islam in History*, 'Islamic Concepts'. Irwin, *Khaldun. Rasa'il Ikhwan al-Safa*, 'Letters of the Brethren of Purity', tenth century encyclopaedia. Also Polybius, the Greek chronicler of the decline of Greece and of Rome's rise to power.

9 Crone, *Slaves on Horses*.

10 Schopenhauer, *World as Will and Representation*. Irwin, *Khaldun*.

11 Paterson, *China, Trade and Power*.

12 *Spectator*, 6/7 & 21/9/2019.

13 Magnus, *Red Flags*.

14 Hessler, *River Town*.

15 The Panama Papers are 11.5 million leaked documents that detail financial and attorney–client information for more than 214,488 offshore entities. The documents, some dating back to the 1970s, were created by, and taken from, Panamanian law firm and corporate service provider Mossack Fonseca.

16 Camus, *First Man*.

17 Russell, History of Philosophy.

18 Magnus, *Red Flags*.

19 Dubois, *Mysterious*.

20 *Spectator*: O'Malley, 17/11/2018; Daw, 6/7/2019.

21 Ibn Khaldun, *Muqaddima*, Vol. 3.

READING LIST

Abdel Haleem, M A S, translated, *The Qur'an* (Oxford University Press 2010)

Ainley, Henry, *In order to Die* (1955; 2019, Gyan, New Delhi)

Allison, Graham, *Destined For War, Can America And China Escape Thucydides's Trap?* (Scribe, London 2019)

Antonson, Rick, *To Timbuktu for a Haircut, A Journey through West Africa* (Skyhorse, New York, USA 2008)

Auphan, Paul, and Mordal, Jacques, *The French Navy in World War II* (US Naval Institute, Annapolis, Maryland 1959)

Auslin, Michael R, *The End of the Asian Century, War, Stagnation, and the Risks to the World's Most Dynamic Region* (Scroll and Key Society, Yale College, 2018)

Aussaresses, Paul, *The Battle of the Casbah: Terrorism and Counter-Terrorism in Algeria 1955-1957* (Enigma, New York 2005)

Basho, Matsuo, translated Yuasa, Nobuyuki, *The Narrow Road to the Deep North and other Travel Sketches* (Penguin, London 1966)

Behr, Edward, *The Algerian Problem* (Penguin, London 1961)

Boyd, Douglas, *The French Foreign Légion* (Ian Allen, Hersham 2010)

Boye, Alida Jay, and Hunwick, John O, *The Hidden Treasures of Timbuktu, Historic City of Islamic Africa* (Thames and Hudson, London 2008)

Boylan, Kevin, & Olivier, Luc, *Valley of the Shadow, The Siege of Dien Bien Phu* (Osprey, Oxford 2018)

Burchett, Wilfred G, *Vietnam, Inside Story of the Guerilla War* (International Publishers, New York 1965)

Burke, Peter, *Vico* (Oxford University Press 1985)

Camus, Albert, *The Outsider* (1942; Penguin, London 1983); *The First Man* (Penguin, London 1994)

Castle, Timothy, *One Day Too Long: Top Secret Site 85 and the Bombing of North Vietnam* (Columbia University 2000)

Cha, Dia, *Dia's Story Cloth* (Lee & Low, New York 1996)

Colvin, John, *Volcano Under Snow, Vo Nguyen Giap* (Quartet, London 1996)

Conboy, Kenneth, *The War in Laos 1960-1975* (Osprey, London 1989)

Cooper, Robert, edited, *The Hmong, A Guide to Traditional Lifestyles* (Times Editions, Singapore 1998)

Crone, Patricia, *God's Rule, Government and Islam* (Columbia University Press, New York 2004)

Curtin P D, *Economic Change in Precolonial Africa: Supplementary Evidence* (University of Wisconsin 1975)

Danish Broadcasting Corporation, *the cruellest journey*, cd, (Copenhagen, Denmark 2007)

de Gramont, Sanche, *The Strong Brown God* (Granada, St Albans 1975)

Dubois, Félix, translated White, Diana, *Timbuctoo the Mysterious* (1896; Andesite, USA 2019)

Economy, Elizabeth C, *The Third Revolution, Xi Jinping and the New Chinese State* (Oxford University Press 2018)

Economy, Elizabeth C, and Levi, Michael, *By All Means Necessary, How China's Resource Quest Is Changing The World* (Oxford University Press 2014)

Eliot, T S, *Four Quartets* (Faber and Faber, London 1966)

English, Charlie, *The Book Smugglers of Timbuktu, The Quest for this Storied City and the Race to Save its Treasures* (William Collins, London 2017)

Fadiman, Anne, *The Spirit Catches You and You Fall Down, A Hmong Child, Her American Doctors, and the Collision of Two Cultures* (Farrar, Straus and Giroux, New York 1997)

Fall, Bernard B, *Street Without Joy, The French Debacle in Indochina* (1961; Pen & Sword, Barnsley 2005); *Hell in a Very Small Place, The Siege of Dien Bien Phu* (Lippincott, Philadelphia, USA 1967)

Fenn, Charles, *Ho Chi Minh, A biographical introduction* (Studio Vista, London 1973)

Fisher, Allan G B and Humphrey J, *Slavery and Muslin Society in Africa, The Institution in Saharan and Sudanic Africa and the Trans-Saharan Trade* (Hurst, London 1970)

Frankl, Victor E, *Man's Search for Meaning* (Pocket Books, New York 1985)

Gardner, Brian, *The Quest for Timbuctoo* (Cassell, London 1968)

Gerth, Karl, *China Made, Consumer Culture and the Creation of the Nation* (Harvard University Asia Center 2003); *As China Goes, So Goes The World: How Chinese Consumers Are Transforming Everything* (Hill and Wang, New York, USA 2010)

Gertz, Bill, *The China Threat, How the People's Republic Targets America* (Regnery, Washington, USA 2000); *Deceiving the Sky: Inside Communist China's Drive for Global Supremacy* (Encounter, New York 2019)

Gordon, David C, *The Passing of French Algeria* (OUP, London 1966)

Greene, Graham, *The Quiet American* (1955; Penguin, London 1971)

Hallett, Robin, *The Penetration of Africa: European Enterprise and Exploration, Vol. 1, 'To 1815'*; edited (Frederick, London 1965); *The Niger Journal of Richard and John Lander, 1832-4* (Routledge & Kegan Paul, London 1965); *Africa since 1875, A Modern History* (University of Michigan, USA, 1974)

Hamilton-Merritt, Jane, *Tragic Mountains, The Hmong, the Americans, and the Secret Wars for Laos, 1942–1992* (Indiana University Press 1993)

Hammer, Joshua, *The Bad-Ass Librarians of Timbuktu and their race to save the world's most precious manuscripts* (Simon & Schuster, New York, USA 2016)

Harris, Nigel, *The Mandate of Heaven, Marx and Mao in Modern China* (Quartet Books, London 1978)

Harvey, David, *A Brief History of Neoliberalism* (Oxford University Press, New York 2005)

Heal, Chris, *Sound of Hunger* (Unicorn, London 2018); *Disappearing* (Chattaway and Spottiswood, Taunton 2019)

Hennissart, Paul, *Wolves in the City, The Death of French Algeria* (Paladin, St Albans 1970)

Hessler, Peter, *River Town, Two Years on the Yangtze* (John Murray, London 2001); *Oracle Bones, A Journey Through China* (HarperCollins, New York 2006)

Horne, Alistair, *A Savage War of Peace, Algeria 1954–1962* (Penguin, London 1985)

Hunt, Christopher, *Sparring with Charlie, Motorbiking down the Ho Chi Minh Trail* (Bantam, London 1966)

Ibn Khaldun, translated Rosenthal, Franz, *The Muqaddimah, An Introduction to History* (1370; Princeton University Press, USA 2005)

Irwin, Robert, *Ibn Khaldun, An Intellectual Biography* (Princeton University Press, USA 2018)

Jenness, Aylette, *Along the Niger River, An African Way of Life* (Thomas Y Crowell, New York, USA 1974)

Joffre, Joseph Jacques Césaire, *My March to Timbuctoo* (1915; Hardpress, Miami, USA 2019)

Joyce, James, *A Portrait of the Artist as a Young Man* (1916; Jonathan Cape, 1950); *Ulysses* (1922; Bodley Head, London 2008); *Finnegans Wake* (1939; Faber & Faber, London 1992)

Kao, Kalia Yang, *The Latehomecomer, A Hmong Family Memoir* (Coffee House Press, Minneapolis, USA 2008); *The Song Poet, A Memoir of My Father* (Metropolitan Books, New York 2016)

Keenan, Jeremy, *The Tuareg People of Ahaggar* (Sickle Moon 1977)

Kingsley, Mary H, *Travels in West Africa* (1895; Folio Society, London 1976)

Kurlantzick, Joshua, *A Great Place to Have a War, America in Laos and the Birth of the Military CIA* (Simon & Schuster, New York, USA 2016)

Kynge, *China Shakes The World, The Rise of a Hungry Nation* (Phoenix, London 2007)

Lançon, Phillippe, translation Rendall, Steven, *Disturbance, Surviving Charlie Hebdo* (Europa, New York 2019)

Lee, Mai Na M, *Dreams of the Hmong Kingdom, The Quest for Legitimation in French Indochina, 1850–1960* (University of Wisconsin, 2015)

Lewis, Bernard, *Islam in History, Ideas, People, and Events in the Middle East* (Open Court Publishing, Peru, Illinois, USA 1993)

Lewis, Norman, *A Dragon Apparent, Travels in Cambodia, Laos and Vietnam* (1951; Eland, London 2003)

Lieberthal, Kenneth, *Governing China, From Revolution Through Reform* (Norton, New York 1995)

Lien, Vu Hong, *Half a Tiger, Quest for The Nguyen Gold along the Ho Chi Minh Trail* (USA POD, 2012)

Lister, Tracey, and Pohl, Andreas, *Vietnamese Street Food* (Hardie Grant, London 2013)

Lonely Planet, *West Africa* (2009); *Vietnam, Cambodia, Laos and Northern Thailand* (2012)

Lloyd, Christopher, *The Search for the Niger* (Readers Union, Newton Abbot 1974)

Lucretius, trans. Bailey, Cyril, *The Nature of Things* (Wildside Press 1910)

Maalouf, Amin, translated Bray, Barbara, *On Identity* (Harvill Panther, London 2000)

Macdonald, Peter, *Giap, The Victor in Vietnam* (Fourth Estate, London 1993)

Maçães, Bruno, *The Dawn of Eurasia, On the Trail of the New World Order* (Allen Lane, London 2018)

Magnus, George, *Red Flags, Why Xi's China is in Jeopardy* (Yale University Press 2019)

Mann, Thomas, *Buddenbrooks* (1902; Penguin, Harmondsworth 1971)

Mitter, Rana, *A Bitter Revolution, China's Struggle with the Modern World* (Oxford University Press 2004); *Modern China, A Very Short Introduction* (Oxford University Press 2016)

Moore, David, compiled, *A Free People, Tracing Our Hmong Roots* (Master Communications, Cincinnati, USA 2003)

Morris, Virginia with Hills, Clive, *The Road to Freedom, A History of the Ho Chi Minh Trail* (Orchid Press, Bangkok 2006)

Newman, Rick, and Shepperd, Don, *Bury Us Upside Down, The Misty Pilots and the Secret Battle for the Ho Chi Minh Trail* (Ballantine, New York 2006)

Olson, Mancur, *Power and Prosperity, Outgrowing Communist and Capitalist Dictatorships* (Basic Books, New York, USA 2000)

Paterson, Stewart, *China, Trade And Power, Why The West's Economic Engagement Has Failed* (London Publishing Partnership 2018)

Park, Mungo, *Travels in the Interior of Africa* (1795-97; Wordsworth Classics, Ware, 2002)

Penman, Jim, *Biohistory, Decline and Fall of the West* (Cambridge Scholars Publishing, Newcastle-upon-Tyne 2015)

Plume, Christian, and Démaret, Pierre, *Target: De Gaulle, The Thirty-One Attempts to Assassinate the General* (Corgi, London 1974)

Pound, Ezra, *Shih-ching, The Classic Anthology Defined by Confucius* (Harvard University Press, USA 1976)

Pratt, John Clark, *The Laotian Fragments* (Avon, New York 1974); *Vietnam Voices, Perspectives of the War Years 1941–1975* (University of Georgia Press, Athens, USA, 1999)

Rough Guides, *Laos* (2017); *Vietnam* (2018)

Salak, Kira, *The Cruellest Journey, 600 miles in a canoe to the legendary city of Timbuktu* (Bantam, London 2005)

Scruton, Roger, *An Intelligent Person's Guide to Modern Culture* (Duckworth, London 1999); *The West and The Rest, Globalization and the Terrorist Threat* (Continuum, London 2002); *The Uses of Pessimism And the Danger of False Hope* (Atlantic, London 2010)

Shea, Pegi Deitz, *Tangled Threads, A Hmong Girl's Story* (Clarion, New York 2003)

Spengler, Oswald, *The Decline of the West* (1918; Stellar Books, Bowdon 2013)

Steele, Philip, *Ho Chi Minh* (Heinemann, Oxford 2003)

Stuart-Fox, Martin, *A History of Laos* (Cambridge University Press 1997)

Swain, Jon, *River of Time* (Vintage, London 1998)

Townsend, John, *The Légion of the Damned* (The Adventurers Club, London 1961)

Tucker, Jonathan B, 'The "Yellow Rain" Controversy: Lessons for Arms Control Compliance', *The Nonproliferation Review*, Spring 2001

Vater, Tom, *The Cambodian Book of the Dead* (Osprey, Nottingham 2013); *The Man with the Golden Mind* (Osprey, Nottingham 2014)

Waley, Jonathan, translated, *Spring in the Ruined City, Selected Poems of Du Fu* (c 750 AD; Shearsman, Exeter, 2008)

Warbey, William, *Vietnam: The truth* (Merlin Press, London 1965); *Ho Chi Minh and the struggle for an independent Vietnam* (Merlin Press, London 1972)

Warner, Roger, *Shooting at the Moon: The Story of America's Clandestine War in Laos* (Steerforth, Westminster, Maryland 1997)

Windrow, Martin, *The Last Valley, Dien Bien Phu and the French Defeat in Vietnam* (Cassell, London 2005)

Young, John Robert, *The French Foreign Légion, The Inside Story of the World-Famous Fighting Force* (Thames and Hudson, London 1985)

ALSO BY CHRIS HEAL

978-1-911604-41-19. Hardback • 768 pages • 234 x 155 mm
100 B&W illustrations, 12 colour maps • June 2018

Just before throwing off his identity and embracing a nomadic life, Chris Heal published in 2018 an applauded social history of two brothers, u-boat commanders in WWI. He examined their lives and careers against the politics and culture of their day. Applauded that is, until the BBC encouraged him in a radio book programme to explain his views on the European Union and Germany's modern-day role in running the continent. Then the roof fell in.

Plaudits for *Sound of Hunger*

The depth and breadth of this book is staggering. You would have to read a dozen others to get anywhere close to what's given you. The author wants you to know that WW1 was not won by the titanic slaughters, but by the slow starvation of the civilian populations of Germany and Austria. This is mature erudition from a man of three score and five who has produced a magnum opus to which I say, 'Bravo, Sir.' This is the kind of book I love because as soon as you finish it you start reading it again to see what you missed and enjoy it all over again.

Jack V Sturiano

This handsomely produced volume will be recognised as a distinctive and valuable contribution to the history of the First World War. Its author has been very careful in his research and shows both commendable levels of objectivity combined with real imaginative sympathy for his subjects. This is gripping stuff and should not disappoint its audiences. Four years into the publishing jamboree that is the War's centenary, here is a title that stands out and deserves its place on (and one hopes frequently off) the shelf.

Dr Richard Sheldon

Chris Heal's writing is densely packed with a wide variety of subject matter that flows thick and fast, but it rewards the reader with a deeper understanding of this critical period in German and European history. It covers events that are usually recounted at the national and international geopolitical level. It is much rarer to have a social, family and personal viewpoint and that is why Sound of Hunger *makes a valuable contribution to the current literature.*

Dr John Greenacre

A major contribution to WWI military history ... excellent work ... the author writes extremely well and his style is both lucid and engaging ... such a scholarly source book is a welcome addition to my bookshelf ... an objective, dispassionate foreigner's view of German history.

Col John Hughes-Wilson

978-1-9161944 -0-3. Paperback • 324 pages • 210 x 147 mm
55 B&W illustrations, 4 maps • June 2019

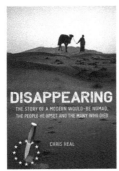

Chris Heal, one of many adopted names, wrote *Disappearing*, an almost-always-true autobiography, to try to save his life. On the run, north of Timbuktu, it looks like it didn't work. The book responds to the columnist Juliet Samuel who called for the 'corrective of a modern Don Quixote, a bolshy pensioner with a mission' and to T S Eliot, 'Old men ought to be explorers'.

Set in today's world, the protagonist, a man in later years, is so upset by his life experiences, the casual death which follows him, his constant brushes with bureaucracy, predatory business, the political establishment and the surveillance culture, that he decides on a great experiment: through careful and sometimes illegal planning, can he rid himself of his identity? When the times comes can he just get up and go, travel and not be found?

Anger at *Disappearing*

This a subversive book that should not receive the breath of publicity. Among other crimes, one can learn how to kill silently, dispose of bodies, hotwire a car, make a Molotov cocktail, fraudulently extract a pension without tax, and evade mechanical and electronic surveillance. These are skills best kept within the purview of government agencies.

Detective Chief Inspector, National Counter Terrorism Security Office

The author is taunting us with his knowledge of the unsolved murders of Juncker and Selmayr. This was a wicked crime; we are dealing with an amoral, calculating mass murderer. Whether alive or not, he should be investigated and brought to book in name or in person.

Secretariat, European Commission

Heal views the European Union as a wicked organisation, but there is no doubt that he is a celebrant of European culture. Squaring the circle that he inhabits is fundamental to the success of the federal project.

Assistant Secretary, Foreign & Commonwealth Office

I assumed that most of this book was fantasy, but the facts check out. I sensed that the author had been there, from rock climbing to Van Gogh, from flamenco to the Biafran war, from begging in Winchester to travelling through the Sahara. I now think much of the story may be true. It could even mostly be true.

Surveillance officer, The Security Service, charged with finding the author

The book explains how an individual can divest themselves of identity, go off grid and use terrorist-supporting Hawala to move money. Heal's success is a direct threat to our banking system and a danger to Western civilisation.

Senior Executive Officer, International Monetary Fund, Informal Funds Transfers

Felt-Hatting in Bristol & South Gloucestershire
I: the Rise

Chris Heal
ALHA Books No 13

Avon Local History & Archaeology. Pamphlets • Both parts
42 pages • 147 x 210 mm
Part 1: the Rise (ALHA 13): 10 illustrations, 3 maps, 1 figure;
Part 2: the Fall (ALHA 14): 3 illustrations, 6 maps, 6 figures •
June 2013, reprint 2015

These books are a pair, both of which are best sellers in the ALH&A series and available through Amazon. The first tells of the beginnings of the felt hat industry in the mid-16th century to its heyday around the end of the 18th century. The second traces and explains the industry's rapid decline in the 19th century. Both books are based on Chris Heal's doctoral thesis, 'The Felt Hat Industry of Bristol and South Gloucestershire, 1530-1909', completed in 2012, aged sixty-five, at the University of Bristol. Copies of the thesis are available for download from the British Library's EThOS web site (ID THESIS00618690). There is a supporting booklet describing a Hatters' Trail, which is available from the Watley's End Residents' Society; over 5,000 have been printed.

Plaudits for *Felt-Hatting*

Chris Heal's immensely impressive scholarship has identified more than 6,000 hatters and their businesses scattered throughout the region's towns and villages ... reminding us of the importance hats once held in English daily life and the considerable contribution the industry once made to the national economy ... Heal traces not only the rise and fall of the industry over three centuries but its culture of association, traced through the development of benefit clubs and unions ... and considers wider social issues in the hatting community; its drinking and recreational customs, its connection to Methodism, and the effect of the manufacturing process upon the health of its workers. 'Stubborn, well-organised, drunk, illiterate, poor, diseased and disposed to violence as they may be,' he concludes, 'the feltmakers of South Gloucestershire supplied work of high quality' ... The real value of these booklets lies not only in what they reveal about the organisation of the hatting trade, but in their strength as a case study of the response of a well-organised craft industry to economic and social change from its early modern origins to the industrial age. They are well written and very thoroughly researched.

Professor Steve Poole

Until well into the 20th century no man, rich or poor, would be about his business without a hat, and although millions of felt hats were made each year for the home market and millions more for export, today it is a largely forgotten industry. Also forgotten is the important role that felt hatmaking played in this part of the West Country for over 300 years, employing many thousands of men in the second largest manufacturing industry in south Gloucestershire after the cloth industry. Being always a 'cottage' industry, dominated by local families who left no substantial industrial or technological remains, it has consequently been overlooked by later researchers. This has now been thoroughly rectified by Chris Heal's study.

Mike Chapman

Lightning Source UK Ltd.
Milton Keynes UK
UKHW022008041121
393396UK00004B/92